DECISIONS AT FREDERICKSBURG

OTHER BOOKS IN THE COMMAND DECISIONS IN AMERICA'S CIVIL WAR SERIES

Decisions at Stones River: The Sixteen Critical Decisions That Defined the Battle
Matt Spruill and Lee Spruill

Decisions at Second Manassas: The Fourteen Critical Decisions That Defined the Battle
Matt Spruill III and Matt Spruill IV

Decisions at Chickamauga: The Twenty-Four Critical Decisions That Defined the Battle
Dave Powell

Decisions at Chattanooga: The Nineteen Critical Decisions That Defined the Battle
Larry Peterson

Decisions of the Atlanta Campaign: The Twenty-One Critical Decisions That Defined the Operation
Larry Peterson

Decisions of the 1862 Kentucky Campaign: The Twenty-Seven Critical Decisions That Defined the Operation
Larry Peterson

Decisions at Gettysburg: The Twenty Critical Decisions That Defined the Battle, Second Edition
Matt Spruill

Decisions at The Wilderness and Spotsylvania Court House: The Eighteen Critical Decisions That Defined the Battles
Dave Townsend

Decisions of the Tullahoma Campaign: The Twenty-Two Critical Decisions That Defined the Operation
Michael R. Bradley

Decisions at Antietam: The Fourteen Critical Decisions That Defined the Battle
Michael S. Lang

Decisions of the Seven Days: The Sixteen Critical Decisions That Defined the Battles
Matt Spruill

DECISIONS
AT FREDERICKSBURG

The Fourteen Critical Decisions
That Defined the Battle

Chris Mackowski
Maps by Edward Alexander

Command Decisions
in America's Civil War
Matt Spruill and Larry Peterson,
Series Editors

The University of Tennessee Press / Knoxville

Each book in the COMMAND DECISIONS IN AMERICA'S CIVIL WAR series introduces a major engagement in the Civil War, focusing not on the what of warfare, but on the why. As the wider drama of the battle unfolds, readers discover how discrete decisions made by Union and Confederate officers create the final outcome. Forthcoming books in the series will investigate decisions made in notable battles both in the Eastern and Western Theaters of the Civil War.

First Edition.

Library of Congress Cataloging-in-Publication Data

Library of Congress Cataloging-in-Publication Data
Names: Mackowski, Chris, author. | Alexander, Edward S., cartographer. Title: Decisions at Fredericksburg : the fourteen critical decisions that defined the battle / Chris Mackowski ; maps by Edward Alexander. Other titles: Fourteen critical decisions that defined the battle
Description: First edition. | Knoxville : The University of Tennessee Press, [2021] | Series: Command decisions in America's Civil War | Includes bibliographical references and index. | Summary: "Early in the Civil War, the Union sought to put a quick end to the Southern rebellion by capturing Richmond, Virginia, the new capital of the Confederacy. The Army of the Potomac, under the recently promoted leadership of Major General Ambrose Burnside moved to take Richmond, but delays in pontoon bridge construction and troop movement allowed General Robert E. Lee's Army of Northern Virginia ample time to entrench his troops and block Burnside's advance. As Burnside finally crossed the Rappahannock River, his troops engaged in direct combat with the Confederate defensive positions, leading to several failed frontal assaults and one of the more lopsided victories for the Confederacy of the entire Civil War. Intended for the Command Decisions in America's Civil War series, Chris Mackowski's study examines the tactical choices at the heart of the Battle of Fredericksburg. Rather than offering a history of the battle, Mackowski focuses on the critical decisions confronting Federal and Confederate leaders and ultimately shaping the battle as we know it today"—Provided by publisher.
Identifiers: LCCN 2021039682 (print) | LCCN 2021039683 (ebook) | ISBN 9781621907008 (paperback) | ISBN 9781621907015 (kindle edition) | ISBN 9781621907022 (pdf)
Subjects: LCSH: Fredericksburg, Battle of, Fredericksburg, Va., 1862. | United States—History—Civil War, 1861–1865—Campaigns. |Strategy—History—19th century.
Classification: LCC E474.85 .M33 2021 (print) | LCC E474.85 (ebook) | DDC 973.7/33—dc23
LC record available at https://lccn.loc.gov/2021039682
LC ebook record available at https://lccn.loc.gov/2021039683

To my cousin, Jack Taber

CONTENTS

ILLUSTRATIONS

Figures

Maps

PREFACE

From Marye's Heights, Confederate artillerists could once look down on the city of Fredericksburg, Virginia, a bustling commerce center known as the jewel on the Rappahannock River. As the highest navigable point on the river, the city's bustling docks thrummed with trade. A network of roads converged from all directions, concentrating trade and travel, and the Richmond, Fredericksburg, & Potomac Railroad shuffled goods and people northward and southward. It's little wonder the armies converged in Fredericksburg late in 1862; the town is situated midway between Washington, DC, to the north and, in a direct line, Richmond, Virginia, to the south. It had only been a matter of time.

Between the city and the heights just to the west stretched nine hundred yards of open ground dotted by a few small houses, the local fairgrounds, and a canal. Fifteen feet wide and ten feet deep, the canal provided free hydropower from the river to a pair of mills built near the canal's mouth. Midway down the canal's course, a millrace branched away and cut across most of the rest of the field, finally to empty back into the Rappahannock on the south end of town. Today, Kenmore Avenue covers the old millrace, and the open field is filled with neighborhoods and shops. It's hard to envision the gentle downhill slope from the base of the heights to the town, obscured as it is by houses.

But the walk to the top of Marye's Heights is still worth the view. From there, one can look across the rooftops and see, rising above them, the distinctive steeples of the Baptist, Presbyterian, and Episcopal churches along

From Marye's Heights, visitors can look down into the Sunken Road, past the Innis House (a wartime structure), and to Fredericksburg beyond. Where an open plain once stretched up from the town, a neighborhood now covers the landscape. Chris Mackowski.

Princess Anne Street. A pair of cannons sit atop the heights, where as many as forty-five guns once lined the crest. Confederate artillerists had such an advantageous perch that one, Edward Porter Alexander, claimed, "A chicken could not live on that field when we open on it."[1]

It would not be chickens, though, but soldiers of the Army of the Potomac that had to cross those nine hundred open yards, advancing toward the heights and the stone wall that skirted its base. At the start of battle, two thousand Confederate infantrymen—mostly Georgians and Tar Heels—waited in a sunken road that ran behind that wall. From the crest of the heights, forty feet above, a modern visitor can look down into that road and along the wall, both of which now serve as centerpieces for Fredericksburg and Spotsylvania National Military Park.

The crunch of gravel beneath one's shoes can easily evoke the sound of soldiers' boots as the men milled about, waiting for the first Federal assault. The quarried granite wall stands almost chest high and offers a sturdy defensive position. An original section of stones, still used as a retaining wall, remains along part of the road; it is from this segment the road gets the name we know it by even now: "Sunken Road." Two center portions, reconstructed in 2004 using modern archeology and Civil War–era photographs, provide a good approximation of the wartime structure. The southernmost stretch of wall is shorter and less sturdy, a relic not of the war but of the Civilian Conservation Corps' labor in the 1930s in building the park.

We speak today of the Stone Wall and the Sunken Road with capital letters, earned by the infamy of the Civil War's most intense struggles. In my years giving tours at Fredericksburg battlefield, I have invited visitors standing in the road to step up to the wall. "Try and put yourself in the Confederates' shoes as they stood here," I tell them. "Try to envision the Federal soldiers coming at you." Sightseers will try to look past the neighborhood that clogs the view and, from the security of the strong defenses, try to imagine that attack approaching across those nine hundred open yards. "Why did Burnside send his men against this position?" they often wonder aloud. "What was he thinking?"

Others ask, "Why did he keep the attacks going? Couldn't he see this was foolish? Why didn't he try somewhere else?" Fans of the movie *Gods and Generals*, which suggests Burnside could have simply shifted a mile or two upriver, ask, "Why didn't he cross where the river was shallower?" It's the movie

Today the restored Sunken Road not only evokes the scene of December 1862 but offers excellent interpretation to contextualize the historic landscape. Chris Mackowski.

that is shallow, I want to tell them. The scene makes for a convenient device showing the later fruitlessness of Federal assaults, but it certainly doesn't give Burnside's reasoning a fair shake.

Years ago, when I first started on my path of Civil War scholarship, scholar Frank O'Reilly shared an invaluable piece of insight with me. A legendary historian at Fredericksburg and Spotsylvania National Military Park and author of *The Fredericksburg Campaign: Winter War on the Rappahannock*, Frank knows more about the battle than anyone (probably ever). He was an important mentor to me and remains a good friend. One day, while walking the length of Hawke Street in the footsteps of the Twentieth Massachusetts—the Harvard Regiment—he told me that Burnside faced a myriad of bad options from the outset. Each choice he made limited the number of subsequent options available to him, all of which remained less than optimal. In effect, each decision funneled Burnside into a narrower set of worse options.

My intent with this volume is to examine the most critical of Burnside's decisions, as well as those most critical decisions of his Confederate counterpart, Robert E. Lee. I'll also look at the most crucial choices some of the people around them made.

As defined by this book series, "a critical decision is a decision of such magnitude that once it was made, it affected the flow and sequence of events of a battle or campaign from that point on." "Critical decisions cover the entire spectrum of war," series coeditor Matt Spruill explains.[2] They can occur on the strategic, operational, and tactical levels or within organizational or logistical structures. They can also involve personnel.

The accompanying chart shows the decision hierarchy.

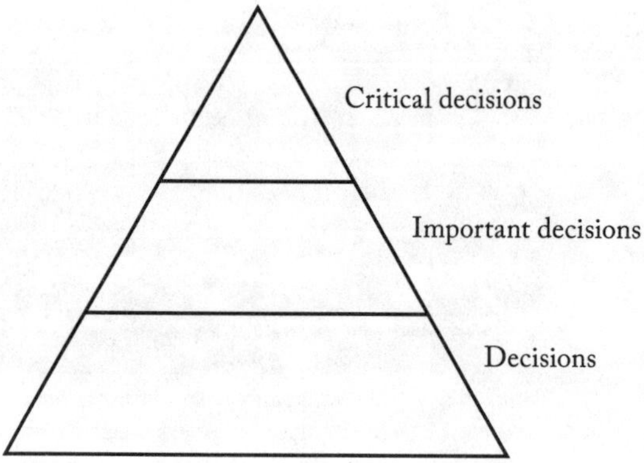

Decisions Hierarchy

Numerous decisions are made on all levels during the course of a campaign. They often deal with issues such as how to carry out an order or whom to assign to a specific duty. These determinations are often routine, but not always. They happen by the hundreds, if not thousands, every day. Far fewer are the important decisions, which perhaps impact the course of events but don't affect the very character and nature of those events. Critical decisions—the most vital of all—are, in effect, turning points or points of no return. Once a critical decision is made, it has an irrevocable impact on everything that follows thereafter.

Based on that definition, I have identified fourteen critical decisions for the Fredericksburg Campaign, eight of which were made by Union commanders and five of which were made by Confederates. The disparity favoring Federal forces here results from the fact that Burnside held the strategic and operational initiative for most of the campaign, forcing Lee to be reactive rather than proactive. As we'll explore, Burnside's predecessor, George McClellan, was fired for dragging his feet, so Burnside clearly understood the consequences of inactivity.

Additionally, the political pressures on Burnside because of the Emancipation Proclamation forced him into action. A multitude of factors impacted the political context in which the Fredericksburg Campaign took place, including rising inflation, a ballooning national debt, and growing antiwar

Maj. Gen. Ambrose Burnside faced an array of bad choices from the outset, and as the campaign and battle unfolded, they limited his options even more. *Frank Leslie's Illustrated Newspaper.*

sentiments among Northern Democrats (known as "Copperheads"), but none was so important as the major gestalt shift precipitated by the Emancipation Proclamation. The proclamation was, far and away, Lincoln's most consequential critical decision of the war. Lincoln scholar Harold Holzer has simply called it "Lincoln's most important act."[3] To that end, the introduction will spend considerable time exploring that context, for it influenced all other events in this book.

Here are the fourteen critical decisions that shaped the Battle of Fredericksburg:

1. Lincoln Replaces McClellan
2. Burnside Moves to Fredericksburg
3. Robert E. Lee Defends Fredericksburg
4. Burnside Crosses at Fredericksburg
5. Lee Lets the Federal Army Commit to Its Plan
6. William Barksdale Contests the Federal Crossing
7. Burnside Delays His Attack Until December 13
8. William Franklin Attacks Without Clarifying His Orders
9. John Pelham Harasses the Union Left Flank
10. Jubal Early Marches to the Sound of the Guns
11. John Reynolds Directs His Artillery
12. Franklin Calls Off the Attack Without Telling Burnside
13. Burnside Does Not Resume the Offensive
14. Lee Does Not Launch a Counteroffensive

I will not attempt in this book to provide a complete narrative history of the battle. For the fullest possible military account, I recommend Frank O'Reilly's *The Fredericksburg Campaign*. George Rable's excellent and highly readable *Fredericksburg! Fredericksburg!* makes a perfect complement to Frank's book. Frank's work focuses on military affairs, while George's offers a more holistic perspective, including social, economic, and political matters. For readers who aren't quite ready for a deep dive, I suggest *Simply Murder: The Battle of Fredericksburg*, a book I coauthored with my longtime friend and collaborator Kristopher D. White.

ACKNOWLEDGMENTS

In 2005, I had the pleasure of starting work at Fredericksburg and Spotsylvania National Military Park (FSNMP) as a volunteer. My relationship with the park has evolved in the fifteen years since—my position changed from front-desk volunteer to tour guide to contractor to seasonal employee to preservation partner. During that time, I've had the privilege of writing about the battle and battlefield on numerous occasions, including 2012's *Simply Murder: The Battle of Fredericksburg*, cowritten with my longtime collaborator Kris White. He more than anyone has helped shape my thoughts and experiences about this battlefield. I am grateful that he was kind enough to review this manuscript.

I owe my biggest debt to my friend and mentor Greg Mertz, who also reviewed this manuscript. Greg retired in 2021 as the supervisory historian at FSNMP and is the person who taught me how to be an effective tour guide and thought-provoking historian. I am grateful for everything he has invested in me.

Park historian Frank O'Reilly has also invested a great deal of time, energy, and patience in me over the past fifteen years. Truly a legend on the battlefields, Frank takes a boots-on-the-ground approach to history—and Fredericksburg in particular—that has profoundly impacted my development as a historian. I cannot recommend highly enough his definitive *The Fredericksburg Campaign: Winter War on the Rappahannock*, which offers a deep dive into the military history of the battle.

National Park Service historians John Hennessy, Don Pfanz, Eric Mink,

Noel Harrison, Steward Henderson, and Peter Maugle have all also made important contributions to my growth as a writer and historian of the Battle of Fredericksburg. I thank historian Will Greene, formerly of FSNMP and Pamplin Park, for his close read of the manuscript and his excellent suggestions for improvement. Outside the NPS, I tip my hat to George Rable, who is not only a great writer and scholar but also great company. His *Fredericksburg! Fredericksburg!* is smooth reading.

Among my Emerging Civil War colleagues, I thank Rob Orrison, Kevin Pawlak, Steve Phan, Dave Powell, and Terry Rensel for contributions that strengthened this manuscript. Terry works with the Central Virginia Battlefields Trust (www.cvbt.org), which has done much to help preserve the Fredericksburg battlefield. In partnership with the American Battlefield Trust (www.battlefields.org), CVBT has helped save the Slaughter Pen Farm in particular. Finally, from ECW, I offer special thanks to my colleague and friend Edward Alexander for not only his excellent maps but also his reading of the book (he, too, once upon a time worked at FSNMP).

I appreciate Matt Spruill, Larry Peterson, and Thomas Wells for asking me to write this book. Doing so offered me a new way to look at a familiar battle, for which I am grateful. I'm also thankful to the University of Tennessee Press for the opportunity to publish this work.

At St. Bonaventure, I thank my dean, Aaron Chimbel, and my former dean, Pauline Hoffmann, for their ongoing support of my writing. Kathy Boser provides administrative help that keeps me plugging along. I also thank the Faculty Committee on Recommendations and Provost Joe Zimmer for supporting a little sabbatical time for me to work on the book.

Finally, I offer my thanks to my family, especially my wife, Jennifer, who endured my late nights as I wrote, and my children, Stephanie and Thomas (and their new addition, Sophie Marie, my first grandchild), Jackson, and Maxwell James. They are my reasons for being.

INTRODUCTION

SEPTEMBER 22, 1862

Wood rasped against wood as Abraham Lincoln opened the drawer of his desk. From within, he lifted a set of notes that had been much on his mind these past two months. The papers rustled against each other lightly, but for Lincoln, they might have been the weightiest sheets he'd ever handled. They outlined his plan, to be enacted as a war measure grounded in his powers as commander in chief, for freeing slaves in all areas still in rebellion. "The executive government of the United States, including the military and naval authority thereof, will recognize and maintain the freedom of such persons, and will do no act or acts to repress such persons, or any of them, in any efforts they may make for their actual freedom," the document proclaimed.[1]

Southerners—and, for that matter, United States law—recognized slaves as property. Based on that premise, Lincoln argued it was within the army's rights "to seize and confiscate property of rebels"—including human property—as a war measure. The proclamation also effectively suspended the Fugitive Slave Act, demanding proof of loyalty to the US government from any slaveholder trying to reclaim a runaway slave. Finally, the declaration signaled Lincoln's intent to seek gradual manumission of slaves in areas still loyal to the Union, i.e., the border states.[2]

Lincoln had first floated the idea of emancipation with members of his cabinet beginning on July 13. Secretary of State William Seward and Secretary of the Navy Gideon Welles were the first to hear. Sharing a carriage with them on the way to a funeral for the youngest son of Secretary of War Edwin

Pres. Abraham Lincoln.
Library of Congress.

Stanton, the president broached the subject. "The slaves were undeniably an element of strength to those who had their service," he explained, "and we must decide whether that element should be with us or against us."[3] Lincoln then elaborated at great length on his ideas about emancipation. "He dwelt earnestly on the gravity, importance, and delicacy of the movement," Welles recalled, "said he had given it much thought and had about come to the conclusion that it was a military necessity absolutely essential for the salvation of the Union, that we must free the slaves or be ourselves subdued."[4]

The president asked both men "to frankly state how the proposition struck us," Welles continued, but both demurred. The subject, said Seward, involved consequences "so vast and momentous" that he wished to have a little time for "mature reflection" before answering. Welles agreed. Lincoln brought the matter up two or three more times on the ride, but neither man rose to the bait.[5] Welles stated, "Before separating the President requested us to give it early, especial, and deliberate consideration, for he was earnest in his conviction that the time had arrived when decisive action must be taken."[6]

Lincoln's mood on emancipation represented a surprising change of tone—a "new departure," the navy secretary called it. "For until this time, in all our previous interviews, whenever the question of emancipation or the mitigation of slavery had been in any way alluded to, he [the president] had been prompt and emphatic in denouncing any interference by the General Government with the subject," the navy secretary explained.[7]

Not only did the full cabinet support that same approach, so did the commander of Lincoln's principal army, George B. McClellan. In a July 7, 1862, letter to the president, McClellan—a conservative Democrat—warned, "A declaration of radical views, especially upon slavery, will rapidly disintegrate our present Armies."[8] The general was still reeling from a series of reverses before the gates of Richmond at the hands of a newly emboldened Confederate army. Rebels forced McClellan to retreat to the safe cover of Union gunboats on the James River, abandoning his previous position thirty-eight miles north on the Pamunkey. Thus he already had his hands full. McClellan felt he did not need the added military, political, and morale complications that would surely arise if Lincoln tampered with the South's so-called peculiar institution.

Yet it was this very series of defeats that crystallized Lincoln's musing into something more concrete, prompting him to finally broach the subject with Welles and Seward during their July 13 carriage ride.[9] Welles, later reflecting on the military and political climate at that moment, understood why the commander in chief tied them together as he did. "We wanted the army to strike more vigorous blows," Welles explained. "The Administration must set the army an example, and strike at the heart of the rebellion."[10]

In the days following the funeral, Lincoln raised the issue of emancipation with various other cabinet members. On July 22, he fully assembled them—with Postmaster General Montgomery Blair arriving late—to lay the subject before them for full discussion. He told them he had already resolved on the matter, so he didn't seek their advice so much as their suggestions.

Reaction was mixed, and several cabinet members expressed significant misgivings. Treasury Secretary Salmon P. Chase asked for stronger language about arming blacks. Atty. Gen. Edward Bates asked that deportation be considered in conjunction with emancipation. Blair warned that Democrats might capitalize on the unpopularity of the measure to make gains in the midterm elections, which might cost Republicans their majority in the House of Representatives. He worried, too, about the effect on the border states. Secretary of the Interior Caleb Smith, unspeaking, privately resolved to resign.

Then Seward spoke up. "Mr. President, I approve of the proclamation," he said, "but I question the expediency of its issue at this juncture." The repulse from the gates of Richmond had upset and depressed the public mind, and he suggested Lincoln postpone the proclamation "until you can give it to the country supported by military success." Otherwise, he said, "It may be viewed as the last measure of an exhausted government, a cry for help . . . our last *shriek*, on the retreat."

Lincoln later admitted, "The wisdom of the view of the Secretary of State struck me with very great force." Realizing that something had been missing from all his thought on the subject, the president confessed, "It [the timing of emancipation] was an aspect . . . I had entirely overlooked."[11]

Lincoln set the draft aside and waited for better news from the battlefield. "From time to time I added or changed a line, touching it up here and there, anxiously watching the progress of events," he told a friend.[12] In public, though, he took pains to maintain his previous stance on the slavery issue. "My paramount object in this struggle *is* to save the Union, and is *not* either to save or to destroy slavery," he wrote on August 22 in response to a goading editorial by *New York Tribune* editor Horace Greeley.

> If I could save the Union without freeing any slave I would do it, and if I could save it by freeing all the slaves I would do it; and if I could save it by freeing some and leaving others alone I would also do that. What I do about slavery, and the colored race, I do because I believe it helps to save the Union; and what I forbear, I forbear because I do not believe it would help to save the Union.[13]

Lincoln added an important caveat, pregnant with what historian James McPherson calls "intentional ambiguity": "I have here stated my purpose according to my view of *official* duty; and I intend no modification of my oft-expressed *personal* wish that all men every where could be free."[14] Greeley and his readers could read into that caution whatever they wanted.

All the while, Lincoln waited for events on the battlefield—any battlefield—that might bolster his ability to issue his proclamation. The successful Union defense of Baton Rouge, Louisiana, on August 5 offered the first glimmer of hope, but a Confederate victory on August 9 at Cedar Mountain, Virginia, much closer to the gates of Washington, erased the good news. On August 16, Confederate brigadier general Carter Stevenson materialized at the entrance to the Cumberland Gap in East Tennessee and shook the staunchly Unionist region. A few days later, on August 21, Braxton Bragg moved his Confederate army across the Tennessee River at Chattanooga on a northward dash that would take them all the way to Kentucky. There, in Richmond, they would win a stunning victory on August 29 and 30. However, an even bigger Confederate victory at Second Manassas from August 28 to 30 overshadowed news from the Bluegrass State.

Yet Robert E. Lee would not be content to rest on the laurels of that victory, and on September 4, he and the Army of Northern Virginia struck into Maryland with an eye on Pennsylvania. McClellan pursued with unusual

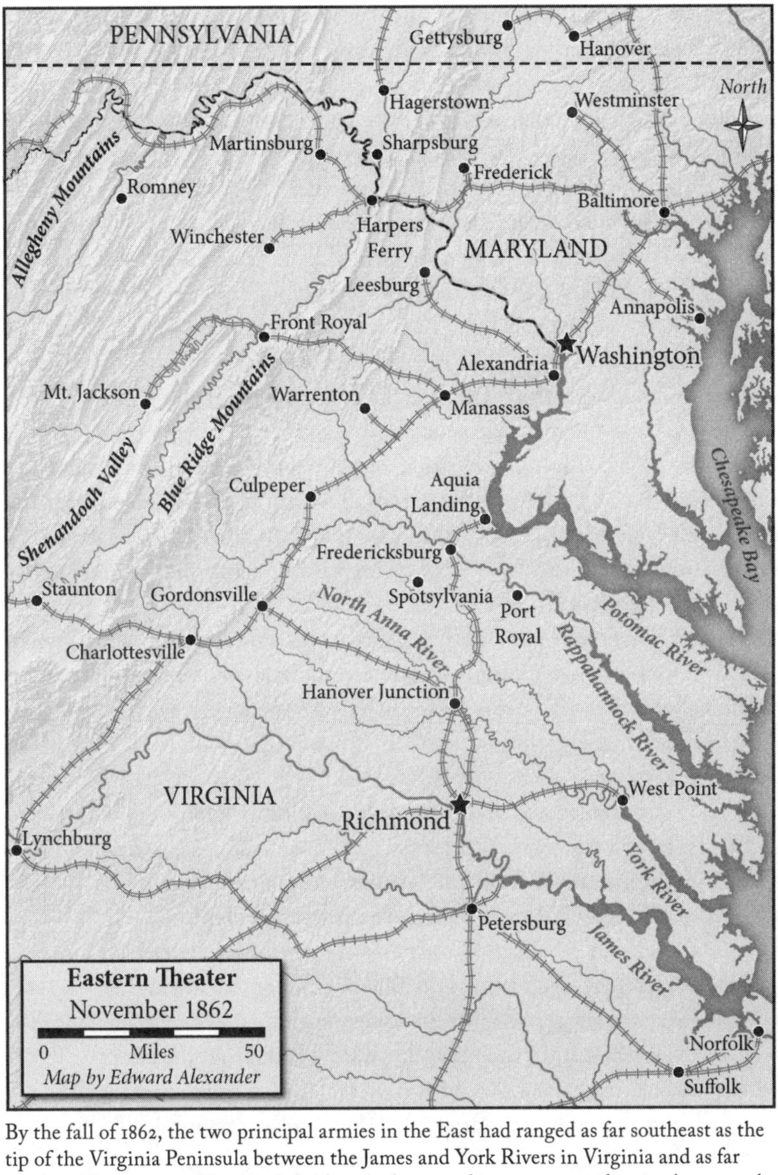

By the fall of 1862, the two principal armies in the East had ranged as far southeast as the tip of the Virginia Peninsula between the James and York Rivers in Virginia and as far north as Hagerstown, Maryland. Soldiers had engaged in concentrated action between the capitals of Washington, DC, and Richmond, Virginia, and secondary action in Virginia's Shenandoah Valley. Edward Alexander.

vigor, though, forcing Lee to scrap his invasion plan and instead consolidate his forces near Sharpsburg, Maryland, along the banks of Antietam Creek. The resulting battle on September 17 would go down in history as the single bloodiest day in American history, with some 23,110 combined casualties.[15] The campaign would also include the largest surrender of American troops during the war—at Harpers Ferry on September 15—and a final bloody nose for Federals at Shepherdstown during the Confederate retreat. It was not a perfect win for McClellan by any means, but the Confederate army did abandon the field in the end. "Our victory is complete," McClellan wrote to his wife, Ellen, on September 19. "Enemy has left his dead & wounded on the field. Our people are now in pursuit."[16]

Lincoln finally got the battlefield victory he'd been looking for.

On Sunday, September 21, Lincoln revisited his proclamation in the privacy of his office, "carefully" writing out a clean copy.[17] With his cabinet reassembled the next day, he slid open the drawer of his desk and removed the sheet so his colleagues could have a look. "For several weeks the subject has been suspended but, the President says, never lost sight of," Gideon Welles wrote in his diary.[18]

For a man who has since been remembered as an elegant literary stylist, Lincoln could not have created a more bureaucratic-sounding proclamation had he had it written by a committee of middle managers. For instance, see this passage:

> It is my purpose, upon the next meeting of Congress to again recommend the adoption of a practical measure tendering pecuniary aid to the free acceptance or rejection of all slave States, so called, the people whereof may not then be in rebellion against the United States and which States may then have voluntarily adopted, or thereafter may voluntarily adopt, immediate or gradual abolishment of slavery within their respective limits; and that the effort to colonize persons of African descent, with their consent, upon this continent, or elsewhere, with the previously obtained consent of the Governments existing there, will be continued.[19]

One radical abolitionist later complained, "The proclamation is written in the meanest and most dry routine style; not a word to evoke a generous thrill. . . . Nothing for humanity, nothing to humanity."[20] Furthermore, Lincoln—in journalism parlance—buried the lead, which doesn't appear until the third paragraph: "All persons held as slaves within any State, or designated part of a State, the people whereof shall then be in rebellion against the United States shall be then, thenceforward, and forever free."[21]

The proclamation was, after all, a legal document, and Lincoln—a lawyer himself—used that fact to full advantage. Couching emancipation in legalese would help de-escalate what would almost certainly be highly emotional reactions by any number of parties. The proclamation would serve as a challenge to the South and a rallying cry for abolitionists in the North. It would also, hopefully, deter intervention by European nations that enjoyed economic ties with Southern states yet cringed at the South's embrace of slavery. By that same token, though, the proclamation could not unduly upset still-loyal border states where slavery remained legal. Nor could it unduly upset Northerners who supported preservation of the Union but who might see a war to end slavery as a bait and switch. Such believers enlisted in the Federal army were of particular concern.

Indeed, much of the subsequent scholarship on the Emancipation Proclamation has focused on its central role in reframing the war's purpose from a political one into a moral one—from "preserving the Union" to "abolishing slavery." However, that interpretation suggests the two aims were exclusive of each other. In fact, Lincoln's adoption of emancipation was long-term

The Preliminary Emancipation Proclamation, issued by President Lincoln in September 1862, provided a context of intense political pressure for the commander of the Army of the Potomac. Library of Congress.

insurance for the Union's preservation. North and South had gone to war over slavery; were the two sides to reconcile with the institution intact, what was to prevent another sectional crisis over the same issue years down the road? Preserving the Union meant purging it of its original sin; only then could it be restored and *stay* restored.

When Lincoln pulled the draft from his desk, he "made a little talk to [his cabinet] and read the momentous document," recorded his secretary, John Hay. "Mr. Blair and Mr. Bates made objections, otherwise the cabinet was unanimous."[22] According to Welles, discussion "was long, earnest, and, on the general principle involved, harmonious." But Lincoln reminded his advisers that he was not asking for permission on the matter. "He remarked that he had made a vow, a covenant, that if God gave us the victory in the approaching battle, he would consider it an indication of Divine will, and that it was his duty to move forward in the case of emancipation," Welles said. "It might be thought strange, he [the president] said, that he had in this way submitted the disposal of matters when the way was not clear to his mind what he should do. God had decided this question in favor of the slaves. He was satisfied it was right, was confirmed and strengthened in his action by the vow and the results."[23]

Hay, who often acted as Lincoln's uncredited publicist in the newspapers, penned a reaction of unbridled enthusiasm. "The President determines the stroke shall be delayed no longer," he wrote. "He has withheld it as long as seemed to him just or expedient. We do not seem to advance as rapidly as we should. Some new step must be taken. This seems the best one possible." Hay's anonymous editorial continued, "The Proclamation of the President . . . flashes over the wires to every quarter of our waiting land, declaring that the Government has done with leniency or paltering with murderous traitors, and has given them but one more opportunity for repentance and safety."[24]

Tucked away in Hay's breathless endorsement of the Emancipation Proclamation was an implied criticism of Union forces: "We do not seem to advance as rapidly as we should." No line could better sum up Lincoln's frustrations than that one, particularly as they related to the commander of his principal army in the East, Maj. Gen. George Brinton McClellan of the Army of the Potomac, and the commander of one of his main armies in the West, Don Carlos Buell of the Army of the Ohio.

In fact, by the time Lincoln issued the Preliminary Emancipation Proclamation, Buell was already on the chopping block, with orders on the way for his removal. Orders to his intended replacement, Maj. Gen. George Thomas, explicitly underscored the need for decisive action: "The Government expects energetic operations by the troops placed under your command. . . . Operate against the enemy; find him and give battle."[25] With Confederate forces moving aggressively in the region, Lincoln postponed Buell's removal, but the War Department harried Buell with such a constant barrage of messages that he complained of "the frequent charges of tardiness that are made against the movements of the Army of the Ohio."[26]

In the East, meanwhile, McClellan had done little to follow up his important victory at Antietam. "McC. was doing nothing to make himself either respected or feared," Hay complained privately in his journal.[27]

Volumes have been written on the turbulent relationship between Lincoln and McClellan.[28] During his early war tenure, the general showed true genius as an organizer of armies and inspirer of men; it is just as true that he showed disrespect and "thorough contempt" for his commander in chief.[29] By late September 1862, Lincoln wrestled at least as much with McClellan and his feelings about McClellan as he did with any Confederate general.

Although Maj. Gen. George McClellan's early war successes came in a minor theater of action, they came at a time when the Union had little else to cheer about. As a result, his reputation inflated so much that admirers called him "the Young Napoleon." Library of Congress.

McClellan first rose to command on the recommendation of the aging general-in-chief of the army, Maj. Gen. Winfield Scott, after early war victories in western Virginia. McClellan repaid the endorsement by actively working to undermine the old war hero and drive him into retirement. "He [Scott] is an imbecile," McClellan wrote to his wife in August 1861. "He understands nothing, appreciates nothing, and is always in my way."[30] A rift also developed between McClellan and another of his early supporters, Secretary of War Edwin Stanton, who would eventually become his bitterest nemesis in the administration. The depth of their animus cannot be overstated.

Adoring newspapers christened the thirty-four-year-old McClellan "the Young Napoleon," and he quickly developed what historian James McPherson describes as "a messiah complex" because of the attention lavished on him.[31] "I seem to have become *the* power of the land," McClellan told Ellen shortly after arriving in Washington.[32] As his responsibilities increased following Scott's departure, he boasted to the president, "I can do it all."[33]

Maj. Gen. Henry Halleck, known as "Old Brains," rode into Washington with an excellent reputation as a military genius. The ballyhoo surrounding his promotion to the East made him all the more reluctant to jeopardize that status, rendering him an ineffective partner for strategizing with the commander of the Army of the Potomac. Library of Congress.

Yet the general soon demonstrated that, in fact, he could not. According to biographer Stephen Sears, McClellan exhibited "a willful stubbornness that was becoming increasingly noticeable."[34] Lincoln tired of having to work around it. He stripped McClellan of his role as general-in-chief and gave the post to Maj. Gen. Henry Halleck, recently transferred from the Western Theater after taking credit for a string of victories largely engineered by Ulysses S. Grant.

McClellan opened the spring campaign of 1862—after much pressure—by inching his way up the Virginia Peninsula from Fort Monroe toward Richmond. All the while, he bickered with his superiors in Washington. When he finally reached the Confederate capital, he declined to move in for the kill, giving besieged Confederates time to take the initiative. After the reverses of the Seven Days Battles from June 25 to July 1, followed by weeks of even more bickering with his superiors, it's little wonder that McClellan finally fell from grace. Lincoln began stripping the Young Napoleon of much of his army. The president then recalled him from the peninsula and transferred many of his forces to the newly formed Army of Virginia under Maj. Gen. John Pope, whom McClellan loathed. However, Pope came to grief at the end of August on the plains of Manassas, and on September 2, Lincoln turned back to McClellan to salvage the scattered and demoralized Union forces. "Mac is back!" soldiers cried with delight.

Lincoln's cabinet largely opposed the appointment—some of them violently—and during a September 1 meeting, a cabal tried to have McClellan removed entirely. Stanton, Chase, Smith, and Bates "did not deem it safe that McClellan should be intrusted with an army," recorded Gideon Welles privately. This was indeed an understatement, considering Stanton wanted McClellan court-martialed and Chase wanted him shot.[35] Welles simply deemed McClellan "deficient in the positive qualities which are necessary for an energetic commander."[36]

"Greatly distressed" during the discussion, Lincoln stuck with McClellan, although with great reluctance. He admitted the general was "troubled with the 'slows' and good for nothing for an onward movement," but he saw no other options.[37] "We must use the tools we have," the president later conceded.[38]

For his part, McClellan saw himself as the best tool, period. "Again, I have been called upon to save my country," he wrote to Ellen on September 5.[39] McClellan had always seen it as his mandate to save his country. "I am fighting to preserve the integrity of the Union and the power of the Govt," he wrote a friend in November 1861. But the officer believed only certain methods would gain that end, stating, "We cannot afford to raise up the negro question." In fact, he implored his friend, "Help me to [dodge] the nigger—we want nothing to do with him."[40] News of the Emancipation Proclamation thus rankled McClellan, a situation made worse by Lincoln's decision a day later to suspend the writ of habeas corpus. "The Constitution and the Union must be preserved, whatever may be the cost in time, treasure, and blood," McClellan had vowed to Lincoln in July. But the twin proclamations in late September, which McClellan privately condemned, went too far.

"The proclamation was ridiculed in the Army," groused Maj. Gen. Fitz John Porter, adding, "[It] caused disgust, discontent, and expressions of disloyalty to the views of the administration and amount, I have heard, to insubordination."[41] As one of McClellan's closest partisans, Porter occupied the same echo chamber as his commander. Although some segments of the army indeed threatened revolt over the measure, others met it with an equal measure of ambivalence. "I can't see what practical good it can do now," wrote Robert Gould Shaw to his abolitionist family back in Massachusetts. "Wherever our army has been, there remain no slaves, and the Proclamation will not free them where we don't go."[42]

The range of reactions within the army matched those without, noted Gideon Welles: "The Emancipation Proclamation has, in its immediate effects, been less exciting than I had apprehended. It has caused but little jubilation on one hand, nor much angry outbreak on the other."[43]

McClellan spent nearly two weeks sorting through his own conflicting reactions. During that span, he dashed off a note to a friend, businessman William H. Aspinwall of New York City, seeking advice. "I am very anxious to know how you and men like you regard the recent Proclamations of the Presdt inaugurating servile war, emancipating the slaves, & at one stroke of the pen changing our free institutions into a despotism," McClellan wrote.[44] Aspinwall responded by visiting McClellan in person to remind the general of his duty "to submit to the Presdt's proclamation & quietly continue doing my duty as a soldier."[45]

Finally, on October 7, McClellan issued a special order to the army that, in effect, said he and they should toe the line. "The Constitution confides to the civil authorities . . . the power and duty of making, expounding, and executing the Federal laws. Armed forces are raised and supported simply to sustain the civil authorities, and are to be held in strict subordination thereto in all respects. . . . The Chief Executive, who is charged with the administration of the national affairs, is the proper and only source through which the needs and orders of the Government can be made known to the armies of the nation."[46] That he felt the need to distribute this civics lesson remains telling.

The message's next passage subtly let the general's feelings slip. "The remedy for political errors, if any are committed, is to be found only in the action of the people at the polls," he wrote. McClellan needn't have written this passage had he not felt Lincoln had committed a political error. However, McClellan's unequivocal conclusion made clear that he and his army would avoid "casting any reflection upon that loyalty and good conduct which has been so fully illustrated upon so many battlefields."[47]

Even as the political situation with the Army of the Potomac de-escalated, the military situation in Kentucky boiled over. Braxton Bragg, who had been moving through the Bluegrass State with impunity, struck a blow on October 8 against Maj. Gen. Don Carlos Buell's Army of the Ohio at Perryville. Always able to pull defeat from the jaws of victory, though, Bragg withdrew from the state shortly thereafter. Confederates had likewise retreated from northwest Mississippi after Maj. Gen. Earl Van Dorn unsuccessfully attempted to retake the important rail junction of Corinth on October 3 and 4.

With the Confederate tide receding across the map, Lincoln knew his own armies had to seize the initiative. If his new vision for a restored Union had any chance at all of success, Federal troops needed battlefield victories. Only then could the president actually enforce his proclamation.

Lincoln's decision to issue the Emancipation Proclamation proved to be the most critical one of his tenure in office—a "momentous decision," as historian Doris Kearns Goodwin describes it, something that "would define both his presidency and the course of the Civil War."[48] But at the time, Lincoln understood what a tenuous thing his decree was. Without battlefield victory to back it up, the proclamation would seem, as William Seward warned, like "the last measure of an exhausted government" too worn down to execute its own will.

To fulfill his plans, Lincoln looked first and foremost to the Army of the Potomac and its troubled, troublesome commander.

CHAPTER 1

BEFORE THE CAMPAIGN, SEPTEMBER–NOVEMBER 1862

1. Abraham Lincoln Replaces McClellan

Situation

Abraham Lincoln surveyed the panoramic view of the army spread across the hills around Sharpsburg. It was "a great city of white tents and sleeping soldiers," said Ozias Hatch, Lincoln's sole companion on his walk to the battlefield. A former political associate from the president's home state of Illinois and its wartime secretary of state, Hatch had come east to visit his old friend and had agreed to tag along on the trip. Daylight was just purpling the eastern horizon when they set out. Here and there they met a guard and passed a quiet greeting, but otherwise, only early morning birdsong and distant farmyard voices broke the stillness. "Lincoln seemed to be peculiarly serious, and his quiet, abstract way affected me also," Hatch recalled.

Lincoln had come to Sharpsburg to visit his men and their officers in the wake of their September victory over the Army of Northern Virginia. In the two weeks since, army commander George McClellan had spent his time reorganizing and reequipping, even as the ANV slipped farther and farther into Virginia and out of reach. Lincoln had used the triumph as his excuse to release the Emancipation Proclamation, but privately, he knew he had reasons to be less than thrilled with McClellan's performance.

The relationship between Abraham Lincoln and George McClellan was never easy. Their meeting in the field following the Battle of Antietam was fraught with tension. Library of Congress.

For instance, Lincoln had learned that McClellan had withheld the army's reserves on the afternoon of the battle, fearing an overwhelming Confederate counterattack. No one even realized that McClellan had overinflated Lee's numbers by a factor of two, but the general's overcautiousness frustrated the president. McClellan's ongoing case of "the slows" also irritated Lincoln. After all, in the wake of Lee's victory at Second Manassas, the Confederate commander waited less than five days before launching his campaign into Maryland. McClellan showed no such initiative after Antietam.

By this time, McClellan's inactivity had become the stuff of legend in Lincoln's inner circle. Lincoln had prodded his general mightily in the spring in an attempt to get the army to move on Confederate forces in northern Virginia. McClellan first blamed his stillness on Winfield Scott, then blamed it on overwhelming—that is, grossly overinflated—Confederate numbers, then on the weather, then on illness. By March 3, 1862, Benjamin Wade, chairman of the Joint Committee on the Conduct of the War and a former McClellan supporter since soured, urged Lincoln to replace McClellan.

"With whom?" Lincoln asked.

"Why, anybody!"

"Wade," Lincoln replied, "anybody will do for you, but not for me. I must have somebody."[1]

Thus McClellan kept his job but ever seemed in need of prodding. After the disasters during the Seven Days, Lincoln finally looked to westerner John Pope as a viable alternative—until Robert E. Lee routed him. The president turned back to McClellan with great reluctance, fearing, among other things, more overcautiousness. But the Federal commander's skills as an organizer had outweighed at that particular moment the many strong negatives he brought with him, foremost his "hesitancy and reticence," according to Gideon Welles.[2]

McClellan had responded to Lee's invasion of the North with alacrity, but since the battle, he had settled back into his old habits. Lincoln thought an in-person visit to the army might inspire the men and spur McClellan to action. The meeting went poorly, though, and the tension between army commander and commander in chief was palpably felt by everyone around them.

Reflecting on his visit, and with the army stretched out before him on his early morning walk with his friend from Illinois, Lincoln asked, "Hatch—Hatch, what is all this?"

"Why, Mr. Lincoln," Hatch replied, "this is the Army of the Potomac."

Hesitating a moment, Lincoln then straightened. "No, Hatch, no," he said, raising his voice from its previous whisper. "This is *General McClellan's body-guard.*"[3]

Lincoln returned to the capital on October 5. "The Presdt was very kind personally," McClellan wrote to his wife that day. The general continued, "[He] told me he was convinced I was the best general in the country etc etc. He was very affable & I really think he does feel very kindly toward me personally. I showed him the battle fields & am sure he departed with a more vivid idea of the great difficulty of the task we had accomplished."[4]

McClellan did have a point. He had taken command of a demoralized Federal force on September 5 and, before having any real time to rally and reorganize the troops, faced the emergency Lee's invasion triggered. Thrown into battle, the Federals won a bruising fight on South Mountain and then survived unprecedented slaughter around Sharpsburg. With Lee on the retreat, McClellan hoped for a period in which to finally get his army in order and tend to its now-urgent supply needs. He tried mightily to make this case to Lincoln even as the president tried to convey the necessity for movement.

Brig. Gen. George Gordon Meade, placed in temporary corps command after the battle, wrote to his own wife, Margaretta, the same day McClellan wrote to his. The generals shared much the same impression of the president's visit. "I think . . . he was informed of certain facts in connection with this army which have opened his eyes a little," Meade wrote, "and which may induce him to pause and reflect before he interferes with McClellan by giving positive orders."[5] It's doubtful, though, that McClellan and Lincoln were actually hearing each other by this point—such was their mutual frustration and distrust. Lincoln returned from the visit thinking McClellan "would move at once," he later told John Hay. To Lincoln's thinking, his army commander was "a ruined man if he did not move forward, move rapidly and effectually."[6] To his astonishment, though, as soon as the president got home, McClellan "began to argue why he ought not to move."[7]

On October 6, General-in-Chief Henry Halleck sent McClellan a peremptory order on the matter: "The President directs that you cross the Potomac and give battle to the enemy and drive him south. Your army must move now while the roads are good."[8] McClellan disagreed. "I can't go far," he admitted in a letter to Ellen, "for the reason that I cannot carry many supplies."[9] The general followed this missive by taking leave without permission on October 9 and 10 to meet up with her. During McClellan's absence, Confederate cavalryman Jeb Stuart led a raid into Chambersburg, Pennsylvania, then circled back into Virginia unscathed. "It is a burning disgrace," groused Union artillerist Charles Wainwright, "that . . . he [Stuart] should have been permitted to ride rough-shod through so well settled a country, and not a shot fired at him, as it is that our cavalry should have allowed it."[10]

"This will be a mortifying affair to McClellan, and will do him, I fear, serious injury," Meade wrote. "I am getting very tired of inactivity, and though I am not fond of fighting, yet if we have to do it, I think the sooner we get at it and have it over the better."[11] It didn't seem likely, though. Meade thought that his boss "errs on the side of prudence and caution, and that a little more rashness on this part would improve his generalship."[12]

A week after Halleck's order, when McClellan still hadn't moved the army, Lincoln sent his general a letter of his own. "You remember me speaking to you of what I called your over-cautiousness," the president said, reminding the commander of their meetings during Lincoln's visit to the army.[13] McClellan promised to give Lincoln's correspondence "the fullest & most unprejudiced consideration," stating, "It is my intention to advance the moment my men are shod & my cavalry are sufficiently remounted to be serviceable."[14]

Lincoln finally lost his cool. "Will you pardon me for asking," he wrote, "what the horses of your army have done since the battle of Antietam that fatigues anything?"[15] McClellan, who found offense nearly anywhere he looked, was stunned. He had informed anyone who would listen, including his in-

The Army of the Potomac's supply issues after the Battle of Antietam were real, made acute by strains on the rail system. Library of Congress.

dulgent wife, "I am just as anxious as anyone, but am crippled by want of horses."[16] Telling Ellen of Lincoln's snarky note, the officer confided, "[It] was one of those dirty little flings that I can't get used to when they are not merited."[17]

McClellan again had a point. The correspondence of two of his subordinates, George Gordon Meade and Charles Wainwright, provides independent confirmation. "They do not, or will not, send from Washington the supplies absolutely necessary for us to have before we can move," Meade complained. "I have *hundreds* of men in my command without shoes, going barefoot, and I can't get a shoe for man or beast. . . . Our artillery horses and train animals have been literally starving, and have been suffering for the want of forage, and our men for the want of clothing, and yet we can't get these things."[18]

On October 7, Meade had telegrammed the Clothing Department that his division needed three thousand pairs of shoes; by October 23, nothing had yet arrived. "And it is the same thing with blankets, overcoats, etc., also with ammunition and forage," he said.[19] Newspapers reported the army had been "fully supplied with everything as fast as [McClellan] called for it," but Meade stated categorically, "This is false."[20]

Wainwright, too, protested his troops' lack of provisions: "This corps as yet has received next to no supplies, and is just as badly off as directly after the battle. None of my batteries have yet had their ordinance requisitions filled, nor have we drawn any horses, and though there are standing requisitions at both Hagerstown and Harper's Ferry for horseshoes, we have not got a single shoe."[21] By October 19, he noted that the situation hadn't materially improved: "This corps got a certain amount of clothing last week, the first we have received worth speaking of; still the men are very badly off for shoes and blankets. . . . I have been unable to procure any horses yet, and have received but one keg of shoes. Not a single battery has yet got their ordinance requisition filled."[22]

The complaints of Meade and Wainwright were common refrains. When John Reynolds returned to the army to command the First Corps, he complained about the lack of supplies still plaguing his men. William Franklin, too, objected to deprivations in his Sixth Corps.[23] Historians have since debated where the crux of the matter lay. "No one was prepared for the sheer scale of the problem posed by supplying forces in western Maryland," points out McClellan biographer Ethan Rafuse. "Regardless of the source of the difficulties, McClellan's complaints regarding the difficulties simply supplying his army, much less preparing it for an offensive movement, were based in reality."[24] Another biographer, Stephen Sears, agrees that there was plenty of blame to go around, but he offers a Trumanesque reminder of where the buck stopped:

> A less obvious factor in the supply crisis was the commander of the Army of the Potomac, probably the best military administrator in the United States Army. It was not until three weeks after Antietam that McClellan even informed Washington of supply difficulties that were by then of long standing. He had applied no strong pressure for timely and rapid resupply for the reason that he had no immediate plans for a campaign that depended upon it; the army was unprepared for an advance simply because General McClellan had not ordered it to be prepared.[25]

McClellan himself claimed, "Everything has been done that can be done at the Head Qtrs to accomplish the desired result." But as Sears elsewhere concludes, "Had his heart been in this advance, McClellan would surely have stepped in with his unmatched organizational skills to sort out the tangles and get the army's logistics running smoothly."[26]

Meanwhile, in Washington, fingers drummed on desks. "It is just five weeks since the Battle of Antietam," wrote Gideon Welles on October 18, "and the army is quiet, reposing in camp. The country groans, but nothing is done. Certainly the confidence of the people must give way under the fatuous inaction. We have sinister rumors of peace intrigues and strange management."[27] Welles might have been referring to an incident a few weeks earlier involving Maj. John J. Key, a War Department staffer and brother of one of McClellan's staff officers, Col. Thomas Key. The junior-ranking Key had allegedly said McClellan "did not mean to make any decisive victory but to keep things running on so that . . . the army might manage things to suit themselves."[28] Lincoln investigated the matter and, on September 27, called Key to his office and fired him. "I dismissed major Key for his silly treasonable talk because I feared it was staff talk & wanted an example," Lincoln explained.[29]

Simultaneously, another thread of conversation suggested McClellan wasn't looking to go after Lee, but instead looking to go *around* him. The Federal commander was bucking for a promotion that would let him avoid any more direct conflict with his Confederate counterpart. After a McClellan partisan discussed the matter with Salmon Chase, the treasury secretary wrote in his diary, "McClellan would like to retire from active command if he could do so without disgrace—which could be accomplished and a more active general secured by restoring him to the chief command."[30]

Such machinations puzzled John Hay. "I always thought that McClellan's fault was a constitutional weakness and timidity which prevented him from active and timely exertion, instead of any such deep laid scheme of treachery & ambition," he later told Lincoln. The president confirmed Hay's assessment.[31]

As intrigues swirled and deprivations prevented movement, pressure on McClellan mounted. "The papers are full of reports of McClellan's removal," Wainwright wrote, "and I fear they will prove only too true. His enemies are very bitter, and will see no good in him, though there is not a doubt that no other man in the country could have saved Washington last month."[32] Meade described McClellan's position as "most precarious," concluding, "If he does not advance soon and do something brilliant, he will be superseded."[33]

When the ax came down on October 24, though, it came down not on McClellan but on Don Carlos Buell for his failures following the Battle of Perryville. In a scenario eerily similar to the situation in Maryland, Confederates had been turned back from their invasion of Kentucky, but the Federal commander had done little to capitalize on the success. "Neither the Government nor the country can endure these repeated delays," Halleck warned Buell the day before the latter's firing. "Both require prompt and immediate movement."[34] Lincoln chose Maj. Gen. William S. Rosecrans as Buell's replacement. "I need not urge upon you the necessity of giving active employment to your forces," Halleck reminded Rosecrans. "Neither the country nor

Maj. Gen. Don Carlos Buell lost his job commanding the principal Union army in Kentucky and central Tennessee—a clear signal to McClellan in Virginia. Library of Congress.

the Government will much longer put up with the inactivity of some of our armies and generals."[35]

The message to McClellan was clear.

"McClellan clearly would have preferred not to undertake a major campaign before winter and instead wait until 1863 to return the army to its proper line of operations on the Peninsula," explains historian Ethan Rafuse.[36] Many of McClellan's chief subordinates agreed. George Gordon Meade, for instance, called the James River "the true and only practicable line of approach to Richmond."[37] But it was battle with Lee, not the capture of Richmond, that Lincoln saw as the true and only line.

Following the fight at Sharpsburg, Lee had slipped back into the friendly confines of Virginia and moved toward Winchester at the mouth of the Shenandoah Valley. His position there gave him flexibility of movement depending on McClellan's route of advance, with apt room to escape, maneuver, intercept, or even threaten the Federal flank and/or rear.

On October 26, with the shadow of Buell's removal hanging heavy over McClellan, the Army of the Potomac began crossing into Virginia east of the Blue Ridge Mountains—the "inside track" to Richmond—keeping between Lee and Washington. Even as the troops did so, McClellan worried about the safety of Harpers Ferry in his rear. Fretting to his superiors, "A great portion of [Braxton] Bragg's Army [from the west] is probably now at liberty to unite itself with Lee's command," he pointed out that "the very great reduction of numbers that has taken place in most of the old regiments of this command" necessitated that he "fill up these skeletons before taking them again into action."[38]

McClellan's concerns rang hollow to Lincoln as just more excuses. "McClellan is not accused of corruption, but of criminal inaction," Gideon Welles wrote privately.[39] McClellan, meanwhile, seethed, also in private. "If you could know the mean & dirty character of the dispatches I receive you would boil over with anger," he wrote his wife. He further told Ellen, "The good of the country requires me to submit to all this from me whom I know to be greatly my inferiors socially, intellectually, & morally! There was never a truer epithet applied to a certain individual than that of 'Gorilla.'"[40]

The army took a full six days to cross the Potomac—a river Lee had crossed overnight on September 18–19. Soldiers then inched up the Loudon Valley. By that time, the ersatz "gorilla" had decided it was time to throw his weight around. "I saw how [McClellan] could intercept the enemy on the way to Richmond," Lincoln said. "I determined to make that the test. If he let them get away I would remove him."[41] And, indeed, Robert E. Lee divided his forces and slipped away, well out of McClellan's reach yet able to suddenly threaten him from two directions. One portion of Lee's army under

The Army of the Potomac used a pontoon bridge to cross the Potomac River at Berlin, Maryland (later called Brunswick). The presence of the pontoons in Berlin would come back to haunt the army. Library of Congress.

Lieut. Gen. Thomas "Stonewall" Jackson stayed in the Shenandoah Valley, while another under Lieut. Gen. James Longstreet actually moved into position between the Army of the Potomac and Richmond, effectively negating Lincoln's hope for the inside track.

The final thing staying the president's hand had been the North's midterm elections. Firing McClellan, a popular Democrat, would have only worsened things at the polls for Lincoln's Republicans. On Tuesday, November 4, 1862, in the last major election of the season, New Yorkers handed the governor's office to a Democrat—but untied Lincoln's hands at the same time.

Options

Option 1: Retain McClellan

Technically, Lincoln had two options when it came to McClellan: promote him out of his position—as Chase had earlier written that the general desired—or fire him outright. "We have many rumors in regard to changes in the commanding general of this army," George Meade wrote to his son, John Sergeant. "Some say McClellan is again to be commanding general of the whole army at Washington, and Halleck is to return to the West, but I can hardly believe this."[42]

In both practical and political terms, though, McClellan's fate was sealed. His fitness for command had been litigated daily—seemingly endlessly—at least since the fall of 1861. As early as January 13, 1862, according to McClellan biographer Stephen Sears, Lincoln "realized he must closely monitor his stubbornly uncooperative general and press him for information and action. . . . Thereafter nothing would come easy in the relationship of president and commanding general."[43] Opinions about McClellan had only soured and hardened since.

As recently as early September following the Union loss at Second Manassas, McClellan's fitness for command came into sharp relief. During those days of intense debate, General-in-Chief Henry Halleck contended he "had no other officer whom he thought capable and said he consequently was left with no alternative but McClellan."[44] No viable new player had emerged on the scene since to shake up the cast of characters.

Complicating matters, the men of the Army of the Potomac continued to hold McClellan in deep affection. "The men have the most implicit faith in him," wrote Robert Gould Shaw, "and he never appears without being received with cheers."[45] That didn't necessarily blind the men to their commander, though, as Charles Wainwright attested:

> I am not so strong an admirer of McClellan myself but that I can see he falls short of being a really great general, such as one we ought to have in command of this army, but I do think he is head and shoulders above any other man we have. Indeed, if you put the question "Who is better?" to any of those who are most bitter, it silences them at once. Burnside and Hooker are the only two I have heard of as his successor; the first has been offered the position and has declined it, stating fairly that McClellan was better fitted for it than he was. Hooker I do not think is at all capable of filling the position.[46]

Option 2: Joseph Hooker

Joe Hooker—"Fighting Joe" Hooker, as the press had dubbed him—was as aggressive a self-promoter as anyone in the entire Federal army. A graduate of the West Point class of 1837, he had distinguished himself during the war with Mexico before leaving the army to seek his fortune out west. He returned in time to witness First Manassas, but he couldn't get a commission because of a prewar spat with general-in-chief of the army Winfield Scott. However,

Maj. Gen. "Fighting Joe" Hooker claimed the Union army would have decisively crushed Confederates at Antietam had he not been injured during the battle. Library of Congress.

with the help of well-placed advocates, Hooker caught Lincoln's ear soon thereafter. "I was at the battle of Bull Run the other day, and it is neither vanity or boasting in me to declare that I am a damned sight better general than you, Sir, had on that field," he told Lincoln. The president took note—and believed Hooker—and recommended him for a brigadier generalship.[47]

Hooker proved as good as his word, too, excelling on the battlefield with such distinction that he rose to corps command by the fall of 1862. At Antietam, after his men were cut down scythe-like in the Miller Cornfield, a wounded foot knocked him out of action. "Had you not been wounded." McClellan told him, "I believe the result of the battle would have been the entire destruction of the rebel army."[48] Recovering in Washington, Hooker took advantage of his proximity to the seat of power to share McClellan's testimonial with anyone who would listen. "All indications are, that Hooker is playing a game to overthrow McClellan," surmised Provost Marshal Marsena Patrick.[49]

"It seems to be generally conceded that if McClellan is removed, Hooker will succeed him," Meade wrote to his son. "Hooker is a very good soldier and a capital officer to command an army corps, but I should doubt his qualifications to command a large army. If fighting, however, is all that is necessary to make a general, he will certainly distinguish himself."[50] Meade and Hooker were "old acquaintances," having served together at West Point and in Mexico. "He is a very good soldier," Meade told his wife. The general continued as follows:

> [Hooker is a] capital general for an army corps, but I am not prepared to say as to his abilities for carrying on a campaign and commanding a large army. I should fear his judgment and prudence, as he is apt to think the only thing to be done is to pitch in and fight. . . . Now he is made, and his only danger is the fear that he will allow himself to be used by McClellan's enemies to injure him. Hooker is a Democrat and anti-Abolitionist—that is to say, he was. What he will be, when the command of the army is held out to him, is more than any one can tell, because I fear he is open to temptation and liable to be seduced by flattery.[51]

Despite Hooker's reputation for being "ambitious and unscrupulous," his name seemed to circulate most frequently and most openly, although he remained Lincoln's third choice.[52] That might have been because the officer still remained in Washington, recovering from the foot wound he had sustained at Antietam.

Option 3: Ambrose Burnside

By the fall of 1862, affable Ambrose Burnside had amassed one of the most impressive records of any Union general thus far in the war. A graduate of the West Point class of 1847, he had served time in the prewar army and the Rhode Island militia. He also devoted time to his interest in firearms, inventing a carbine that would bear his name. Burnside was involved in the fighting at First Manassas, where he neither distinguished himself nor embarrassed himself, and by February of 1862, he found himself in charge of an expeditionary force that ended up capturing the Outer Banks of North Carolina, sealing off much of the state's coastline. Following McClellan's embarrassment at the gates of Richmond, Burnside's Ninth Corps joined the Army of the Potomac as reinforcements. A good friend of McClellan's, Burnside was glad for the opportunity to serve with him. However, sometime on July 26–27, Montgomery Meigs, acting on behalf of Lincoln, offered Burnside command of the army. No record of the conversation exists, but we know Burnside demurred in deference to his friend.

After McClellan's fall from grace later that month, and after Pope's drubbing at Second Manassas, Henry Halleck called on Burnside once more to take overall command. "But Burnside declined and declared himself unequal to the position," Gideon Welles noted with disappointment.[53] Burnside understood corps command and performed well in that capacity; he worried that army command would promote him beyond his abilities. Today, we would call that the "Peter Principle," and to the general's credit, he recognized it. The men of the army seemed to sense it, too, as did members of Lincoln's cabinet. "I have my fears that he has not sufficient grasp and power for the position given him, or the ability to handle so large a force," Welles later wrote; "but he is patriotic, and his aims are right."[54]

Option 4: Somebody Else

At various times, Lincoln and his advisers considered Ambrose Burnside, Samuel Heintzelman, George Sykes, and Nathaniel Banks for the command of the army. All were deemed estimable officers in their "proper place, under orders," said Gideon Welles, but the president's counselors always decided "the War Department must hunt up greater men, better military minds, than these to carry on successful war."[55]

The other danger was what has since become known as McClellanism: the ingrained influence of George McClellan on the hearts, minds, attitudes, and habits of the officers who served under him. Of the army's highest-ranking commanders, William Franklin and Fitz John Porter were the most

McClellanesque. Porter had the added taint of a growing controversy in the wake of Second Manassas, where he'd been accused of intentionally withholding help to the Army of Virginia to sabotage John Pope and defer to McClellan. The other most senior commander, Edwin V. "Bull" Sumner, was sixty-five. McClellan had intimated that the career officer's "age, state of health, and the many exposures he has undergone" made it "doubtful whether he can stand the fatigues of another campaign." (Indeed, Sumner's health would give out terminally almost five months to the day of McClellan's prediction.)[56]

McClellanism infected the army in both obvious and insidious ways. "The soldiers whom McClellan has commanded are doubtless attached to him," Welles noted. "They have been trained to it, and he has kindly cared for them while under him. With partiality for him they have imbibed his prejudices, and some of the officers have, I fear, a spirit more factious and personal than patriotic."[57] That worry manifested itself most acutely in early September, when Lincoln finally called on McClellan after Second Manassas. "To have placed any other general than McClellan, or one of his circle, in command would be to risk disaster," Welles observed. "It is painful to entertain the idea that the country is in the hands of such men. I hope I mistake them."[58] Events over subsequent weeks would only add to Welles's pain.

Col. Henry A. Morrow of the Twenty-Fourth Michigan articulated a different take on the situation. "The best course," he told a reporter, "would be to put at its head some general who had never been mixed up with its quarrels and rivalries, in whom all would have confidence, and who should bring with him the prestige of success. General Rosecrans seemed to answer this description better than any other man."[59] After Buell's late-October sacking, however, Rosecrans found himself in command of the newly rechristened Army of the Cumberland and would soon have his hands full in Tennessee.

Meanwhile, Welles knew something had to give with the Army of the Potomac: "[I] am sad, sick, sorrowful over this state of things, but see no remedy without change of officers."[60]

"Oh," wrote infantryman Josiah Favill of the Fifty-Seventh New York, surely summing up Lincoln's own thoughts, "for a military genius to take command!"[61]

Decision

Lincoln had seen an opportunity for McClellan to cross the Potomac and intercept the Army of Northern Virginia on the way to Richmond. "I determined to make that the test," he explained. "If he let them get away I would remove him. He did so & I relieved him." As Lincoln explained to one confidant who tried to change his mind, he had "tried long enough to bore with an auger too dull to take hold," so it was finally time to let Little Mac go.[62] In fact, Welles admitted, "I had expected it might take place earlier."[63]

On November 5, Lincoln ordered Halleck to relieve McClellan and replace him with Burnside. With the same lack of urgency that would bring Burnside to ruin within weeks, Halleck finally had the order ready for delivery on November 7. The task fell to Brig. Gen. Catharinus P. Buckingham, an Ohioan with a pip-pip, old chap–sounding name who would ever after be best remembered for the mission he was about to undertake. On assignment as special assistant to Secretary of War Stanton and carrying the full authority of the president, Buckingham set out into a snow squall and made his way to the Army of the Potomac. He carried General Order 182, which relieved McClellan of command. A companion order named Ambrose Burnside as McClellan's successor.

Upon his arrival, Buckingham first went to Burnside, interrupting the Ninth Corps commander's evening downtime. Burnside balked at the news—he had demurred twice before when offered army command, and he tried to do so again. On those previous instances, though, Burnside had been *offered* command; this time, he was *ordered* to accept. Besides, Buckingham said, McClellan was being relieved whether Burnside took the job or not—and, if not, perhaps the job would go to Joe Hooker. According to Burnside biographer William Marvel, Burnside—who could get along with just about anyone—loathed Hooker and found him "arrogant, devious, and dangerously selfish."[64] To prevent his rival from getting the job, Burnside accepted.

The pair then traveled to McClellan's headquarters so Buckingham could carry out the primary part of his mission. "As I read the order, " McClellan told his wife, "I am sure that not a muscle quivered nor was the slightest expression of feeling visible on my face." Though he admitted to Ellen, "I must have made many mistakes," he also said he did not see "any great blunders." "But no one can judge himself," McClellan then added. Mostly, the general seemed disappointed: "They have made a grave mistake—alas for my poor country—I know in my innermost heart she never had a truer servant."[65]

Resigned to his fate, McClellan noticed that his friend Burnside seemed anything but. "Poor Burn feels dreadfully, almost crazy," he told Ellen. "I am sorry for him, & he never showed himself a better man or truer friend than now."[66] Later, McClellan would comment on "the cordial feeling" he and Burnside shared, stating, "His is as sorry to assume command as I am to give it up. Much more so. Be sure that all will yet come out well. Old Burn is true & honest—his future will be all that you can wish."[67]

Historian James M. McPherson rightly judges that "nothing in McClellan's tenure of command became him like the leaving of it."[68] At Burnside's request, McClellan stayed on with the army for a few days to make sure his successor understood the deployment of the troops and the strategic and operational situation he'd inherited. But he admitted to his closest circle that his recall pained him. "I feel as if the Army of the Potomac belonged to me," McClellan told a gathering of officers. "It is mine. I feel that its officers are my brothers, its soldiers my children. This separation is like a forcible divorce of husband and wife."[69]

The feeling, at least among most of the officer corps, was mutual. "The Army is in mourning & this is a blue day for us all," said Provost Marshal Marsena Patrick.[70] Artillerist Charles Wainwright, who described the mood as "terribly blue," said some men even went so far "as to beg [McClellan] to resist the order, and saying that the army would support him":

> These last he reproved gently but strongly. To everyone personally he expressed his high opinion of General Burnside, and begged them to transfer to him all the devotion and zeal they had ever shown for himself. Whatever might be their opinion of McClellan as a general, no one who saw and heard him today as I did could help pronouncing him a good and great man: great in soul if not in mind.[71]

Troops gathered for grand reviews so their former commander could say good-bye. McClellan "rode slowly along the lines, the men all saluting as he passed," said Wainwright, who noted, "There was hardly a dry eye in the ranks. Very many of the men wept like children, while others could be seen gazing after him in mute grief, one may almost say despair, as a mourner looks down into the grave of a dearly loved friend."[72] Lieut. Robert S. Robertson of the Ninety-Third New York called the event a "funeral of departed hopes."[73]

"In parting from you I cannot express the love and gratitude I bear for you," McClellan told the men.[74] He said as much to Ellen just before his final departure. "It made me feel very badly yesterday when I rode among them & saw how bright & cheerful they looked & how glad they were to see me," he wrote of the "poor fellows." Later, McClellan admitted, "I did not know before how much they loved me nor how dear they were to me. . . . The scenes of today repay me for all that I have endured."[75]

Results/Impact

Burnside would prove to be a spectacularly vanilla choice. "Burnside is a pure man and a man of integrity of purpose," McClellan told Brig. Gen. Oliver Otis Howard, "and such a man can't go far astray."[76] Others weren't so sure. "Those of us who were well acquainted with Burnside knew that he was a brave, loyal man," wrote Maj. Gen. Darius Couch, "but we did not think he had the military ability to command the Army of the Potomac."[77] Artillerist Charles Wainwright captured the mood expressed by many:

> I am inclined to think . . . that Burnside is not just the man they want, and that they only use his popularity on the country to counter-balance McClellan's. I know that Burnside does not want the command, and that before long it will be turned over to Hooker or Meigs, as more pliable tools. The greatest indignation is expressed by everyone here, even those who have blamed McClellan. Most say the change is a bad one, and the time chosen worse. Yet none of them can say who they would like to have in command of this army, while any change just at this time will have the effect of dampening the ardour of the men, and causing much delay.[78]

Michigander Henry Morrow, speaking to Henry Raymond of *Scribner's Monthly,* explained the lack of confidence in Burnside: "Because he had no confidence in himself; he had said more than once that he did not feel competent to command that army. I spoke of this as only the natural modesty of a truly capable man. Yes, he said, that was true; but he (General B.) had not only *spoken* of his incompetency, but had gone before the Congressional Committee and *sworn* to it."[79] In Raymond's final assessment, "There was a good deal of dissatisfaction—or, rather, of despondency—among the officers and men."[80]

George Meade seconded that assessment. "The army is filled with gloom and greatly depressed," he confided to his wife. "Burnside, it is said, wept like a child, and is the most distressed man in the army, openly says he is not fit for the position, and that McClellan is the only man we have who can handle the large army collected together."[81] As the days passed, this last point seemed to gnaw at Meade:

> With all my respect, and I may almost say affection, for Burnside—for he has been most kind and considerate towards me—I cannot shut my eyes to the fact that he was

> not equal to the command of so large an army. He had some very positive qualifications, such as determination and nerve, but he wanted knowledge and judgment, and was deficient in that enlarged mental capacity which is essential in a commander. Another drawback was a very general opinion among officers and men, brought about by his own assertions, that the command was too much for him. This greatly weakened his position.[82]

Meade also predicted—incorrectly, as it would turn out—the consequences of McClellan's removal: "[It will] keep Hooker away, if he can possibly avoid coming, as I know he will not serve voluntarily under Burnside. Still, it is said Hooker has injured himself very much by his prolonged stay in Washington, where he has talked too much and too indiscreetly, and that he is not now half as strong as when he went there."[83] Despite the dislike between the two men, Hooker returned to the army on November 10 as one of Burnside's top lieutenants; his new placement only made Hooker's tongue wagging more discreet. In one such surreptitious conversation, he told Meade "he expected to have the Army of the Potomac. . . . Hooker gave one or two hints at Burnside and rather hinted it might not be very long yet before he was in command."[84] Events at Fredericksburg would embolden Hooker even more.

As McClellan departed for his home in Trenton, New Jersey, and Burnside settled in, the army tried to put its best face forward for their new commander. "[We] received him—[Burnside] handsomely—but not enthusiastically," wrote Marsena Patrick. "He was well pleased & all seemed gratified. . . . He appeared well—very well, but all seemed to think there was one they liked much better."[85]

Not that everyone was sad to see McClellan go. A Pennsylvania officer said "very many thought that the President had good cause for his removal."[86] New Yorker Josiah Favill conceded, "The change is undoubtedly for the best," but he added, "Nobody expects much from Burnside."[87] However, William Taylor, an infantryman in the One Hundredth Pennsylvania, suggested they didn't expect worse from Burnside, either. "Burnside is a good general too & will do us well enough," he said.[88] In fact, remarked Isaac Morrow of the 122nd Pennsylvania, "The majority of our regiment are better pleased since Burnside has the command of the army of Virginia," although he admitted, "Weather [*sic*] it is for the better I do not know."[89] Other units exhibited a similar ambivalence. "The new change in commanders of the army of the Potomac we hope will prove beneficial," wrote J Henrie of the Fifteenth Connecticut. "It is not for us to form an opinion, yet many are glad that Burnside has command, and others are sorry."[90]

That ambivalence over Burnside, coupled with the wider sense of aggrievement over McClellan, would cause morale problems for the new army commander that would never quite go away. "It is quite plain that until this feeling is allayed, no commander will likely to succeed with this army," warned Pvt. John Haley of the Seventeenth Maine. "It is the theme at all times and all places, growled out at the mess table, around the campfires, and on picket. We think 'little Mac' the smartest and most ill-used person on earth and are convinced that nothing can crush the Rebellion unless he is in command. No stone is left unturned to keep alive this feeling of distrust among the privates and lower-grade officers. Burnside has to contend with all this festering and fomenting."[91] As events unfolded under Burnside's leadership, the downhill slide would eventually turn into freefall.

CHAPTER 2

THE CAMPAIGN BEGINS, NOVEMBER 7–DECEMBER 10, 1862

2. Ambrose Burnside Moves to Fredericksburg

Situation

On the night George McClellan was relieved from command, Brig. Gen. Herman Haupt, the chief of the Union army's Bureau of Railroads, had joined McClellan for supper. Assistant Secretary of War Peter H. Watson had confidentially advised Haupt of the pending change in leadership, and so as the generals dined, Haupt knew what the army commander did not: this was McClellan's last supper. "He seemed to be entirely ignorant at the time of the fact that, within one hour, he would be relieved," Haupt later noted. "He was speaking to me of proposed operations, which I knew he would have no opportunity to carry into effect."[1]

Haupt figured very much into those proposed operations. During the inexhaustible exchange of messages and telegrams between Washington and the Army of the Potomac's headquarters, McClellan shone a stark spotlight on the army's sore lack of supplies. While Quartermaster General Montgomery Meigs, General-in-Chief Henry Halleck, Secretary of War Edwin Stanton, President Lincoln, and General McClellan all had fingers to point and

Brig. Gen. Montgomery Meigs, as quartermaster general of the United States Army, is one of least appreciated architects of Union victory. Library of Congress.

questions to ask, the railroads ran through the heart of the discussion. The Army of the Potomac was roughly equivalent in population to 1860 Chicago; having what amounted to a small city's worth of men encamped in western Maryland taxed the railroads' infrastructure. However, as long as Washington provided the supplies and the army provided the manpower to load and unload them, Haupt kept the trains running. A serious-looking man with a Brillo beard and domed forehead, the forty-five-year-old Haupt was, by any measure, a genius at his work.

The brigadier general had proved to be a steady voice of reason in the hypercharged communications between Washington and the Army of the Potomac. For instance, in early October, McClellan settled on a movement of limited scope against Lee's army then hovering around the safety of Winchester. "On no other line north of Washn can the Army be supplied nor can it on any other cover Maryland and Penna," McClellan told Halleck, once more expressing his litany of supply concerns.[2] Lincoln, in contrast, preferred a line of advance to the east of the Blue Ridge Mountains that would cut off Lee's line of communication. McClellan dismissed this route as having little strategic value: "It is important only so long as the enemy remains near Win-

Brig. Gen. Herman Haupt was a genius when it came to railroad operations. Library of Congress.

chester & we cannot follow that line far beyond that point simply because the country is destitute of supplies & we have not sufficient means of transportation to enable us to advance more than 20 or 25 miles beyond a railway or canal terminus."[3]

Haupt's assessment certainly backed McClellan up on this point. "It appears that the [railroad to Winchester] is in very bad order; that even with good ordinary repair and good management, its capacity would not exceed about sixty cars per days," Haupt remarked.[4] "If the object of our military operations should be simply to expel the enemy from Winchester and hold it ourselves without following the enemy further," he argued, reconstructing the road might be feasible. "But I cannot suppose that our armies, if successful in obtaining Winchester, would stop there," Haupt added.[5] Even so, that's what McClellan intended: "[I want] to fight the enemy if they remain near Winchester, or failing in that to force them to abandon the valley of the Shenandoah—then to adopt a new & decisive line of operations which shall strike at the heart of the rebellion."[6] What that decisive line would be, he did not say.

An October 13 rebuke from Lincoln made it clear that McClellan needed to think bigger. "I certainly should be pleased for you to have the advantage of the Railroad from Harper's Ferry to Winchester," the president wrote, "but it wastes all the remainder of autumn to give it to you; and, in fact, ignores the question of time, which can not, and must not be ignored."[7] McClellan then began to cast a wider net for options. By October 24, as he finally prepared to move his army across the Potomac, he asked Haupt to "be ready to supply this Army via the Orange and Alexandria and Manassas Gap Railroads." Haupt was also to be ready to rebuild the railroad from Aquia Landing along the Potomac River southward, and "to be prepared to rebuild the Railroad bridge over the Rappahannock at Fredericksburg, and to supply that road with rolling stock."[8] The Orange and Alexandria (O&A) angled southwest, away from Washington and Richmond. The Potomac–Fredericksburg stretch of the Richmond, Fredericksburg, & Potomac (RF&P) railroad, which McClellan could reach by a march eastward, arrowed straight south toward the Confederate capital. McClellan ordered his army to concentrate around Warrenton, Virginia, which kept his options open.

Haupt, ever a realist, had little good to say about either route. "The road by which your army is to be supplied [the O&A] is a single track, without siding sufficient for long trains, without wood and with insufficient supply of water," he wrote. For good measure, he added that, in the spring, the line had failed to adequately service an army one-fourth the size of the Army of the Potomac. "If you advance far," Haupt remarked, "the operation of the road will present greater difficulty; its protection against raids will be almost impossible, and the breaks of connection will become frequent from various causes."[9]

Once in great shape, the railroad from Aquia to Fredericksburg had been wrecked—ironically, as it would turn out—by Burnside's Ninth Corps during an occupation prior to the Maryland Campaign. "The destruction of this road was an unfortunate piece of vandalism on the part of our troops," Haupt lamented. "If it is absolutely necessary to use this road, extraordinary efforts will be required to reconstruct it in time to be available. . . . The reconstruction of the Rappahannock bridge at this season will be difficult, and the structure, if rebuilt, precarious. Timber at this time is very scarce. Would it not be best to rely on boat and pontoon bridges at Fredericksburg?"[10] Haupt knew Confederates had destroyed the city's railroad bridge the previous spring during a Federal occupation. Confederates had also demolished a wagon bridge between Commerce Street—today known as William Street—and Stafford Heights and another between the north end of town and Falmouth. Nothing remained of them except for "their blackened piers," which a Federal infantryman called "melancholy monuments of the devastation of war."[11]

Burnside, familiar with the absence of bridges at Fredericksburg, apparently proposed the idea of a pontoon bridge to McClellan on two occasions: when it first became apparent the army had to move after Antietam, and again after the movement started. "If he proposed to go to Richmond by land," the Ninth Corps commander said, "he would have to go by way of Fredericksburg." And in this, Burnside added, McClellan "partially agreed with me."[12] To that end, McClellan sent orders on November 6 for the army's pontoon train to move immediately to Washington. He still had not committed to a move toward Fredericksburg, but he wanted to marshal resources that would let him do so if he so desired. However, Brigadier General Buckingham arrived on the snowy evening of November 7, interrupting McClellan's supper with Herman Haupt and disrupting McClellan's plans.

The order that promoted Burnside as McClellan's successor carried a brusque and urgent directive: "Immediately on assuming command of the Army of the Potomac, you will report the position of your troops, and what you propose doing with them."[13] To McClellan's credit, he did not just spend his last days with the army parading before the men so they could cheer for and cry over him. Rather, he spent considerable time conferring with Burnside so that "Ol' Burn" would understand the strategic situation he was inheriting, the dispositions of the army, and the location of the enemy. "I probably knew less than any other corps commander of the positions and relative strength of the several corps of the army," Burnside admitted.[14]

Burnside knew a portion of Lee's army—Longstreet's First Corps—hovered nearby, with the rest of the Confederates still in the valley and potentially able to threaten his rear if he misstepped. Should he try to crush them in detail or slip away from them entirely and make a dash at the Confederate capital? "The taking of Richmond, I think, should be the great object of the campaign," Burnside declared after his consultations, "as the fall of that place would tend more to cripple the rebel cause than almost any other military event, except the absolute breaking up of their army."[15] The question was, How to get there?

Options

<u>Option 1: Go Into Winter Camp</u>

According to historian Frank O'Reilly, "Burnside inherited a strategic situation that had befuddled George McClellan."[16] As such, the simplest choice might have been to beg off doing anything at all. He had never been shy about "unreservedly" expressing to the government that he was "not competent to command such a large army as this," and so he might try to play that card, claiming he needed time to get his head around the situation.[17] Everyone expected the change in command to be tumultuous, so a delay would help smooth over the transition. "The general opinion is that [the new change] hardly does justice to either general," noted Orlando Willcox of Burnside's Ninth Corps, "relieving one while succeeding & putting the other in his shoes to take up his plans, substantially without having time to form new or different ones of his own."[18] Burnside could also contend he needed time to ensure the supply issues that had plagued the army all fall were, indeed, resolved.

But all of these would rightly be seen as nothing more than shabby excuses. Doing nothing wasn't really an option. Burnside knew his predecessor had been fired for having "the slows." So had Don Carlos Buell out west. Furthermore, the Emancipation Proclamation hung like the Sword of Damocles over the army's head. Burnside had to do *something*, he had to be successful at it, and he had to do it *soon*—as the snowstorm that accompanied Buckingham to the army reminded him.

Option 2: Move Toward Culpeper

In his October 13 letter, President Lincoln had urged McClellan to move along the east face of the Blue Ridge Mountains in an attempt to isolate Lee from the Confederate capital. "One of the standard maxims of war, as you know, is 'to operate upon the enemy's communications as much as possible without exposing your own,'" Lincoln wrote. By crossing the Potomac below instead of above the Blue Ridge Mountains, McClellan could immediately menace those Confederate communications. If the opportunity presented itself, McClellan could "press closely to him [Lee], fight him if a favorable opportunity should present, and, at least, beat him to Richmond on the inside track." After all, the Union commander would be closer to Richmond than Lee was. "Why can you not reach there before him, unless you admit that he is more than your equal on the march," Lincoln asked, prodding McClellan. "His route is the arc of a circle, while yours is the chord."[19]

With its discussion of communication lines, interior versus exterior lines, pressing the campaign toward a decisive point, and logistics, the content of the letter might have come from military theorist Antoine-Henri Jomini himself.[20] However, Lincoln's tone sounded more like fatherly advice, and he even closed by saying, "This letter is in no sense an order." But as he'd told a confidante, "I saw how [McClellan] could intercept the enemy on the way to Richmond. I determined to make that the test." McClellan obviously failed.

Balanced against this course of action was Haupt's pertinent warning about the state of the army's supply line. He assessed the situation thus: "The

Orange & Alexandria Railroad alone will be a very insecure reliance."[21] Burnside further understood that a move down the railroad toward Culpeper or even Gordonsville amplified those supply issues because he'd be following "a retreating army, well supplied with provisions."[22] Burnside further stated, "The enemy, in my opinion, would not give us a decisive battle at any place this side of Richmond."[23] The general might be able to get a fight out of the Confederates at Gordonsville—perhaps "until such time as they felt they had given us a check," he figured. But even with results in his favor, Burnside predicted benefits for the rebels. "The enemy will have many lines of retreat for his defeated army," he stated, noting that Confederates would be apt to reach Richmond ahead of him "with enough . . . force to render it necessary to fight another battle at that place."[24]

An even greater complication would arise if Lee retreated not toward Richmond but into the Shenandoah Valley toward Staunton, or farther southwest toward Lynchburg. Both options would draw the Army of the Potomac deeper into enemy territory and much farther away from dependable supplies. "The difficulty following them would be very great," Burnside testified.[25]

Finally, a move by Burnside toward the southwest might give Lee enough room to maneuver and an opportunity to slip past the Army of the Potomac on a dash at Washington. Lee had done this in the summer of 1862, culminating in the Battle of Second Manassas. Perennial fear of a repeat engagement would keep the Army of the Potomac tethered to the capital for much of the war.

Option 3: Move to Fredericksburg on the North Bank of the Rappahannock

Burnside had already suggested to McClellan a move toward Fredericksburg because it promised a more secure and more efficient supply line. It also provided two more direct paths to Richmond—the Telegraph Road and the Richmond Road—which would allow the army to advance southward along parallel routes. This would ease congestion while keeping wings of the army close enough to mutually support one another. Fredericksburg also allowed the army to stay between Lee and Washington. Finally, as if having an afterthought inspired by the recent snowstorm—and so requiring no additional explanation—Burnside added, "A great reason for feeling that the Fredericksburg route is the best is, that if we are detained by the elements it would be much better for us to be on that route."[26]

To pull this off, Burnside explained what the Federals would need to do after continuing down the Orange and Alexandria Railroad toward Culpeper: "Make a small movement across the Rappahannock, as a feint, with a view to divert the attention of the enemy, and lead them to believe we were going to move in the direction of Gordonsville."[27] The feint would tie Lee to the upper Rappahannock while the rest of the Army of the Potomac dashed eastward toward Fredericksburg along the river's north bank. There, Burnside could get across the river with the help of pontoons—since, as Haupt had warned, repairs to the railroad bridge would be almost impossible on such short notice at this time of year. Burnside knew McClellan had, fortuitously, already sent orders to mobilize the army's pontoon trains.

To steal a march on Robert E. Lee required speed—not a given, considering the reputation of the army's former commander for "the slows." If Burnside could get across the river before Lee could react, though, the road to Richmond lay open.

Option 4: Move to Fredericksburg on the South Bank of the Rappahannock

A feint toward Culpeper could also potentially open a route to Fredericksburg along the south bank of the Rappahannock River. That would avoid the potential difficulties of a river crossing in the city. The downside to this movement was that it could potentially pin the Federal army between the Rappahannock and its southerly sister the Rapidan, which converged into a *V* several miles upriver of Fredericksburg. The army could make use of a number of fords to get across both rivers, but effective opposition by Lee's cavalry could easily tangle the Federal advance. In that case, not only would Burnside lose any initiative, but portions of his army could also become isolated from one another and more vulnerable to attack. His whole force could become bottlenecked.

A movement on the south bank would also keep the army tied to its inadequate supply line along the O&A. Burnside would have to occupy the city before he could reestablish the Richmond, Fredericksburg, & Potomac Railroad as a line of supply, and to do that while also staving off attacks from Lee might open the door to unnecessary complication under urgent circumstances.

Alternatively, Lee could let Burnside go and instead make a dash at Washington. Burnside would be trapped south of the Rappahannock, while Lee could move with impunity north of the river.

Decision

On November 9, before McClellan had even left the army, Burnside forwarded his plan to the War Department. He would feint toward Culpeper, "then make a rapid move of the whole force to Fredericksburg, with a view to a movement upon Richmond from that point."[28]

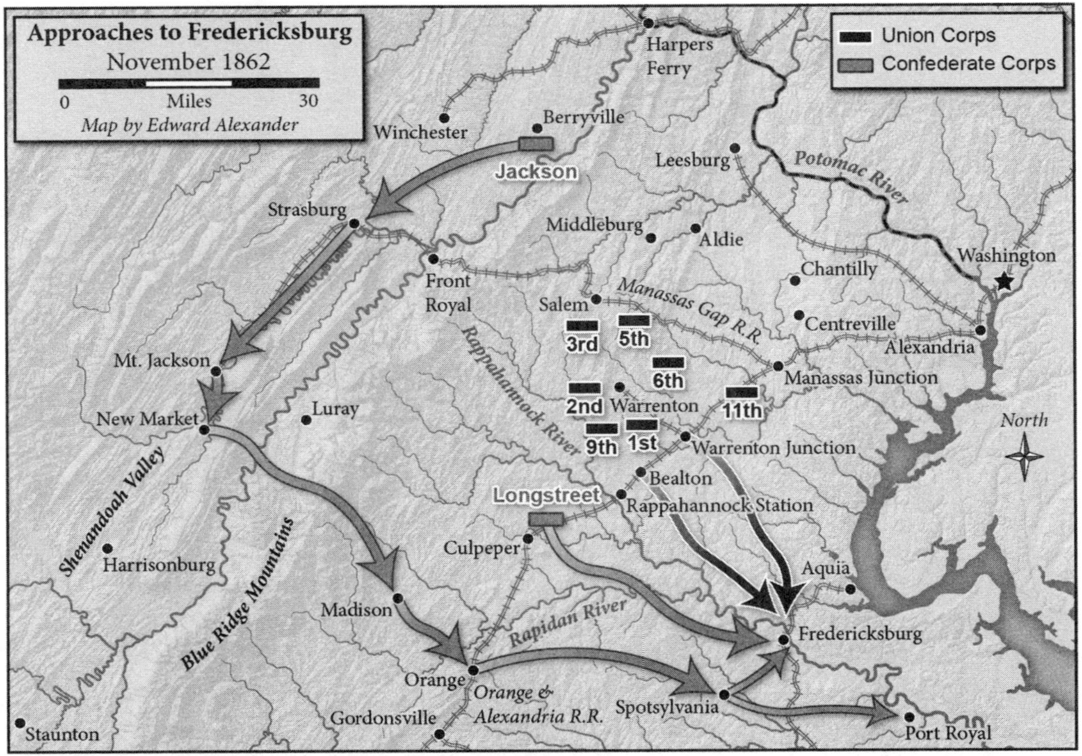

Federals had an inside track to Fredericksburg, from which they could make a dash due south at Richmond. However, this plan would first require getting across the Rappahannock River. With his smaller army split into two wings, Lee had to play defense. Edward Alexander.

"This plan had been fully matured," he said, "and was at the time understood to be in accordance with the views of most of the prominent officers in the command."

Haupt agreed. "Will do all in my power to carry out your wishes, and keep things moving," he wired Burnside. "Movement in everything and everywhere is essential."[29]

Despite the plan's internal support, Lincoln balked. He wanted his O&A plan, and he sent Halleck to Warrenton on November 13 to impress his view on the new army commander. Halleck brought Haupt and Meigs for support. "During that night and the next morning, we had long consultations," Burnside reported. "General Halleck was strongly in favor of continuing the movement of the army in the direction of Culpeper and Gordonsville, and my own plan was as strongly adhered to by me."[30]

Meigs and Haupt, keenly aware of the logistical issues involved, apparently threw their weight behind Burnside. Haupt went so far as to describe the Fredericksburg route as "a military necessity."[31] Burnside stated his impression when the meeting concluded: "If the President approved my plan, I was to move the main army to Falmouth, opposite Fredericksburg, and there cross the Rappahannock on pontoon bridges, which were to be sent from Washington."[32]

Halleck recounted a different story a year later, ostensibly to deflect from his own culpability in the disaster that eventually unfolded. Burnside, he said, "finally consented to so modify his plan as to cross his army by the fords of the Upper Rappahannock, and to move down and seize the heights south of Fredericksburg, while a small force was to be sent north of the river to enable General Haupt to reopen the railroad."[33] In other words, Halleck claimed to leave the meeting with the impression that Burnside would move to Fredericksburg on the south bank of the Rappahannock (Option 4). Ever covering his own back end, Halleck also went so far as to discredit any role in approving the plan Burnside adopted—apparently against Halleck's will:

> It has been inferred . . . his plan of marching his whole army on the north of the Rappahannock, from Warrenton to Falmouth, had been approved by authorities in Washington, and that he expected, on his arrival there, to find supplies and pontoons, with gunboats to cover his crossing. In the first place, that plan was never approved, nor was he ever authorized to adopt it.[34]

Unfortunately, says historian Frank O'Reilly, "Records are sketchy on what was discussed or promised, and we are left with conflicting testimony given after the fact, and colored by the outcome of the campaign."[35] What we do know is that Halleck wired to Burnside on November 14, "The president has just assented to your plan. He thinks that it will succeed, if you move very rapidly; otherwise not."[36]

Results

With that ambivalent blessing, Burnside set his army in motion at daylight on November 15. He had not been idly waiting for the order to move. In the intervening time, he had reorganized his army into so-called grand divisions, with each one containing several corps. The idea was to reduce the number of direct reports to the army commander while also outsourcing some of the annoying administrative duties that encumbered army headquarters. Maj. Gen. Edwin "Bull" Sumner oversaw the Second and Ninth Corps. Maj. Gen. Joe Hooker oversaw the Third and Fifth Corps, and Maj. Gen. William Franklin oversaw the First and Sixth Corps. John Haley of the Seventeenth Maine described the officers as "a trio of veterans no less celebrated that [*sic*] the bumptious individuals who command the other side:

> General Franklin is considered an especially able officer, and Hooker a very dashing one. Summer is the soul of

Maj. Gen. Edwin V. "Bull" Sumner and his staff, photographed in Warrenton, Virginia, just before the start of his movement to Fredericksburg. Library of Congress.

> patriotism and not given to jealousies and growling as some others we know. As for Franklin, he is very envious of Burnside and exceedingly angry over McClellan's removal. Burnside might, with reason, suspect Franklin of treachery. Instead, he has entrusted Franklin with a highly important part of his plan (if he has a plan) and put him in command of nearly one-half of our army.[37]

This army reorganization, while important, qualifies as an important decision rather than a critical decision because it didn't affect the flow of the campaign in a material way. Burnside would still have moved toward Fredericksburg, for instance, or down the O&A, regardless of the structure of his army. The reorganization would affect the battle on a tactical level, though. Burnside's choice of Franklin would prove fateful, but not for the reasons John Haley worried about.

On November 15, Sumner's grand division led off the march toward Fredericksburg. Hooker and Franklin followed the next day. By the seventeenth, Sumner's lead elements marched into Falmouth, opposite Fredericksburg. Artillery opened on them from the south bank but were quickly silenced. "The enemy do not seem to be in force on the opposite side," Burnside observed.[38]

He had beaten Robert E. Lee to Fredericksburg.

Impact

It's worth noting that Burnside identified Richmond as "the great object of the campaign" because he thought the fall of the Confederate capital would

Fredericksburg on the far side of the Rappahannock, as viewed from Falmouth on the north bank. Library of Congress.

have a "crippling effect." The only thing more devastating, he said, would be "the absolute breaking up of their [the Confederacy's] army." Yet Lincoln's suggested plan to operate along the Orange and Alexandria Railroad—a move that would cut the Army of Northern Virginia off from Richmond and, ideally, bring it into combat with the Army of the Potomac—could have broken up the rebel force. Burnside seems to have discounted that outcome, though, choosing instead a course of action he literally defined as the next-best thing. For a general who'd earned a reputation as a man of action, this could seem a curious choice.

Combat surely would have awaited him down the O&A. Robert E. Lee understood that the farther along that line the Army of the Potomac advanced, the more vulnerable it would be. "The enemy's strength will . . . decrease the farther he removes from his base," Lee wrote to Richmond on November 7, the very day McClellan was relieved. The rebel commander added, "I hope an opportunity will offer for us to strike a successful blow."[39]

On the surface, it might be hard to judge the results of Burnside's choice versus the results had he followed Lincoln's plan. However, hindsight lets us see a year into the future, to the fall of 1863. By then, George Gordon Meade had risen to command of the Army of the Potomac, and he sparred with the Army of Northern Virginia for months along the axis of the Orange and Alexandria Railroad. After the November 7 Battle of Rappahannock Station, Meade faced a choice similar to the one Burnside confronted in November 1862: continue moving along the O&A, or move east to Fredericksburg and the many logistical advantages it offered.

Lincoln expressly forbade Meade from moving to Fredericksburg. "He does not see that the proposed change of base is likely to produce any favorable result," Halleck replied to Meade on Lincoln's behalf, "while its disadvantages are manifest."[40] The president said the country could scarcely survive another end-of-the-year defeat there. With his hands thus tied, Meade made the best of his situation but quickly found his ability to maneuver severely hampered. After the failed effort to get into Lee's rear that ended along the banks of Mine Run, Meade returned to the Culpeper area and settled in to winter camps. By that time, the O&A had undergone significant improvements. Although Mosby's Rangers always made security an issue, the infrastructure of the line could finally support the necessary traffic to adequately supply the army—but it took the strains of the fall of 1862 to realize the work that needed to be done.

One final bit of context bears discussion: as Burnside considered his options, he seems not to have worried about Stonewall Jackson's corps in the valley beyond its ability to assault his flank or harass his supply line. That is,

Jackson, who'd earned his fame with lightning-fast movements and unexpected offensives, could have easily launched a northward invasion from his position in Winchester. Yet Burnside discounted the possibility. He believed enough Federal forces stretched along the Potomac from Harpers Ferry to Washington to discourage any sortie by Stonewall against the capital. Beyond that, Burnside predicted, "It is hardly probably that he [Jackson] would attempt any serious invasion of Pennsylvania at this season of the year." "And even if he should," the Federal officer added, "the destruction of that force would be the result very soon after winter set in." Oddly, though, Burnside seemed willing to make a trade-off. "The destruction of property by [Jackson] would be small in comparison with the other expenses of the war," he said, adding, "The loss of a half a dozen of our towns and cities in the interior of Pennsylvania could well be afforded" if Richmond were captured.[41]

3. Robert E. Lee Defends Fredericksburg

Situation

"We will . . . endeavor to confuse and confound [the Army of the Potomac] as much as our circumstances will permit," Robert E. Lee wrote to Stonewall Jackson on November 14.[42] He intended to embarrass and retard the movements of the enemy and "baffle his designs by maneuvering, rather than . . . resist his advance by main force."[43]

Jackson, at the time, remained in the Shenandoah Valley with the army's Second Corps, blocking any Federal movement in that direction and hovering as a vague threat to the Army of the Potomac's right flank and rear. Meanwhile, the army's First Corps under James Longstreet lurked in the vicinity of Upperville "to observe the enemy's movement in front."[44]

Combined, the two wings of the army would be able to muster some seventy-eight thousand men—a dramatic improvement compared to the depleted Confederate force that had fought at Sharpsburg, which might have totaled thirty-seven thousand men. As more soldiers returned to the ranks, keeping the wings separated made supply problems easier to deal with. The separation also gave Lee options for movement. However, depending on Federal intentions, Lee might need to unite the army quickly—something he began to worry about more and more as bad weather made roads less dependable.

The problem, of course, was that Lee didn't know when the Army of the Potomac would move or in which direction. "Whether he [Burnside] will cross the Rappahannock or proceed to Fredericksburg I cannot tell," Lee

By November 1862, Gen. Robert E. Lee had strung together a series of victories for the Confederacy that changed the momentum of the war. Library of Congress.

informed Jackson. "In the apparent & probable need of all our forces southward, the force under you is too far from the scene of action. If an advance toward Fredericksburg is discovered it is plain that you cannot delay longer and you must be prepared to move at any time."[45]

Indeed, the man who intended to befuddle his enemy seemed befuddled himself.

Itching for something to do, and with no word of any Federal movement, Lee began eyeing the O&A and the RF&P. "If I could ascertain that he [Burnside] would pursue either of these routes, I should commence [breaking up the railroads] at once," he said. Lee refrained only because of his "reluctance to perpetuate what might prove an unnecessary injury to the community" by destroying any railroad needlessly.[46] This practice fell in line with his general belief that the army should be as easy on the civilian populace as possible. For instance, Lee warned his son Rooney, who commanded a cavalry brigade, "to permit no . . . depredation upon the citizens" and to pay for any articles the men consumed on their journeys.[47]

On November 15, Lee ordered the Sixty-First Virginia Infantry and the "Norfolk Blues" Light Artillery toward Fredericksburg to glean what they could. If Federals weren't occupying the city, the detachment was to occupy it themselves. If the Federals did occupy the city, the Confederates were to move southward and take possession of the RF&P where it crossed the North Anna River. [48]

But the very next morning, Burnside set his army into motion, first with a feint along the O&A. Lee remained in the dark as to the Federals' intentions: "Whether [Burnside acts] with a view of massing them on that line of communication, to threaten Gordonsville, or to fall down upon Fredericksburg, or to retire towards Alexandria, to be transferred by water south of the James River, I cannot yet discover."[49] That day, the Confederate commander reported to Jefferson Davis that he'd originally expected a move toward Fredericksburg. But the general also declared, "There is nothing to show his [the enemy's] purpose in that direction beyond the guards established on the roads leading to Fredericksburg."[50] Furthermore, Lee hadn't received news about any repairs to the railroad between Aquia and Fredericksburg, "which would naturally precede such a movement" in order to supply the Federal army.[51] "I should think some provision would be made for subsisting a large army if a movement upon Fredericksburg was designed," he told Davis. Word of Haupt's urgent work, only days underway, hadn't yet reached the Army of Northern Virginia.

Word of Sumner's arrival in Falmouth arrived much quicker. The Federals had stolen a march on him, Lee realized—but at least now he knew their plan.

Options

Lee's November 15 order to his son W. H. F. "Rooney" Lee directed the cavalry detachment's movements and laid out the two options available, depending on the location of the Federals: Fredericksburg or the North Anna River.

Option 1: Fredericksburg

The Rappahannock River provided a natural barrier that Lee could incorporate as part of any defense he set up in the city. Just before it reached the Fredericksburg, the Rappahannock ran through a valley of high bluffs before spilling over its fall line and bending from an west–east course into one that flowed more south–southeast. As it did so, the river valley widened. On the north/east bank, Stafford Heights towered over the waterway and dominated the city, which sat just past the riverbend on a low shelf of land about forty feet above the water. The heights on the city side of the river—the south/west bank—didn't hug the water, instead standing anywhere from a mile to

Landscape restoration in 2014 allows visitors to Chatham Manor to see a view of Fredericksburg similar to the one enjoyed by Federal forces in late 1862. Chris Mackowski.

a mile and a half away from it. "The hills . . . rise 300 or 400 feet higher and make a quarter circle back of and above the town, reaching to the river about three miles up," a Federal artillerist later described. "Just below the town . . . I could see a vast flat of apparently fine land with the range of hills running along its south side, but more broken, and lower than they are back of the town itself."[52]

With his engineer's eye, Lee had reason to be leery of the topography. "If the enemy attempt to cross the river I shall resist it, though the ground is favorable to him," Lee told Richmond.[53] He also had the city and its citizens to consider. The war in the East had largely skirted towns or passed through them on the march, but the pending crisis threatened to place Fredericksburg squarely between the two armies. Lee's concern for civilians would have weighed heavily on his conscience.

Option 2: The North Anna River

Located some thirty miles south of Fredericksburg and running in a west–east course, the North Anna River offered the same steep banks as the Rappahannock but without similar topographical disadvantages on the south bank. The North Anna was not as wide as the Rappahannock, but in bad weather, that added to its effectiveness as a barrier. The river's narrow course and steep banks meant water rose dramatically and flowed quickly in inclement conditions.

As seen here, where modern Route 1 crosses the North Anna River, the riverbanks are steep and high, posing a logistical problem for crossing. Chris Mackowski.

Hanover Junction sat just behind the North Anna River, which meant Lee's army would have a ready source of supplies from both the RF&P, running up from Richmond, and the Virginia Central Railroad, running in from the northwest. Lee knew Burnside would make the rail junction a target of any campaign toward the Confederate capital, which lay only twenty miles beyond. This proximity to Richmond also meant supplies and reinforcements would reach Lee quicker than if they had to go all the way to Fredericksburg.

The North Anna line had its disadvantages, though. According to Southern historian Henry A. White, writing in 1897, "The Richmond authorities were anxious to save Virginia's territory from devastation." They therefore discouraged Lee from taking up an initial position along the North Anna because "the Confederate Government held the corn crops between the Rappahannock and North Anna rivers." White contended that the Davis administration's "fatal defensive policy" prioritized the cornfields as being "of more importance than the strategic advantage of luring Burnside as far as the Anna, where a Federal defeat, so far from water communication, would most probably result in the destruction of the Army of the Potomac."[54] It's hard to say whether the flaw in logic was Davis's or White's, but in late November, there would have been no corn in the fields to worry about, so this seems a moot point, although history has nonetheless remembered it.

Regardless, as a military commander, Lee was not deaf to political concerns. He certainly would have understood the drawbacks of giving up thirty miles of Virginia real estate without a fight.

Decision

"At the first disclosure," recalled James Longstreet, "[Lee] was inclined to move for a position behind the North Anna, as at that time the position behind Fredericksburg appeared a little awkward for the Confederates. . . . Defence behind the Anna would have been stronger, but the advantage of the enemy's attack would also have been enhanced there. Then, too, anticipation of the effect of surprising the enemy in their intended surprise had some influence in favor of Fredericksburg."[55]

Lee split the difference by sending the division of Maj. Gen. Lafayette McLaws to Fredericksburg and the division of Brig. Gen. Robert Ransom toward the North Anna. The rest of Longstreet's Corps soon followed, first toward the North Anna. However, once Lee realized the Federals had not yet crossed the Rappahannock, he redirected the corps to Fredericksburg. Longstreet's men remembered the terrible weather during the movement. "Night rainy and 'dark as Erebus,' roads deep with mud," wrote artillerist William Miller Owen of the circuitous march. "[It was] raining in torrents."[56]

Confederates filed into town in the midst of a flood of civilians leaving. "A grand exodus is going on," Owen wrote, describing the scene as follows: "All day long we met people, old and young, leaving the city, carrying their household gods with them. Carts and wagons containing their bedding, etc., going to the rear. Children and women all in the procession." Harried initially by the Fifteenth Virginia Cavalry, four companies of Mississippi infantry, and a light battery of field artillery, then later by the Sixty-First Virginia Infantry and the Norfolk Blues, Federals had retaliated by demanding the surrender of the city under threat of bombardment. Lee withdrew his men, but he warned that he would resist any Federal attempt at occupation. Soon, Confederate wagons and ambulances joined in to assist the evacuation of the city. "It was a piteous sight," Lee told his wife, Mary. "But they have brave hearts."[57]

Lee did not understand why Burnside had not yet forced a crossing, but with half of the Army of Northern Virginia now ensconced atop Marye's Heights, the Confederate commander intended to block the way if he could. "The longer we can delay him [Burnside] and throw him into winter, the more difficult will be his undertaking," Lee wrote to Davis. "It is for this reason that I have determined to resist him at outset, and to throw every obstacle in the way of his advance."[58] Delaying Burnside at the river's edge also offered the additional advantage of buying time for Jackson to arrive from the valley.

All the while, Lee kept an eye toward the North Anna. Any advance by Burnside, once across the Rappahannock, would be in that direction. Ideally, Lee could fall back, coaxing Burnside to follow. He could tear up the railroad as he withdrew, too, which would force Burnside to depend on a large wagon train and, in turn, slow the Army of the Potomac and limit its supplies. Destroying the railroad would have a negative impact on the local citizenry, though, and Lee worried about their reaction. "I therefore do not wish to undertake it without due consideration," he told Davis, "and should you think it preferable to concentrate the troops nearer to Richmond, I should be glad if you would advise me."[59]

On the Federal side of the Rappahannock, George Meade expected Lee to take this very course or something quite similar:

> Their policy is to draw us as far as possible from the Potomac and then to attack our rear, cut off if possible our lines of communication and supply, and compel us, in order to keep these open, so to weaken our force in front as to prevent our attacking them, and enabling them, if they can collect sufficient for, to attack us. Of course, they will dispute every available point on the road, and hold us in check at each place as long as they can, but I do not look for any general engagement till we get to [Hanover Junction].[60]

In the meantime, Lee hunkered down with the forty thousand men of Longstreet's First Corps along the heights beyond Fredericksburg. Keeping in close contact with Jackson still in the valley and a close eye on Burnside across the river, the Confederate commander waited for the Federals to make the next move.

Results/Impact

Lee's aide Walter Taylor saw the officer's occupation of Fredericksburg through the lens of adoration: "Again, General Lee gave 'check!'"[61] However, Lee clearly lost the race to Fredericksburg, and Burnside stayed out of the city through no effort or genius of Lee's. Burnside *would* eventually come to grief in Fredericksburg, in no small part because of the dominating topographical advantage Lee secured by occupying the heights, but until Burnside made a move, the heights offered Lee little more than a tall perch from which to worry.

History also allows us to assess, at least partially, the possible outcome of a move to the North Anna. As fate would have it, Lee and Burnside would meet along the banks of that river in May 1864 as part of Ulysses S. Grant's Overland Campaign. Burnside's Ninth Corps would make up the center prong of Grant's push across the river, and the unit was given the task of crossing at Ox Ford. Lee created his opposing defenses in an inverted *V*, with the apex on the commanding high ground overlooking that ford. "The enemy's side of the river is densely wooded along its bank," Burnside reported, "with high ground in rear, with one battery in position, flanked by rifle pits, and it is reported that there is another line of rifle pits in front." The ford itself was rough and deep. "The prospects of success are not all that flattering," Burnside admitted, "but I think the attempt can be made without any very disastrous results, and we may possibly succeed."[62]

He did not—and neither did the rest of the Union army. However, Lee fell ill and couldn't take advantage of the trap he'd laid, allowing the Federals to escape.[63]

Lee's inverted *V*—his strongest and most ingenious defensive position of the war—resulted from a bit of inspired improvisation by his chief engineer, Maj. Gen. Martin Luther Smith, who was not with the Army of Northern Virginia in November 1862. Therefore, it's hard to know exactly what kind of defensive line Lee would have established along the river had he moved there instead of Fredericksburg.

4. Burnside Crosses at Fredericksburg

Situation

On May 24, 1863, just a day after his thirty-ninth birthday, Ambrose Burnside sat comfortably ensconced in his Cincinnati headquarters as the commander of the Department of Ohio. Surrounded by the men of his beloved Ninth Corps, Burnside felt relieved to be well away from the political viper's nest that was the Army of the Potomac. His former army, now under Joe Hooker's management, had recently suffered another loss—this one at Chancellorsville—but word had reached Burnside that some officers were still refighting the Battle of Fredericksburg from the previous December. Drawn into the controversy even from faraway Ohio, Burnside sat down to pen a reply.

"I have always felt and said," he wrote, "it was the wish of the government that I should be successful in every enterprise that I have undertaken, and it was their intention to give me all the support in their power. It is true that my views have not always coincided with theirs, but they were the superiors, and I hope that I have always cheerfully obeyed."[64]

A word most often associated with Burnside is *affable. Amiable* and *good-natured* also come to mind—and if nothing else, this passage reflects Burnside's good nature. Perhaps, too, it reflects the softening of attitudes that comes with the passage of time and the resulting distance from events.

On November 18, 1862, with his army prepared to strike at Fredericksburg—which was guarded by only a token Confederate force—Burnside was unable to get across the Rappahannock River because of a lack of bridging materials. As a result, the Union general felt anything but fully supported by Washington's power. His movement on Fredericksburg, which he had clearly outlined to Halleck and Lincoln, had "contemplated . . . the prompt starting of the pontoons from Washington." The pontoons would meet Sumner's grand division as it arrived in Falmouth, allowing Sumner to immediately cross the river, capture the town, and occupy the heights beyond.

"This was not a private conversation," said Joe Hooker, who sat in on Burnside's meeting with the delegation from the War Department. Halleck or Meigs—Hooker couldn't remember which—said everything could be ready in three days, a point Hooker repeated in his testimony to an investigative committee days after the battle. "They said that they thought they

Brig. Gen. Daniel Woodbury failed to act with alacrity when ordered to move the pontoons from the upper Potomac to Burnside's army. Library of Congress.

Lieut. Cyrus Comstock, Burnside's chief engineer, bore responsibility for getting the pontoons, although he had little control over the actual process. Library of Congress.

Maj. Ira Spaulding of the 50th New York Engineers had the woeful task of getting pontoons to the Army of the Potomac through bad weather and high water. Library of Congress.

could have the pontoons ready, stores landed, and everything in readiness to advance in three days," Hooker attested. "I remember that I thought that was marvellous [*sic*] at the time; that it was within the range of human possibility to do that."[65]

"I supposed this would be attended to," Burnside said. But on November 14, just before his army started on its march and at a time when he was "feeling anxious to know something definite," he asked his chief engineer, Lieut. Cyrus Comstock, to follow up with Brig. Gen. Daniel Woodbury, commanding the Engineer Brigade. When Comstock did not receive an immediate reply, Burnside had him telegraph again, urging Woodbury to forward the pontoons as promptly as possible.[66]

The engineer finally replied the following day. The pontoons, he said, had just begun to arrive in Washington from Harpers Ferry and Berlin on the upper Potomac, and they should be ready to head south by the sixteenth or seventeenth. This was Burnside's "first information of delay," and it must certainly have flabbergasted him: he knew McClellan had ordered the mobilization of the pontoon train on November 6.[67] Because of security concerns, though—and unbeknown to Burnside or McClellan—the order went by packet boat rather than some quicker means of transmission. Maj. Ira Spaulding, who was responsible for the pontoons, didn't get the message until

November 12, "when I took immediate measures to carry it out."[68] That same day, Halleck—who knew of Burnside's intentions because of the November 9 memo—told Woodbury, "Transport all your pontoons and bridge materials to Aquia Creek."[69]

When Spaulding reached Washington on the fourteenth and reported to Woodbury, a communication mix-up led the young officer to infer "that the plan for the campaign had been changed with the change of commanders," which caused additional delay. Burnside gave Spaulding the benefit of the doubt for due diligence in prosecuting his work, "but he was not impressed with the importance of speed," and "neither was he empowered with any special authority that would hasten the issuing of the necessary transportation."[70]

Burnside later admitted to the investigating committee, "I could have sent officers of my own there to attend to those matters, and perhaps I made a mistake in not doing so, as General Halleck afterwards told me that I ought not to have trusted them in Washington for the details."[71] The slippery Halleck went far beyond that, in fact, resorting to great contortions to deflect blame for the debacle onto anyone but himself. So much for "all the support in their power."

Burnside knew that Lee now knew the whereabouts of the Army of the Potomac, and he expected the Confederate commander to respond with alacrity. If the pontoons got underway as promised, Burnside thought he might yet get across the river before Lee could stop him. Doing so would also present an excellent opportunity to engage Longstreet's Corps in detail. "We wanted to meet this force and beat it before Jackson could make a junction with them," Burnside hoped, "or before Jackson could come down on our flank and perhaps cripple us."[72]

However, Spaulding had difficulty equipping the pontoon train, which delayed his departure until November 19. Poor weather and bad roads then delayed him on the march. "It rained a dull, heavy, sleeting rain, just enough to make us all feel lonely, cheerless [and] desolate," Capt. Wesley Brainerd of the Fiftieth New York Engineers recalled of the journey.[73] "The Army was waiting for us and obstacles seemed to accumulate as they had never done before. The situation was extremely unpleasant. . . . Messengers continued to arrive with orders for us to 'hurry up.'"[74]Spaulding tried to speed things along by sending half the pontoons by water, but Burnside didn't get his bridging material until the night of the twenty-fifth.[75]

"By this time the enemy had concentrated a large force on the opposite side of the river," Burnside wrote, "so that it became necessary to make arrangements to cross in the face of a vigilant and formidable foe."[76]

Options

Option 1: Cross Upriver by One of the Fords

As soon as Joe Hooker realized the army was bottlenecked on the north bank of the Rappahannock, and days before the arrival of the pontoon train, he suggested a crossing upriver from Fredericksburg. "When a move of that sort should be attempted," he later conceded, "the enemy would know of it as soon as we commenced it, and the fords there are of such a character that a few hours' work with so many men as they have would make those places very formidable." But, Hooker added, that still would have been a much better move than any of the other options Burnside had.[77]

Hooker wanted to provision his men for three days, ford the river, then "beat any force of the enemy in front of him." That would give the rest of the army time to build the bridges once the pontoons finally arrived. However, Burnside worried that rising waters from any sudden foul weather might cut Hooker off. "As I had no means of crossing at Fredericksburg I would be prevented from sending him [Hooker] supplies and assistance," he explained. "It would be a very hazardous movement to throw a column like that beyond the reach of its proper support."[78] Subsequent weather proved the general right. "It commenced raining and the river began to rise, not to any great extent, but I did not know how much it might rise," Burnside recalled.[79] Any force on the far side of the river would be cut off from support and supplies.

Even if the weather held—no sure thing in late November—the upriver fords presented other disadvantages. Although shallow above the fall line, the river had an extremely rocky bed just north of town. Those rocks would have made it impossible for anything dependent on a horse to cross the river: artillery, supply wagons, cavalry, or even officers' mounts. Numerous fords of varying quality were located farther upriver, but the army would have to traverse both the Rappahannock and the Rapidan, and Lee could potentially contest both actions. Burnside explored the fords but found Hooker's prediction true: Confederate resistance would make any upriver crossing costly.

Option 2: Cross Downriver at Skinker's Neck

Skinker's Neck, twelve miles downriver, offered a relatively easy crossing site, with a good road on the far side to facilitate the army's movement toward the town of Bowling Green. A downside was that the river was considerably wider and deeper than at Fredericksburg. The rising and falling tide affected it, which would make bridge building trickier. On the upside, the deeper, wider river meant the navy could play a protective role helping the army cross. The river oxbowed at Skinker's Neck—from the Federal side of the river, the bend curved inward, and from the Confederate side, the bend bulged outward. If the army crossed at the apex of the bow, the navy could position gunboats along both sides of it, effectively outflanking any opposing Confederates positioned on the neck of land between. All things considered, engineer Brainerd, who scouted the position, called it "a most magnificent place for a crossing."[80]

Unfortunately, the twelve miles between Falmouth and Skinker's Neck seemed devoid of any other possibilities. Conditions on both sides of the river needed to be just right to support the passage of huge numbers of men and material, but engineers couldn't find a single spot that filled the bill. "When a good position [with] hard ground [and] easy approaches was found on our side . . . the very reverse would appear on the other," Brainerd said.[81] Brainerd even sneaked over to the far bank of the river under the dark of night to scout out locations, but he had no luck.[82]

Option 3: Cross at Fredericksburg

Like Hooker, when Edwin Sumner found himself waiting for absent pontoons, he suggested a river crossing. The foe on the far bank was weak, and he felt confident he could sweep the Confederates away—if he could first get over there. As he cast about for options, he discovered a ford near the former bridge at Falmouth. "But that ford depends upon the tide, which rises above this town," Sumner explained. "That ford is represented to me as being a deep ford, with deep holes in it. Men can skip from rock to rock—a few men at a time. But there are occasionally deep holes, from six to eight feet deep. Such a ford would never be considered practicable for marching troops over."[83]

A dam north of the city also offered a possible crossing point. Built in 1855 by the Fredericksburg Water Power Company, the eighteen-foot-tall dam diverted water into a canal that bypassed the Rappahannock's rapids above the city. A millrace branched from the canal, running just west of downtown before emptying back into the river at the south edge of the city, providing hydropower to mills along the riverfront.[84] While infantry could slip across—literally—Sumner realized the dam would need to be built up to serve as a useful bridge for horses, wagons, and artillery. Once across, the army would then face the canal system, an additional logistical barrier to navigate that would impede momentum.

In any case, Burnside rejected any crossing by Sumner, citing the same reasons he gave Hooker: a force on the far side could be isolated if bad weather made the river suddenly rise. "On reflection," Sumner admitted, "I myself thought that he was right."[85] Subsequent days of rain proved him so.

Alfred Waud sketched himself into this image of the dam that spanned the Rappahannock just above the city. The dam provided water to the canal system and offered a potential crossing point for Federals. Library of Congress.

The longer Sumner stayed opposite the city, the less he liked the army's chances of crossing there. "Throwing our bridges directly over to the town might be attended with great loss, not only from their [the rebels'] artillery, but every house within musket range could be filled with Infantry," he counseled Burnside.[86]

But the army's position offered the important advantage of keeping its supply lines as short as possible—no small consideration with 122,000 men to feed, clothe, and equip (not to mention the army's horses and mules that needed to be cared for). Until the supply base at Aquia Landing was rebuilt and the railroad restored from there to Fredericksburg, the army relied on an insufficient wagon train. The less stress on those logistics, the better.

Burnside began to enumerate other advantages to crossing at Fredericksburg. "In the first place, I felt satisfied that they [Confederates] did not expect us to cross here, but down below," Burnside thought; "in the next place, I felt satisfied that this was the place to fight the most decisive battle, because if we could divide their forces by piercing their lines at one or two points . . . then a vigorous attack with the whole army would succeed in breaking their army in pieces."[87]

Option 4: Withdraw

Withdrawal was never an option for Burnside because of the political pressure directing him to do something. As Sumner later summed it up for congressional investigators, "I knew that neither our government nor our people would be satisfied to have our army retire from this position, or go into winter quarters, until we knew the force that was on the other side of the river; and the only way in which we could learn that was by going over there and feeling them."[88]

At least some of the men in the army thought a withdrawal might happen, though. For instance, when his Eleventh New Jersey received orders to cook four days' worth of rations and be ready to move at sundown on December 10, Col. Robert McAllister didn't know where he and his unit were off to, but he admitted he would not have been surprised by a move back to the Virginia Peninsula to "take the condemned Chickahominy rought." He thought the army might go down the Rappahannock and cross below. But McAllister admitted, "I can't think that we will move across here [at Fredericksburg]. The loss of life would be terable. I do not think it is or has been the intention of our commanders to cross here. This is undoubtedly only a faint."[89]

Decision

"It was the unanimous opinion," Franklin said, "that if this river could be crossed it ought to be crossed, no matter what might happen afterwards."[90]

Sumner, who'd had longer to study the scene than anyone, waved Burnside away from a crossing at Fredericksburg. "Throwing our bridges directly over to the town might be attended with great loss," he warned his commander, "not only from their [Confederates'] artillery, but every house within musket range could be filled with Infantry." His warning would prove prophetic. Sumner instead urged a movement downriver to outflank the Confederate right.[91]

Preparations got underway for a crossing at Skinker's Neck. "But our demonstration in that direction concentrated the enemy at that place, and I finally gave up the idea of crossing there," Burnside later revealed. "I still continued operations at Skinker's Neck by way of demonstration, simply for the purpose of drawing down there as large a force of the enemy as possible."[92] Then, on the evening of December 9, Burnside made a game-time call to change his troops' location. "I think now that the enemy will be more surprised by a crossing immediately in our front than in any other part of the river," he informed Halleck.[93]

The decision provoked "a great deal of division of opinion among the corps commanders," Burnside recounted. He continued, "But, after all the discussion upon the subject, the decision to cross over here [in front of Fredericksburg] I understood was well received by all of them."[94] Sounding either pragmatic or ambivalent, Franklin offered a succinct summary: the potential spots for pontoon crossings in Fredericksburg "were as good as the point further down" at Skinker's Neck.[95]

"It is also possible that we would have done better to have crossed at Skinker's Neck," Burnside later admitted. "But, for what I supposed to be good reasons, I felt we had a better cross here."[96]

Brainerd, with his engineer's eye, wondered about that. "It has long been a question in my mind whether General Burnside fully realized the value of that position or had been fully informed of it superior advantages," he reflected years later. Brainerd elaborated,

> By allowing those boisterous demonstrations to be made when the work could just as well have been done quietly, it soon became the general belief that he intended the whole operation to be a ruse, intending to draw the attention of the enemy in that direction while he perfected his arrangements for the real attack.

Brainerd and his fellow engineering officers thought so little of the Fredericksburg option that, when informed about Burnside's decision, they expected the worst: "We all came to the conclusion that we might now return to our quarters and with great propriety execute our last Wills & Testaments."[97]

Results

George Gordon Meade, writing to his wife on November 22, worried about crossing the river at all:

> I do not see how we can advance from the Rappahannock unless the weather should turn cold and freeze the ground. . . . I question if we can get in the neighborhood of Richmond this winter, on this line. I have no doubt the attempt is to be made and an effort to force us on, but I predict, unless we have a cold spell, freezing the ground, that we will break down, lose all our animals, experience great suffering from want of supplies, and if the enemy are at all energetic, meet with a check, if not disaster.[98]

Events didn't quite play out that way, but only because the army didn't advance far enough for things to get mired and break down. The army did meet a check, though, and by most assessments it met a disaster.

Edwin Sumner went to his dying day—only three months after the battle, as it would turn out—believing that things could have been different. He declared, "I could have taken that city and the heights on the other side of it any time within three days after my arrival here if the pontoons had been here."[99] Hooker and Franklin, who didn't agree on much, agreed on that. "This whole disaster," accused Franklin, "has resulted from the delay in the arrival of the pontoon bridges. Whoever is responsible for that delay is responsible for all the disaster which have followed."[100]

The dominos could be traced all the way back to McClellan's order to move the pontoons back to the capital. Even so, Burnside initially placed the blame on Woodbury and, with Halleck's blessing, placed the engineer under arrest on November 23—two days before the pontoons arrived. When Burnside cooled off, though, he released him. For his part, Woodbury seemed to express as much consternation as Burnside. "Had the emergency been made known to me in any manner I could have disregarded the forms of service—seized teams, teamsters, and wagonmasters for instant service wherever I could find them," he swore. "Then, with good road and good weather, they might have possibly been in time. But I had no warrant for such a course, which, after all, could only have been carried out by the authority of the general-in-chief."[101] If Halleck had authorized Woodbury's arrest as a way to deflect blame down the road, he only made Woodbury throw him under the bus all the quicker. Halleck would get the last lick, though, eventually banishing Woodbury to duty at the Dry Tortugas off the Florida Keys.

"Who was to blame for the disastrous failure at Fredericksburg?" asked engineer Wesley Brainerd. "Investigations were commenced and testimony was taken [but] nothing ever came of it except that General Halleck and the *Pontons* [*sic*] were finally in some indefinite manner held accountable. . . . I suppose the matter would still be under investigation if General Burnside had not promptly stepped forward and assumed the entire responsibility and blame. But everyone knew that he assumed more than he deserved."[102]

Impact

In January, Burnside would try offensive operations once again, turning this time to the fords upriver. However, the weather he so often worried about came into play before the troops could even get across the Rappahannock. A pounding rainstorm turned the roads to muck, and the army bogged down to its wagon axles. Confederates on the south bank mocked the Federals with signs that said, "Burnside stuck in the mud." The so-called Mud March would effectively end Burnside's seventy-seven-day tenure as commander of the Army of the Potomac

In the spring, Joe Hooker, as Burnside's replacement, would replicate much of his predecessor's plan, crossing the army at the upriver fords in an

The Rappahannock River north of the city was shallow enough for soldiers to ford, but the rocky bottom would have proved nearly impossible for artillery or supply wagons, let alone the horses that drew them. Terry Rensel.

attempt to swing behind the Army of Northern Virginia, which was still ensconced in the heights outside Fredericksburg.

The longest-term impact of Burnside's decision echoes down through Civil War memory, and it is best exemplified by a scene in the movie *Gods and Generals*. On a frosty morning, Maj. Gen. Winfield Scott Hancock sees a cow cross the Rappahannock. "Sir, we can cross the river," he tells his corps commander, Darius Couch. "Upstream, a quarter mile. It's shallow enough to ford."

"Ford the river?" Couch asks skeptically. "It's a long way across, General, and it's damned cold. You sure it's shallow?" When Hancock assures him it is, they try to convince Burnside of the opportunity.

"General Hancock, I certainly appreciate your efforts at reconnaissance, but that possibility has been considered and rejected," Burnside says, poo-pooing him. "The pontoons will be here at any time, and then we will be able to not only send the men across, but the wagons and supplies as well. It would be foolhardy to send the men without the wagons." Burnside goes on to warn about the weather—just as he did in real life—and then dismisses Hancock. Hancock is one of the movie's protagonists, so the scene is intended to make him look like a good guy foiled by a bad army bureaucracy and inept generalship. Hancock's solution seems so obvious, Burnside's opposition so thickheaded and *wrong*.[103]

The movie, as a box office dud, didn't do much to besmirch Burnside's reputation with the general public, but it did reinforce Burnside's stereotype among Civil War buffs. Because of the events that followed his decision to cross at Fredericksburg, the general is remembered as a bonehead (or worse). Looking more closely at his options, though, shows that Burnside made what he thought was the best call based on the information he had from the choices before him.

CHAPTER 3

THE FIRST DAY OF FIGHTING, DECEMBER 11, 1862

5. Lee Lets the Federal Army Commit to Its Plan

Situation

"All was quiet, peaceful, calm," said Wesley Brainerd as he stood on the bank of the Rappahannock River on the evening of December 10. "Who could have dreamed that a *terrible tragedy* was soon to be enacted there?"[1]

The engineers had parked their pontoons in a ravine far enough back to conceal them from observers across the river. "As we passed through the different Divisions of the Army every man knew that the moment for action had arrived, for the *Pontons* were moving for the river," Brainerd said. He and his colleagues shared a hearty cup of coffee and, as the sun set, made their way past the Lacy House, today known as Chatham Manor, directly across the river from Fredericksburg. Brainerd and his crew would try to effect a crossing at the north end of the city in the morning; another crew would try to force a crossing at the south end of the city, while a third tried to cross a mile downriver.

Brainerd and his companions descended from Stafford Heights to bottomlands that ran along the river's edge for one final view of their objective. "The moon shone with a quiet light which was reflected from the sparkling snow which scarcely covered the ground," Brainerd recalled. "[Reflections from] little fires here and there on the opposite side of the river glimmered and sparkled from the ice which bordered the stream. On our side of the Stream everything was as quiet as if no enemy or Army had an existance."[2]

Later, under the cover of darkness, the engineers brought the pontoons to the river's edge. "We marched as quietly as possible so as not to disturb the enemy," Brainerd said, "who were expecting us to strike someone but could form no idea of the spot."[3] Burnside, in fact, chose to cross in three spots: two bridges would span the Rappahannock at the upriver edge of town, one at the lower edge of town, and one a mile or so downriver. These would eventually become known as the upper, middle, and lower crossings, respectively.

As Brainerd's team worked, Federal infantry began to mobilize as quietly as possible, and a pair of regiments descended to the riverbank as the engineers' support. Artillery soon began to arrive as well; these took the form of a long line of black cannon, "shotted and ready," their muzzles pointed over the engineers' heads. As carefully as possible but at "a lively rate," teams guided the pontoons down the hill—no small task for boats that measured thirty-one feet long and five and a half feet wide and were packed with bridging materials and tools.[4]

"Then," said Brainerd, "the little fires on the opposite side of the River were one by one extinguished but not a word was spoken or a shout made."[5] The ominous sign spurred the engineers. "Our men sprang to their work as if their lives depending upon their efforts," Brainerd recalled.[6]

For Lee, situated on the far riverbank, the appearance of the bridge builders finally tipped Burnside's hand. For weeks the rebel commander had pondered the Army of the Potomac's inactivity. "They seem to be hesitating, but are very numerous," he wrote to his wife in late November.[7] To Jackson, Lee wondered whether the force in Falmouth might be a diversion while other troops moved to some other quarter. He ordered Jackson east, directing him toward Massaponax, where he could draw supplies from the railroad. "Another storm, which may be anticipated at any time at this season, would render roads impassable and subject . . . troops to labor and suffering," Lee told his subordinate, suggesting that Jackson hustle.[8] November had brought rain aplenty already and "produced a great effect upon the roads."[9]

By November 28, Lee told Jackson, "[I am] of the opinion that the enemy will not attempt to cross the Rappahannock in front of Fredericksburg, but at some point below, if he crosses at all." Lee added, "I have examined the river some ten or twelve miles down, and find the banks generally abrupt and requiring work to make a practicable ingress and egress for their pontoon bridges."[10] This was the same conclusion Brainerd and his scouting parties had come to. However, down at Port Royal, access to the river was easier and gunboats could protect Burnside's crossing—as Brainerd had discovered at nearby Skinker's Neck. The road from Port Royal to Bowling Green, which would lead on to the strategic rail hub of Hanover Junction that Lee worried about, was in good condition.

Upriver, meanwhile, scouts had reconnoitered as far as the Rappahannock's juncture with the Rapidan and found "no favorable points for throwing over a pontoon bridge."[11] Nonetheless, Brig. Gen. Wade Hampton's cavalry kept careful watch on the fords.[12]

By December 2, reports reached Lee that Burnside had divided his forces and sent "a large body" nearly opposite Port Royal. These were actually the work crews preparing Skinker's Neck. "This division of the enemy's force seems to me very strange," Lee admitted, "but so many reports may indicate some movement of the enemy."[13] He responded by ordering D. H. Hill's division of Jackson's Corps toward Port Royal to contest any crossing and raise the alarm to the rest of the Confederate army. This essentially spread Jackson's Corps over a twenty-mile expanse from Hamilton's Crossing, where the Richmond, Fredericksburg, & Potomac passed around the end of the line of hills that stretched south from Fredericksburg, all the way to Port Royal. However, Lee's orders also gave him eyes all along the Rappahannock.

But Burnside still didn't move. "His apparent inaction suggests the probability that he is waiting for expected operations elsewhere," Lee mused to Davis a few days later, but the Confederate commander admitted he had no reliable intelligence about where those operations might be.[14] He noted that he might be able to get some reinforcements from other theaters of the war to bolster his chances against Burnside; alternatively, Davis might still approve a move southward toward the North Anna. Lee quickly added, though, that his army "was never in better health or in better condition for battle than now." He didn't want Davis to mistake his suggestions for signs of trouble or weakness.[15]

But Lee was, indeed, starting to have some non-Burnside-related troubles. In his November 6 note to Davis, he hinted, "Some shoes, blankets, arms, and accoutrements are still wanting." At the same time, Lee remarked that the army was occasionally "receiving small supplies and he stated, "[I hope] all will be provided in time."[16] Two days later, he sounded a more ominous note: "Unless the Richmond and Fredericksburg Railroad is more energetically operated, it will be impossible to supply this army with provisions, and oblige its retirement to Hanover Junction."[17]

As he worried about supplies and about Burnside, Lee considered the options before him.

Options

Option 1: Fall Back to the North Anna

When Jackson rejoined the rest of the Army of Northern Virginia in early December, he objected to the army's position, preferring the North Anna line. "He held that we would win a victory at Fredericksburg, but it would be a fruitless one to us," James Longstreet later recounted, "whereas at North Anna, when we drove the Federals back, we could give pursuit to advantage, which we could not do at Fredericksburg."[18]

Lee had, of course, already given this option a great deal of consideration when he first chose his position on the Rappahannock. Whether he summarized those deliberations for Jackson is not known, but the Second Corps commander, ever obedient to his superior, moved his men into their assigned position and let the North Anna option drop—even as Lee continued to hint about the possibility to officials in Richmond.

Option 2: Go On the Offense

Lee is often remembered for his aggressiveness and offensive-mindedness—particularly early in the war, before his numbers were so drained that the 1864 campaign forced him into a mostly defensive posture. So, even when he first chose to defend Fredericksburg, he must have contemplated ways to take the fight to Burnside rather than passively wait for Burnside to bring the fight to him. However, the topography of the river valley strongly discouraged any such offensive movement. At Fredericksburg, Federal artillery atop Stafford Heights controlled the Rappahannock, making a Confederate crossing from the city impossible. Upriver, Lee would face all the same concerns about the fords that kept Burnside from trying them. Downriver, Lee would not be able to cross undetected, and he would have Union gunboats to worry about. Up or down, he would have to extend a supply line that was already proving weak.

Fresh in Lee's mind, too, was his recent reversal in Maryland. He had taken the strategic initiative only to have George McClellan turn him back. While he had since rebuilt his army—bringing it up to an impressive 78,000 men—Lee still had fewer men than Burnside's 122,000, which meant he had to shepherd his manpower carefully, even with his home-field advantage.

In the end, going on offense was no real option at all.

Option 3: Determine an Appropriate Defensive Strategy

When he chose Fredericksburg, Lee initially determined he would resist Burnside "at the outset." How to do that, though, remained an important tactical decision.

If Lee contested any crossing at the outset, Burnside could call it off and try his luck elsewhere. That would, in turn, keep Lee guessing—and keep draining Lee's resources. In the longer term, the rebel general thought time was on his side because ongoing delays would eventually force Burnside into winter quarters, but in the more immediate term, the uncertainty of Burnside's intentions imposed continual strain on Lee and prevented him from formulating the strongest possible response. Paradoxically, then, in order to figure out where Burnside was going to cross, Lee would have to let him do so.

Option 3A

If Burnside crossed at Fredericksburg, the hills behind the city would give Lee an especially strong defensive position and keep his men out of the reach of Federal artillery. However, Lee wouldn't be able to move his army close enough to the river's edge in enough force to resist the crossing itself for any length of time. "Our position was, therefore, selected with a view to resist the enemy's advance after crossing," the general explained, "and the river was guarded only by a force sufficient to impede his movements until the army could be concentrated."[19] Burnside would have to come at him, and Lee's concentrated army could then make good use of its own position. If necessary, Lee could also fall back toward Richmond after an initial battle.

Option 3B

If Burnside crossed upriver, Lee's cavalry could defend the fords long enough for infantry to shift from the heights to the threatened fords. Lee's position along the hills was strong enough that he could leave a light force to occupy the area while he shifted men. (He would ultimately employ a similar strategy during the Chancellorsville Campaign in the spring.)

Option 3C

If Burnside crossed downriver, portions of Jackson's Corps could slow any subsequent advance while the rest of Lee's army fell south to avoid being outflanked. These outcomes fell in line with Lee's overall plan of luring Burnside's army away from the river and its own base of supplies and toward the North Anna.

Decision

According to historian Frank O'Reilly, "Lee never considered evacuating Fredericksburg without a show of force."[20] Having staked out a position outside the city, the Army of Northern Virginia would not just fall back unless

Lee called Lieut. Gen. James Longstreet his "Old Warhorse" and depended on his advice, which served as an important counterbalance to Lee's aggressive spirit. When Lee reorganized his forces in the wake of Antietam, he placed Longstreet in charge of the army's First Corps—its largest—and dated his commission one day earlier than Jackson's to establish Longstreet as the army's second-in-command. Library of Congress.

Lieut. Gen. Thomas Jonathan Jackson earned his nickname "Stonewall" at First Manassas. Lee depended on his aggressiveness and unrelenting drive. Jackson commanded the army's Second Corps, which often acted in independent capacities as a strike force. Library of Congress.

either Burnside outflanked it or Davis ordered it to do so. In the meantime, as Lee tried to divine Burnside's motives, he kept his men busy and on the watch. His soldiers posted along the riverbank would give him as much advanced warning of Burnside's crossing as possible. Lee also flashed his army's strength anytime Burnside made rumblings toward the water. Confederate cavalry continued to collect intelligence, and friendly civilians on the north bank of the river funneled Lee information.

Confederate sharpshooters hid themselves in ravines and pits along the river, ready to bushwhack any attempts at bridge building. "After driving off working parties they were to seek cover till again needed," James Longstreet later explained. "By such practice they were to delay the bridge-builders till the commands had time to assemble at their points of rendezvous."[21]

Behind Fredericksburg, Longstreet occupied the heights and set sentries along the riverbank. "[William] Barksdale's Mississippi brigade is in the town on picket, and the enemy's pickets across the river only a biscuit's toss," said artillerist William Miller Owen. "There is no firing, so they 'chaff' each other fearfully."[22] Barksdale's division commander, Lafayette McLaws, said, "Detachments were immediately set at work digging rifle-pits close to the edge of the bank":

> [The pits were] so close that our men, when in them, could command the river and the shores on each side. The cellars of the houses near the river were made available for the use of riflemen, and zigzags were constructed to enable the men to get in and out of the rifle-pits under cover. All this was done at night, and so secretly and quietly that I do not believe the enemy had any conception of the minute and careful preparations that had been made to defeat any attempt to cross the river. . . . No provision was made for the use of artillery, as the enemy had an enormous array of their batteries on the heights above the town, and could have demolished ours in five minutes.[23]

"McLaws was about the best general in the army for that sort of job," attested artillerist E. Porter Alexander, "being very painstaking in details, & having a good eye for ground. He had fixed up his sharpshooters all along the river to the Queen's taste."[24] Also one with a good eye for ground, Alexander oversaw artillery posted along the heights behind the city, well out of effective range of most of the Federals' guns. Burnside would eventually have to advance against his position. "We cover that ground now so well that we will comb it as with a fine-tooth comb," Alexander boasted to Longstreet, his direct supervisor. "A chicken could not live on that field when we open on it."[25]

Finally, on December 10, "the stir and excitement about the enemy's camps . . . as well as the reports of scouts, gave notice that important movements were pending," Longstreet wrote.[26] "Notice was given the command, and the batteries were ordered to have their animals in harness an hour before daylight of the next morning."[27]

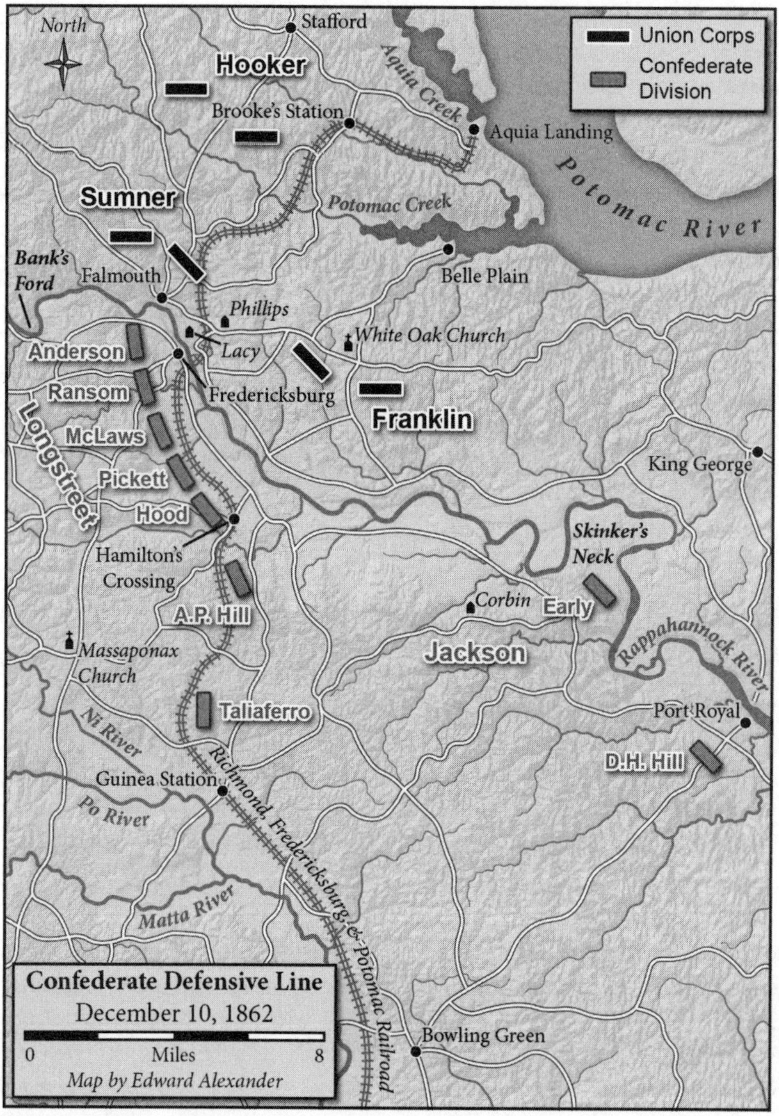

While Lee concentrated Longstreet's First Corps in Fredericksburg, he hedged his bets by extending Jackson's Second Corps to cover possible crossings downriver. William Taliaferro's Second Corps division remained in a reserve position to swing into action where needed depending on Federal movements. Edward Alexander.

Still unsure of the exact point of crossing, Confederates received orders to allow Federal bridge builders to get well underway with their work—thus committing the US troops to a particular course of action—before any Confederates started shooting. "The signal is to be two guns fired in quick succession, and the army will go into the works without further orders," said artillerist William Miller Owen.[28] However, that would require the troops spread out at their different campgrounds to form up and march to their positions along the line—something that would take time.[29] The more of an advanced notice Barksdale's men could provide, the better.

As quiet as Brainerd and his colleagues tried to be, the jig was up just as soon as it started. "The first noise made by the enemy's bridge-builders was understood by the picket guards, as was all of their early work of construction," Longstreet revealed.[30] Along the river, McLaws conferred with Barksdale. "I told him to let the bridge building go on until the enemy were committed to it and the construction parties were within easy range," McLaws said.[31] Barksdale's sharpshooters waited in silence as the fog around them thickened.

That fog provided welcome cover to the engineers. Ice had hampered "rapid construction," so by 5:00 a.m., the Federals' bridges extended only to midriver. Standing at the extreme outer end of one of them, Wesley Brainerd cast his eyes to the far shore just as the fog lifted a little. "I saw, what for the moment almost chilled my blood," he remembered. "A long line of arms moving rapidly up and down was all I saw, for a moment later there were again obscured by the fogg. But I knew too well that line of arms was *ramming cartridges* and that the crisis was near."[32]

Somewhere on the heights behind the city, a cannon boomed. Then another. "The enemy had been committed to that point, by having used half their pontoons," Longstreet explained.[33] Then "there rose from the river the merry popping of Barksdale's rifles," recalled Alexander.[34] "In an instant we were in the midst of a perfect storm of bulletts," Brainerd said. "The battle was now fairly opened."[35]

Results/Impact

According to Alexander, the guns that served as a signal to Confederates "were also taken as a signal by most of the population of Fredericksburg to abandon the town." "By every road there came numbers generally on foot, with carts loaded with bedding, &c., preparing to encamp in the woods back of our lines until the battle was over. The woods were full of them, mostly women & children," he recollected.[36] Other civilians would try to ride out the storm in their homes. By the end of the fighting, the battle would trigger a refugee crisis felt for dozens of miles around.

Meanwhile, along the river, Barksdale's men drove the engineers off the bridges. Bullets whistled "like bees let loose from a hive," Brainerd said.[37] Fire eventually slackened, and the engineers tried to resume work. "We rushed on and were speedily driven off again," Brainerd stated. "Our situation was now dreadful in thc cxtreme." Woodbury appeared on the scene and told his men, "General Burnside had said that our bridge *must* be completed at whatever cost and that the whole army was waiting for us."[38]

Federal artillery tried to silence the sharpshooters. The intensity of the cannon fire, said Lafayette McLaws, was "enough to appal the stoutest hearts!"[39] Federal infantry advanced to the riverbank to lend their weight to the battle, but their exposed positions made them easy targets. Barksdale's men "were prepared and resumed firing with increased ferocity."[40]

"I expected the bridges would be built in two or three hours after they were unloaded, which was about daylight," a deflated Burnside later said.[41] Instead, the back-and-forth between riverbanks continued for hours, with Confederates enjoying the protection offered by houses and stone walls on the Fredericksburg side of the river. "The army is held by the throat by a few sharpshooters!" the Federal commander complained.

In the course of the melee, Brainerd took a bullet in the left arm; he would survive but be knocked out of the rest of the day's action. At the time of his wounding, he was one of eleven men working at the end of the bridge; all were shot down.

On the heights above, Bull Sumner recognized the toll the fight was taking on his engineers. Not only was the loss of life alarming, but the engineers possessed special skills the army could not easily replace. Were they wiped out, no one else could readily build the bridges. When Sumner told Burnside it was impossible to finish the structures, Burnside replied, "They must be built." He continued, "Some plan must be devised for getting these sharpshooters out of the way, so that out men could get to work."[42]

Around 12:30 p.m., Brig. Gen. Henry Hunt, the Federal chief of artillery, brought more than 147 cannon to bear on the city itself in an attempt to drive out Barksdale's men. It was, attested an awed Alexander, "the most impressive exhibition of military force, by all odds, which I ever witnessed."[43] Longstreet, watching from the heights, said, "It seemed that all the cannon within a mile of the town turned their concentrating fire of shot and shell upon the buildings of the devoted city, tearing, crushing, bursting, burning their walls with angry desperation that must have been gratifying to spirits deep down below."[44]

The bombardment didn't work, though, so Hunt turned to a plan forwarded by engineer Ira Spaulding: ferrying infantry across the river in pontoon boats to establish a beachhead and drive the Confederates away (see the next critical decision).

As Federal engineers struggled under heavy fire to complete their bridges at the north and south ends of the city, at the crossing site below Fredericksburg, another detachment of engineers started work on another pair of bridges. The Fifteenth New York Engineers finished their span around 9:00 a.m., and the US Engineer Battalion finished a span next to it by 10:30. Confederates had tried to resist, but once the fog began to thin, they lost the benefit of what little cover they had and could not withstand the Federal artillery brought to bear on them.

Brainerd later condemned Burnside for not making better use of the downriver bridges. Maj. Gen. William Franklin, in command of the troops there, asked Burnside for permission to cross the Rappahannock and then move at Fredericksburg from the south, outflanking the Confederates contesting the other bridges. Burnside, though, worried the Federals would be cut off from reinforcements. He therefore told Franklin to wait until the bridges in the city were finished. "Why did General Burnside not allow troops to cross at these lower bridges?" Brainerd later asked. The army could have gained "many precious hours of time in which many thousands of troops could have been crossed and, [coming] up by the flank, drive[n] the enemy away from the position in front of us or capturing them," he contended.[45] While that might have been true, Franklin's column certainly would have been exposed to fire on its own left flank from artillery posted along the Confederate line as Franklin moved across its front. Burnside chose to avoid this serious likelihood.

As it was, the Army of the Potomac ended up having to bull its way across the upper and middle pontoon crossings and then spend hours fighting for the city. A rueful Brig. Gen. Oliver Otis Howard, whose men would find themselves embroiled in that fight, later said, "Lee, who could hardly before this have dreamed of our crossing in his direct front, must have smiled at our folly."[46]

But Lee had not yet fully bought into Burnside's movement. He sent an early note to Jackson to inform him of Burnside's attempted crossing, but he did not order Jackson to close up with the rest of the army. As nakedly obvious as it was and as tortured as it would become, the crossing might only be an elaborate ruse, with a stronger thrust coming elsewhere. Lee decided to let the situation play itself out more. Jackson responded by alerting his farthest divisions—Jubal Early's and D. H. Hill's—to remain on guard against a downriver crossing, but he also warned Hill to "be in readiness to move in any required direction."[47]

6. Barksdale Contests the Federal Crossing

Situation

The morning wore on, "calm, clear, & cold," and from A. P. Alexander's perch atop the heights behind Fredericksburg, the sound of the fight "rose & fell from time to time."[48] "And I could not but laugh out heartily, at times," Alexander said, "to catch in the roar of the Federal guns the faint drownded pop of a musket which told that Barksdale's men were still in their rifle pits & still defiant. The contrast in the noises the two parties were making was very ludicrous."[49] In fact, Barksdale was so defiant that he sent the following word back to Lee: "If he wants a bridge of dead Yankees [I] can furnish him with one."[50]

Prior to the outbreak of war, the forty-one-year-old Barksdale had been as rabid a fire-eater as had ever served in the US Congress, where he'd earned a national reputation for the vehemence of his proslavery views. When Mississippi, his adopted state, seceded, Barksdale left the Congress for a post with the state militia. He then earned a colonelcy with the Thirteenth Mississippi volunteer infantry and, through meritorious service on the battlefield, worked his way to brigade command.

A fire-eater from Mississippi, Brig. Gen. William Barksdale conducted an excellent defense of the city for the Army of Northern Virginia. Library of Congress.

With Confederate artillery out of effective range from the river, Lee knew he could not prevent the Federals from crossing, even with the stiff resistance the Mississippians offered. Barksdale and his 1,500 men needed only to delay the Army of the Potomac long enough for Longstreet to finish preparations along the heights to receive the attack that would inevitably follow the river crossing. "Hold the enemy in check until ordered to retire," Lee told him.[51]

Sometime before noon, Barksdale received word "that the army was in position, and that he could withdraw his troops at any moment," said James Longstreet, writing years later, "but he preferred his little fight in Fredericksburg."[52] As the contest wore on, the Mississippian lunched with his staff in downtown Fredericksburg beside the Market House, where he'd stationed most of his reserves because of its central location. Cacophony began to rage around them as Hunt launched his 147-gun barrage from across the river. "The town caught fire in several places, shells crashed and burst, and solid shot rained like hail," observed Longstreet. "In the midst of the successive crashes could be heard the shouts and yells of those engaged in the struggle, while the smoke rose from the burning city and the flames leaped about."[53] Near the Market House, a Federal artillery shell ricocheted off a rooftop and plummeted to the ground right in the middle of Barksdale's group. A falling piece of roof tile bruised Barksdale, but the shell itself proved a dud and spun to an impotent stop.[54]

"In the midst of all this fury, the little brigade of Mississippians clung to their work," Longstreet marveled.[55] They remained hunkered in their rifle pits, in the cellars of houses along the riverbank, and behind backyard walls and whatever else offered concealment.[56]

On the Federal side of the river, Hunt began to recruit volunteers willing to ferry across the river and storm the Confederate bank. To support the riverine crossing, Federal artillery and infantry redoubled their efforts. "The concentrated fire from all arms, directed against Barksdale's men in the rifle-pits, became so severe that it was impossible for them to use their rifles with effect," McLaws remembered.[57] In addition, Longstreet pointed out, "The enemy's fire over the west bank was so sweeping that Barksdale could not reinforce at the point of landing."[58]

Barksdale had already held out longer than anyone had expected him to. Now, with Federal infantry on the way across the river, the fiery Mississippian had to decide whether it was finally time to withdraw as his corps commander had suggested.

Even as Federal soldiers stormed the banks to secure beachheads, engineers continued to extend the bridges that would allow the army to cross in force. Library of Congress.

Options

Option 1: Withdraw

Lafayette McLaws had noted a strong position "along a sunken road cut through the foot of Marye's Hill and running perpendicular to the line of the enemy's advance."[59] This sat some nine hundred yards to the rear of the city, just below the ridgeline occupied by the Confederate artillery. If Barksdale withdrew his 1,500 men before the Federal infantry landed, he could pull back to the secure position, and artillery could protect him from the pursuit that would inevitably come. In turn, though, his own men would have to run the gauntlet of Federal artillery fire, which still dropped an incredible barrage of shells into the city.

Option 2: Continue to Fight

Although artillery fire had harried the Mississippians all day, the sharpshooters had easily given better than they'd gotten in their ongoing dual with enemy infantry, and their efforts had completely bottlenecked the entire Federal army. Maintaining that bottleneck could only help buy Lee more time to prepare his position along the heights. His own men seemed to be holding, and the city offered plenty of cover for a fighting withdrawal, thus maximizing his ability to keep delaying the Federals.

Decision

Barksdale's men had already taken the worst the Federals could shell out—literally—so he kept them in position to contest the enemy infantry crossing in the pontoon boats. At the upper crossing, the Seventh Michigan floundered its way across the Rappahannock, paddling flat-ended boats built for stability, not speed or agility. The Seventeenth Mississippi shot at them almost the entire time—but then discovered that once the vessels got close enough to the near shore, the riverbank protected them. Because of the angle, the Mississippians couldn't shoot from their positions beyond the crest of the bank, which shielded the Federal landing.

At the middle crossing, men of the Eighteenth and Twenty-First Mississippi encountered a similar problem while firing from warehouses and residences: as Federals got closer, the topography of the riverbank protected them. The Eighty-Ninth New York disembarked from its pontoons and quickly cleared the area so the engineers could finish their bridge. The Forty-Sixth New York soon joined the Eighty-Ninth, although the two regiments remained content to guard the bridgehead and not push into the city to clear out Confederates.

Not so at the upper crossing, where Barksdale's men fell back from Sophia Street, which lined the riverbank, toward Caroline Street, which ran parallel to Sophia one block west. Hawke Street ran between Caroline and Sophia, and Mississippians flowed into the houses and yards along Hawke to continue contesting the Federal infantry, which pushed into the city after securing its bridgehead. "Barksdale, however, engaged him [the enemy] fiercely at every point, and with remarkable success," Longstreet said.[60]

For the first time in the Civil War, the armies waged large-scale urban combat. Oliver Otis Howard, leading the division tasked with driving out Barksdale's men, recalled "shots to meet from roofs, corners, alleyways, and from every conceivable cover."[61] The fighting went house by house, street by street, block by block, teetering back and forth as attacks and counterattacks swayed the balance of momentum. Howard's corps commander, Maj. Gen. Darius Couch, called it "desperate fighting."[62]

The arrival of the Federal infantry, although a harbinger of rough times for the Army of Northern Virginia, did carry a silver lining for Barksdale: Federal artillery let up. "When the landing was made by the boats, he thought the city safe against artillery practice," Longstreet said, "and was pleased to hold till night could cover his withdrawal."[63]

Federals eventually pushed the Mississippians another block to the east, to Princess Anne Street, where Barksdale set up his final defense near the

Market House and the ridge that ran behind it. Confident his brigade commander had done all he could, McLaws ordered Barksdale to withdraw. Barksdale, waiting for the cover of darkness, ignored McLaws's order and continued his defense. "Genl Barksdale ordered his men to hold their fire until the enemy came up very close to them and pour a deadly volley into their ranks, which they did effectually," said James Beaty, the quartermaster of Barksdale's Brigade. "A close combat then ensued in the streets, which resulted in the enemy getting most terribly whipped and being compelled to 'skedaddle.'"[64] But it turned out that the Federals merely fell back far enough to regroup and then come on again.

"The general was so confident of his position that a second order was sent to him before he would yield the field," Longstreet said.[65] By then, darkness had indeed fallen. Also, Federals occupied the three blocks of the city closest to the river and, on the south end of Fredericksburg at the city docks, the high ground that dominated downtown, making Barksdale's position around the Market House more tenuous. Barksdale finally ordered his men to retire to the position McLaws had staked out along the base of Marye's Heights.

Result/Impact

In his after-action report of the battle, James Longstreet freely shared his praise for what the Mississippians achieved on December 11. "Brigadier-General Barksdale with his brigade held the enemy's entire army at the river bank for sixteen hours," he wrote, "giving us abundance of time to complete our arrangements for battle. A more gallant and worthy service is rarely accomplished by so small a force."[66] Outnumbered almost three to one, the brigade suffered 242 casualties out of 1,500 men.

Because Lee didn't know exactly where Burnside intended to cross until the pontoon bridges started reaching across the Rappahannock, the early warning Barksdale's men provided proved extremely useful. This became more of a moot point as the day wore on, though, because Barksdale's efforts along the riverbank stalled the Federal advance for so long that Longstreet's Corps had ample time to get into position.

The real value of Barksdale's delaying action wouldn't be seen until December 13, on the south end of the field in what would become Stonewall Jackson's sector. According to Union major general Bull Sumner, Barksdale's effort "gave the enemy time to accumulate their forces, which were stretched along the river from Port Royal up to the battle-field."[67] Jackson's first two divisions moved into place on December 12, and his second two divisions would complete Lee's consolidation early on December 13—a move made possible, in part, by Burnside (see critical decision number seven).

"It may be supposed that Lee did all he could to prevent our army from crossing, but this is a mistake," bemused Mainer John Haley, wrote on December 11. "He wanted us to cross, expecting to destroy us or drive us into the river."[68]

It's worth noting that in the course of trying to salvage the situation on December 11, Burnside had to rewrite the rules of war. Hunt's afternoon barrage marked the first time American artillery intentionally bombarded a city. The Seventh Michigan's riverine crossing represented the first time American infantry had ever secured a bridgehead under fire. The street fighting witnessed the first urban combat of the war. For an army trained by George McClellan to be generally risk averse, and for a commander who had thus far in the campaign also proven to be risk averse, these were significant achievements that could (and would) later be built on.

Burnside also recognized the value of the "gallant work" done by his engineers. "No more difficult feat has been performed during the war than the throwing of these bridges in the face of the enemy by these brave men," he wrote in his official report.[69]

The longest-lasting impact of Barksdale's resistance would be to Fredericksburg itself. The artillery barrage and street fighting left the city in shambles. "All the buildings more or less battered with shells, roofs & walls all full of holes & the churches with their broken windows & shattered walls looking desolate enough," wrote the Army of the Potomac's provost marshal, Marsena

The area of Fredericksburg known as Sandy Bottom stood near the middle crossing site. While many of the homes were destroyed by the bombardment, a number of them were rebuilt and still stand today. Library of Congress.

Patrick.[70] This devastation would combine with other factors—such as the exodus of formerly enslaved people from the city—to stunt Fredericksburg's future growth. "The physical impact weighed on the community for decades," says historian John Hennessy.[71] It would take a century before the city's population would rebound to its wartime level of five t thousand. Hennessy further notes, "Fredericksburg would not regain a trajectory toward true prosperity again until the 1960s, when engineers built Interstate 95 along the town's western boundary, paid for with Federal dollars."[72]

"It is probable that if the inhabitants of the city had requested the Rebel army to vacate, it would have done so," supposed John Haley. "Instead, the inhabitants of Fredericksburg chose to be very patriotic. Result: ruin!"[73]

7. Burnside Delays His Attack Until December 13

Situation

In the predawn chill of December 11, with the Rappahannock Valley filled with so much fog that only church steeples rose above it, Ambrose Burnside had gathered with his top lieutenants to finalize the day's plans. His headquarters were situated in "a new brick house, just built by a Mr. Phillips . . . in the cottage gothic style, and supplied with furnace, bathroom, and other luxuries unknown in Virginia generally."[74] The house sat a mile and a quarter back from the crest of Stafford Heights, so Burnside could not see down into the river valley even if the fog offered a view. However, he was not so far away that he could not hear the boom of a Confederate artillery piece, followed by a second. Then musket fire from the far bank, then the near.

While the men listened to the sound of the fighting getting underway, Burnside's staff began scribbling out written copies of the orders he'd just issued. The army's provost marshal, Brig. Gen. Marsena Patrick, had sat in on the meeting. He was already worried about the day's duties ahead of him, but Burnside had just laid an extra assignment before him. The previous spring, Patrick's brigade had occupied the city and Patrick had served as military governor. Because of the familiarity with Fredericksburg that experience had given Patrick, Burnside asked him to find guides from his former command who could serve as guides for each of the grand divisions as they crossed the Rappahannock.

Everything depended on speed. Once the engineers completed their pontoon bridges, Burnside intended to push his entire army across the river and storm the Confederate position quickly and powerfully. Sumner's Right Grand Division, crossing in the city, would assault Marye's Heights on the

Brig. Gen. Marsena Patrick had the unenviable job of provost marshal—the chief law-and-order enforcer of the army—which pulled him in many directions during the Federal army's occupation of the city. Library of Congress.

Confederate left. "The extent of your movement to the front beyond the heights will be indicated during the engagement," Burnside told Sumner.[75] Hooker's Center Grand Division would cross after Sumner as support, ready "to press the enemy in case the other command succeeded in moving him."[76] Hooker could also be available to support Franklin if necessary. Franklin's Left Grand Division, crossing below the city, would hit Prospect Hill on the Confederate far right. Burnside told Franklin, "[Be] governed by circumstances as to the extent of your movements."[77] Burnside gave each grand division commander a specific objective but also considerable flexibility to adapt as the situations in their fronts developed.

Except the situation didn't develop, and Burnside didn't show much flexibility. And thus, December 11 evaporated like the morning's fog without any substantial infantry crossing.

As Burnside mulled his options, night settled over the city and surrounding hills. Infantry on both sides lit campfires, and in Fredericksburg, buildings set afire by the day's cannonade filled the streets with an eerie flickering light and smoke that only added to the darkness. "The sky," wrote John Haley of the Seventeenth Maine, "was lit by the glare of shells."[78]

Burnside had already decided that he wanted the entire army to cross the river all at once so the separated portions could protect one another. Time and time again during his tenure, he had denied requests from subordinates who asked to take unsupported portions across the Rappahannock. On November 17, he had denied Sumner's request to cross at Falmouth if he could find a suitable ford. Soon thereafter, Burnside rejected Hooker's appeal to cross using upriver fords. On December 11, when Franklin had part of his Left Grand Division across the Rappahannock and asked whether he could try to outflank Confederates in the city, Burnside said no. Only after all the bridges were completed would he assent to a full crossing, with just enough force in the city to hold the bridgeheads in the meantime.

Beyond that single choice—already made—Burnside faced two other interrelated critical decisions: when to cross the army and what to do with it once it had crossed.

Options

Option 1A: Cross the Army on the Night of December 11

Confederate resistance in the city had already cost Burnside the element of surprise and dashed his plans for a speedy crossing. While he might not be able to make up for lost time, he didn't have to squander any more of it. Traversing the river at once would allow Federals to launch an attack first thing in the morning. It would also guard against any possible Confederate preemptive strike. "This seems to me of vital importance," wired Henry Halleck from Washington.[79]

However, crossing at night would also risk confusion. Units could get jumbled, and unit cohesion on the regimental, brigade, and division levels could all suffer, making it hard to coordinate any early morning assault. In addition, the men had spent a tense day waiting for the bridges, and their nerves were on end even if most of them weren't engaged in any fighting. "Our imaginations ran riot and we expected every moment to be ordered in," said John Haley, who called it "a day of terrible suspense."[80] Already stressed out by that ordeal, soldiers marching across the river overnight would not get much chance to rest before finally going into battle in the morning.

Option 1B: Cross the Army on the Morning of December 12

Crossing in the morning would avoid the potential confusion of doing so at night because, quite simply, men could better see what they were doing and where they were going. Officers could better organize their men once they took up assigned positions. The troops would also be a little more rested—even if, with battle pending, they might not actually sleep or sleep easy.

However, if the crossing took too long, the army might not have enough time in the short December day to launch an afternoon attack. And, of course, every hour of delay—for any reason—offered the Army of Northern Virginia more time to consolidate and fortify. Burnside still anticipated that Confederates might retreat in the face of his full army. To that end, he hoped a daylight crossing offered the Federals a slight psychological advantage: Confederates, seeing the size of his complete force, might think better of a fight and withdraw.

Option 2A: Stick with the Original Plan

Once across the Rappahannock, Burnside could still send Sumner against the Confederate left and Franklin against the Confederate right, with Hooker still in support. The merit of the plan was that it wouldn't take long to organize and execute because everyone already knew their assigned tasks. The downside was that Burnside would have to strike a prepared foe who could literally see the Federals coming from a mile away.

Option 2B: Modify the attack

Burnside had broadcast his intentions; Confederates reacted. If Lee didn't pull back, he might feel confident enough in his army's position that he believed his men could withstand a Federal assault.[81] For that reason, it might be wise to formulate a different strategy. Unfortunately, Burnside had done little to develop any kind of Plan B and so had no ready options. As soon as Federals breached the city and secured their position on the evening of December 11, Burnside began looking for new information that might lead to viable alternatives to his original plan.

Burnside also needed to consider that, *whenever* he crossed his army, he would have to jam upward of one hundred thousand men into a narrow slice of land along the Rappahannock until he decided on a course of action. Crowding anxious soldiers—troops primed for a battle and itching for payback after the delays of the eleventh—into a relatively confined space would be asking for trouble. The longer they stayed crammed together, the more their tension would build. Add to that the possibility that Confederate artillery could open up at any time, and Burnside would be packing a powder keg of his own making.

Decision

"Our troops now occupy Fredericksburg," Burnside said in his initial wire to Washington. "I expect to cross the rest of my command tomorrow."[82] A little over an hour later, he clarified the time slightly to "early to-morrow."[83] A few hours later, Burnside seemed to indicate an even faster timetable. He authorized Franklin to construct a third pontoon bridge at the lower crossing, then said, "His command ought to cross, and, as soon as he and Sumner are over, attack simultaneously."[84] But, oddly, no follow-up orders went out to either Sumner or Franklin. "The delay in laying the bridges had rendered some change in the plan of attack necessary," Burnside later explained—but, at the time, he wasn't quite sure what the change should be.[85]

According to Francis Walker, a Second Corps staff officer who would later serve as the corps' historian, Burnside had a "sanguine belief" that Lee would "slink away at the sight of his splendid army, and that the immediate problem was not how to win a battle, but how to make the most of Lee's retreat."[86] No record exists of whether that conviction relieved Burnside's sense of urgency or whether he felt confident in his hoped-for psychological edge. But for whatever reason—and despite his apparent first instinct to immediately cross and attack—Burnside waited until the morning of December 12 to move his army to the far bank of the river.

"All are resting until an early hour tomorrow to cross & begin a terrible fight," Marsena Patrick wrote during that long nighttime of waiting. He felt less sanguine than Burnside about the army's prospects, expecting instead to face Lee's entire consolidated army. "The whole will then be upon us," he remarked, "& we must carry their position at whatever cost."[87]

Federals began crossing at 8:00 a.m.—hardly "early," as Burnside promised—and it took them five hours to finish. From the heights beyond the city, Confederate artillery harassed them the entire time, while Confederate infantry hung back. "But little fighting was going on during the day," said Marsena Patrick, "except to keep the town clear."[88]

At Franklin's Crossing, the Federal infantry had an easier time of it. "I cannot understand why the rebs spent so few shot on us," pondered artillerist Charles Wainwright. "The deployment on the open plain of 35,000 men certainly afforded a good mark; and, it seems to me, might have been made an ugly job."[89] Franklin feared the longer US soldiers milled about inactive, the greater the mark they'd become. "We were in such a position that if the enemy had at any moment opened upon us," he later testified, "our men would have been so scattered that it would have been impossible to rally them."[90]

Once the Army of the Potomac finished fording the river—and once the Army of Northern Virginia remained in place—Burnside didn't seem to know what to do next. "After getting in the face of the enemy, his intentions seemed to be continually changing," complained Second Corps commander Maj. Gen. Darius Couch, who realized Burnside "had no fixed plan of battle."[91] "As a matter of fact," attested Francis Walker, "General Burnside had no plan of operations whatsoever when he crossed the river; and all through the day of the 12th, and even through the following night, he was vacillating in purpose."[92] Walker elaborated on this point:

> How came it that . . . the earliest hour of the morning was not seized to make up, as far as might be, for the loss of the 11th? Surely if anything was to be done, in the face of a powerful and intrenched army, it should be undertaken at once; and that this might be, every detail of the plan should have been carefully studied before the crossing, the result reduced to writing in a form so precise and clear as to be literally incapable of misconstruction or misapprehension.[93]

Burnside crossed the river himself to look at Confederate positions. He conferred with subordinates and authorized Franklin to build a third pontoon bridge at the lower crossing site. Burnside also ordered Couch to move to the left to support Franklin, then countermanded the order. The commander was simultaneously a flurry of activity and indecision.

Biographer William Marvel points out that Burnside was on "the brink of exhaustion" at this point and blames that for the general's indecisiveness at this critical moment.[94] "Burnside had been working feverishly at all hours since General Buckingham consigned him that accursed appointment," Marvel writes.[95] Burnside's aide Daniel Larned worried about this almost from the start. "He is working night & day and has been sick ever since he took command," Larned wrote on November 22. "He has slept but little and is most arduous in his labors and does not spare himself even for the common necessities of health."[96] This behavior persisted. In the mornings leading up to and including the battle, Burnside was up in time to wake Marsena Patrick by 4:00 a.m.[97] December 11 ticked into the critical early morning hours of December 12, marking the culmination of weeks of accumulated stress and two days of manic activity and combat. At this point, Marvel argues, Burnside's diminished condition showed enough that Franklin alluded to it in a note to headquarters: "I shall be glad to see General Burnside, but do not wish to deprive him of rest."[98] The circumstantial evidence suggests there was more to Marvel's interpretation than just apologism. Yet critics argue Old Burn just wasn't up to the task, as Burnside himself had forewarned.

At some point in the day, Burnside received word—brought to him by "a colored man from the other side of town"—concerning a new road Confederates had cut behind their line. The route "connected the two wings of their army, and avoided a long detour around through a bad country."[99] Instead of assaulting both ends of Lee's line at once, Burnside realized he could potentially concentrate his strength on one end or the other, break through, and then use the military road to roll up or down the line, outflanking Confederates and forcing them to evacuate. "I wanted to obtain possession of that new road," he later explained.[100]

A plan began to coalesce in Burnside's mind. After one last check of his position in town, he rode south to Franklin's headquarters to confer with his Left Grand Division commander. Together, the two men inspected the Confederate line to the west as the sun set beyond. Even in the gloaming, they could tell that the formation, which ran along a low ridge called Prospect Hill, looked less daunting than the Confederate position atop Marye's Heights. There also appeared to be room enough to maneuver and get around Prospect Hill, outflanking it, whereas the other end of the Confederate line anchored on the Rappahannock. The army could more easily achieve a breakthrough and access the military road here.

Burnside and Franklin subsequently met with Franklin's corps commanders, John Reynolds and William "Baldy" Smith. During the meeting, Franklin argued that "a very strong attack could be made there at daybreak the next morning" using "a column of at least 30,000 men."[101] Smith envisioned that such an assault could "carry the ridge, and turn Lee's right flank."[102] In their combined judgment, Smith added, the plan was "the only one that . . . offered a fair hope of success."[103] Burnside apparently agreed with the triumvirate and indicated written orders would soon come down from headquarters.

Finally, after twenty-four hours, Burnside had come to a decision—but his delay in doing so would prove to be the most critical component of the process. "Burnside had proposed to effect a surprise," Smith recalled, "and now before Lee could be attacked he would have had forty-eight hours for concentration against us and for fortifying his positions on the hills."[104]

Results/Impact

An immediate crossing on December 11 followed by a morning attack on December 12 would have afforded Burnside an opportunity to catch Lee when he was not at full strength. Stonewall Jackson's first two divisions didn't arrive on the battlefield until later on December 12, and his second two divisions didn't arrive until the morning of December 13, just before Franklin finally launched his assault.

What's more, a December 12 assault against Prospect Hill would have pitted Franklin's Left Grand Division—some 40,000 men—against John Bell Hood's lone division from Longstreet's Corps—7,300 men. As Jackson's divisions began to arrive, though, Lee reconfigured the Confederate line. Longstreet's force contracted from an eight-mile front to a six-mile front, still covering a disproportional share of the distance, but his corps enjoyed considerably stronger topography for defense. In his newly acquired two-mile

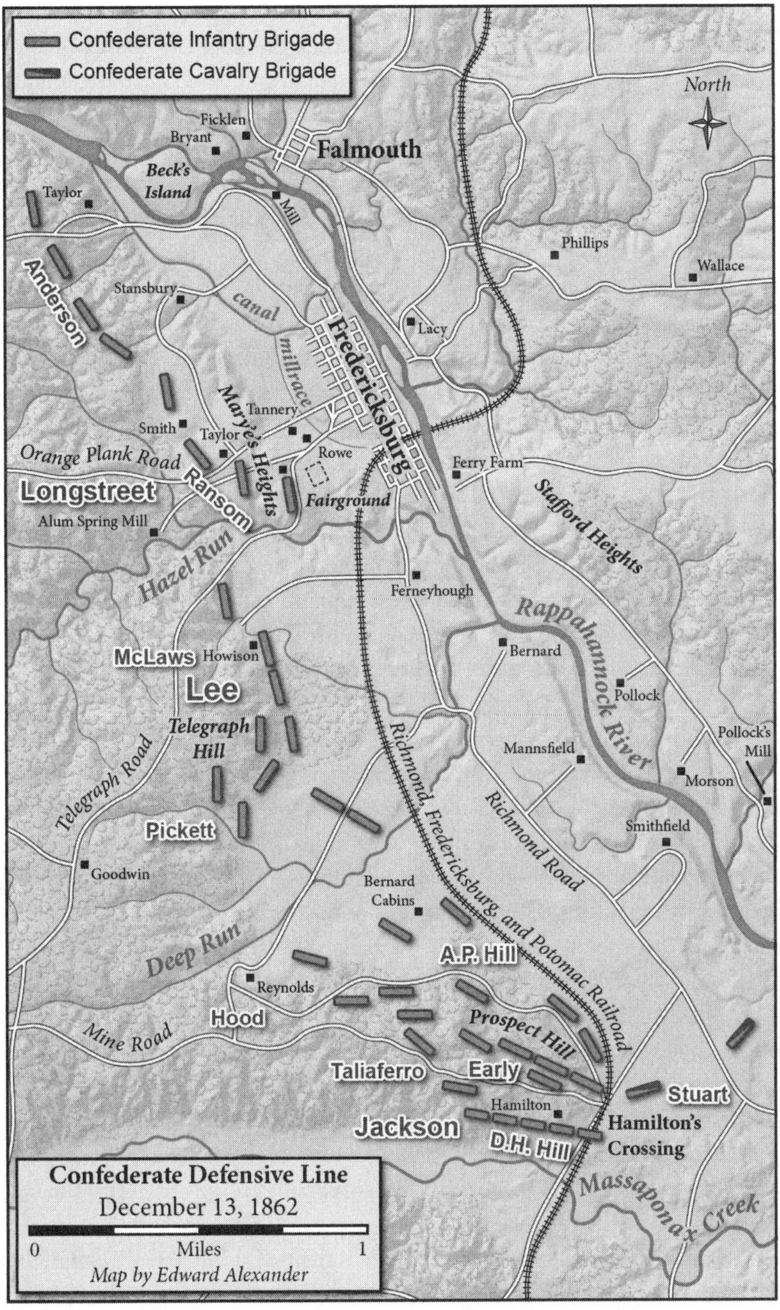

Burnside's delay on December 12 gave Lee the opportunity to consolidate his position, concentrating Jackson's Corps at the south end of the Confederate line. Edward Alexander.

front, Jackson stacked his divisions—38,000 men—in depth, resulting in more Confederates per square foot than anywhere else on the line. "There is reason to believe that the real attack will be made on our right, and not at Fredericksburg," Jackson told division commander D. H. Hill, passing on intelligence from Lee.[105]

In essence, on December 12, Burnside missed the opportunity to attack the weakest part of the Confederate line. On December 13, he would end up attacking one of the strongest sections.

Burnside's hope that an intimidated Lee would evacuate the battlefield proved how poorly he knew his opponent. "We hold the hills around the town," Lee reported to Richmond on the day Burnside dallied. "I shall try and do them all the damage in our power when they move forward. I believe General Burnside's whole army is at this point."[106] "Lee had no thought of retreating," Second Corps historian Francis Walker later summarized:

> He had watched the crossing or our troops with a stern delight. What, indeed, could he ask more, than that the Army of the Potomac should precipitate itself against this position, strong by nature, rendered doubly strong by fortification, crowded with artillery, and held by seventy thousand veterans?[107]

Conversely, it does not appear Burnside ever contemplated withdrawing his own army once he had secured his crossing. With Jackson's troops now leaving positions at Skinker's Neck and Port Royal, it was not too late to revisit the prospect of crossing a significant body of the army at some location besides Fredericksburg proper. "There was a very fine opportunity for turning what had been done into a feint, and crossing the main army elsewhere," said armchair general Baldy Smith years after the war. "But this was not done."[108]

If the delay netted any benefits for the Army of the Potomac, it should have been that the men in the ranks had the opportunity for one more day of rest before going into battle, but Burnside's indecisiveness seemed to rob them of even that. "We had no news of what our army had accomplished and were in a state of appalling uncertainty," Mainer John Haley lamented.[109] December 12, which he called "dark and overcast so we couldn't tell anything as to our whereabouts," seemed to reflect Haley's mood. "I made coffee and then retired with dismal forebodings," he wrote. "What is before us? Possibly this might be my last night on earth. Even worse, ere the setting of another sun I might be mangled and bleeding. Such thoughts crowd in upon me and prevent me from sleeping."[110]

CHAPTER 4

THE BATTLE OF FREDERICKSBURG, DECEMBER 13, 1862

8. William Franklin Attacks Without Clarifying His Orders

Situation

On September 13, 1862, George B. McClellan, then in command of the Army of the Potomac, received one of the greatest windfalls of the war: a lost copy of Robert E. Lee's plans for his invasion of the North. The information in this "lost order" was four days old, so McClellan mobilized his army for a quick pursuit. As part of that mobilization, he wanted his Sixth Corps commander, William B. Franklin, to march to Harpers Ferry and relieve a garrison there that had been targeted by Stonewall Jackson. To get there, McClellan pointed Franklin toward the South Mountain pass at Crampton's Gap.

"If the pass is not occupied by the enemy in force, seize it as soon as practicable," McClellan wrote; if the enemy did hold the pass, Franklin was to "make all . . . dispositions for the attack." Once he gained the way, Franklin was to descend the far side into Pleasant Valley and "cut off, destroy, or capture" the Confederate troops there who were supporting the siege of Harpers Ferry. Then he could move on to Harpers Ferry itself and join forces with the beleaguered garrison. McClellan detached a Fourth Corps division under Darius Couch to support Franklin's advance. "Without waiting for the whole

Maj. Gen. William Franklin would bear much of the responsibility for what happened at Fredericksburg, although he vehemently denied any blame. Postbattle investigations quickly identified his culpability. However, his subsequent punishment might have owed as much to his status as a staunch McClellanite as to his missteps during the battle. Library of Congress.

of that division to join you, you will move at daybreak," McClellan ordered the commander, referring to the morning of September 14.[1]

Although expressly told not to wait for Couch, Franklin did. Then he marched as far as Burkittsville and stopped. He had dithered, then marched, then dithered, then marched. Confederates in the mountain pass watched the Federals "approaching our gap cautiously and slowly.... They were so numerous that it looked like they were creeping up out of the ground."[2] When Franklin got a good look at the Confederate position, he saw rebels "strongly posted on both sides of the road, which made a steep ascent through a narrow defile, wooded on both sides, and offering great advantages of cover and position."[3]

Historian Brian Matthew Jordan's assessment of the situation will sound eerily prescient in the context of what would later happen at Fredericksburg: "With difficult terrain possibly held by a strong veteran enemy, Franklin struggled to interpret McClellan's broad instructions." An exchange of telegrams with McClellan only confused Franklin more.[4] Flummoxed, the Sixth Corps commander froze.

Franklin finally summoned a committee of subordinates, but they dithered on a plan. Brigade commander Joseph Jackson Bartlett finally broke the impasse. Bartlett led a late-day attack that ultimately charged "up an almost perpendicular steep, over rocks and ledges, through the underbrush and timber, until the crest overlooking the valley below was gained."[5] Although the Federals' action was "decisive and complete," nightfall allowed Confederate forces under Maj. Gen. Lafayette McLaws to fortify a position down in Pleasant Valley beyond.[6]

On September 15, McClellan ordered Franklin to attack McLaws's line, but Franklin hesitated again. As a result, the garrison at Harpers Ferry fell to Stonewall Jackson, and McLaws slipped away untouched. Although Franklin showed more aggressiveness at Antietam once he was back under McClellan's direct gaze, he never adequately explained his South Mountain slows. Rather than hold him accountable for his delays, though, the army promoted him to grand division commander under Burnside.

Although no one knew it, Franklin was once more about to be confounded by instructions he did not understand.

Following the December 12 meeting with Burnside, Generals Franklin, Smith, Reynolds, and their staffs waited anxiously for written orders to arrive from headquarters. The three officers had urged the commanding general to send his instructions as quickly as possible so they'd have the maximum amount of time to prepare. "He stated at one time that I should have my orders . . . before midnight," Franklin later recalled of Burnside, "and at another, that I should have them in two or three hours."[7] But Burnside, who left Franklin's headquarters sometime around 6:00 p.m., did not return to his own until after midnight—"owing to the dense fog and smoke," he explained—and he didn't draft his orders to his grand division commanders until just before daybreak.[8]

Sometime after midnight, Franklin "got very nervous about not receiving any orders" and sent an orderly to the telegraph office to make inquiries. The orderly returned with news that "the orders were then being prepared and would soon come down."[9] At 3:00 a.m., Reynolds threw in the towel for the night. "I know I have hard work ahead of me and I must get some sleep," he said.[10]

Shortly after 6:00 a.m., Brig. Gen. James A. Hardie, a member of Burnside's staff—"known in the service," said Franklin, "as an able and zealous officer"—set out from the Phillips House toward Mannsfield. Morning fog again rose from the river and filled the valley, obscuring Hardie's way as he descended from Stafford Heights toward the lower crossing. Cold temperatures had frozen the muddy road and made travel even more difficult. By some accounts, Hardie stopped for breakfast along the way, which slowed him even more.[11] Not until sometime around 7:30 did the brigadier arrive at Franklin's headquarters with Burnside's long-delayed orders.[12]

Franklin had expected the orders hours earlier with an eye toward starting an attack at daybreak. As he understood the previous evening's discussion, he was to launch a massive assault against the Confederate right flank. Burnside's orders, as he received them from Hardie, seemed to suggest something different:

The bookish-looking Brig. Gen. James Hardie was on hand at Franklin's headquarters as Burnside's emissary, but he underperformed. Library of Congress.

Headquarters Army of the Potomac,
December 13, 1862—5:55 a.m.

The general commanding directs that you keep your whole command in position for a rapid movement down the old Richmond road, and you will send out at once a division at least to pass below Smithfield, to seize, if possible, the heights near Captain Hamilton's . . . taking care to keep it well supported and its line of retreat open. . . .

He has ordered another column of a division or more to be moved from General Sumner's command up the Plank Road to its intersection with the Telegraph road, where they will divide, with a view to seizing the heights on both of these roads. Holding these two heights, with the heights near Captain Hamilton's will, he hopes, compel the enemy to evacuate the whole ridge between these points. He makes these moves by columns distant from each other, with a view of avoiding the possibility of a collision of our own forces, which might occur in a general movement during a fog.

Two of General Hooker's divisions are in your rear, at the bridges, and will remain there as supports. . . . You will

> keep your whole command in readiness to move at once, as soon as the fog lifts.[13]

Burnside's original order came as a single paragraph; paragraph breaks have been added here to facilitate reading and make it easier to parse the text, which we need to do in order to understand Franklin's confusion.

First, Burnside seemed to contradict himself by telling Franklin, "Keep your whole command in position" while also suggesting "a rapid movement" and directing him to send part of the command "out at once." Did the troops stay in position or move?

Second, Burnside specified "the old Richmond road" in his order. He expected Franklin to send an assault column down this road to hit the Confederate right flank. The column was to be led by at least a division, well supported, and the entire rest of Franklin's command was to be ready to follow as reinforcements and exploit any initial successes. But as Franklin looked at his map, he saw that the old Richmond Road didn't go to the Confederate right flank. Historian Frank O'Reilly reveals that Franklin and Burnside were actually working from different maps. On Burnside's, the Richmond Road ran northwest to southeast, roughly in line with the river. But just past the Smithfield Plantation, which was just southeast of Mannsfield, the road curved to the south/southwest toward a rail junction known as Hamilton's Crossing (identified in the order as "the heights near Captain Hamilton's," named for Revolutionary War veteran Capt. George Hamilton). On Franklin's map, the Richmond Road continued on to the southeast, toward Bowling Green, and he was unaware of any curve to the west. O'Reilly points out that both maps, ironically, were mislabeled "since the thoroughfare to Hamilton's Crossing did not go to Bowling Green or Richmond."[14]

Furthermore, Burnside directed Franklin to use "a division at least." "[A] division is theoretically 12,000 men," noted artillerist Charles Wainwright, commenting on the infantry, "but in an army like ours where regiments are not filled up, it may be any number less than that."[15] Meade's division, for instance, had 4,500. However, between the First and Sixth Corps, plus two supporting divisions from the Third Corps and one from the Ninth Corps, Franklin had some 60,000 men on hand—certainly capable of the kind of massive hammerblow he and his corps commanders had discussed with Burnside the previous evening. Why, then, send only a division?

The order also directed the attacking force "to seize" the heights near Captain Hamilton's. "The military man is habituated to use with word seize when an unguarded position is to be occupied," a nitpicking Smith later tried to explain. "When an advantage is to be gained by hard fighting or the weight of a mass of troops, the word *carry* is instinctively used."[16]

In the section of his directive beginning with "he has ordered another column," Burnside spelled out Sumner's role for the day. Was Sumner's attack to go forward in conjunction with Franklin's? Were they coequal attacks, or did one support the other? Did they together constitute the "general movement" the orders referred to?

Burnside then mentioned "holding these heights." He had initially indicated that he wanted to use the military road behind the Confederate position to outflank the rebels and sweep up their line. "Holding" did not necessarily suggest movement beyond the initial seizure. Was Franklin supposed to hold while Sumner did the sweeping, contrary to what had been discussed the previous evening?

"Two of General Hooker's divisions are in your rear, and will remain there as supports," the order further said. Franklin expected significantly more reinforcements than that from the Center Grand Division, but Burnside sent him only two divisions from George Stoneman's Third Corps. And if those units stayed in the rear, how could they serve in a supporting role?

Baffled by virtually every component of the order, Franklin looked to Hardie for clarification, but Hardie had no clarification to give.[17] He had not been at the previous evening's conference and had only Burnside's written order to go by.

Finally, Franklin worried that his assault force was "to move at once, as soon as the fog lifts." The morning sun, up since 7:10, had already begun to burn away whatever protective cover the fog offered. He'd wasted all night, and time was working suddenly and urgently against him.

Options

Option 1: Seek Clarification

The Left Grand Division's telegraph station was located only a third of a mile from Mannsfield.[18] Franklin could send a courier there to wire army headquarters and seek clarification from Burnside. As a brigadier general, Hardie had a level of clout for his mission that no mere orderly would have possessed, so Franklin could also send Hardie to the telegraph office to engender an even quicker response. For that matter, in the interest of time, Franklin might even go to the telegraph office himself.

Franklin could send also a courier, or Hardie, to speak to Burnside personally. This would take longer—only Hardie appreciated just how much longer, considering he'd just made the trip—but Franklin could initiate preparations while awaiting a response.

Option 2: Wait for Clarification

Burnside had promised to send along copies of Sumner's and Hooker's orders. They might contain information that could provide additional context or clarity for Franklin's directives.

Then again, Franklin had spent all night waiting for orders that had only just arrived. How long would he have to wait for the next batch?

Option 3: Demonstrate Initiative and Launch an Attack

If Franklin didn't want to take the time to clarify "incongruous and contradictory orders" because he was worried about lost time and lost fog cover, he could use his judgment and initiate action. After all, he was a former engineer with an exacting and deliberate mind. He was also one of the most senior officers in the army, a position he'd attained because of his own experience and time of service—attributes he could draw on to make an informed decision of his own. Beyond that, Franklin could tap into the experience and insight of Smith and Reynolds if he wanted additional perspectives.

Option 4: Follow the Original Plan as Discussed on the Evening of December 12 and Launch an Attack

Since Franklin and his subordinates were unsure just what the written order meant, they could follow their verbal commands from the previous evening, which they did understand. A generous reading of Burnside's written order might even lead one to interpret it more along those lines. For instance, "a division at least" really meant Franklin could send in a division *or more*—say, a column of thirty thousand. And if Franklin concentrated on intent rather than semantics, he could seize the heights or capture, carry, clear, conquer, storm, or sweep over them, just as the four men had discussed. This option required an aggressive mind-set and an expansive view, neither of which the literal-minded Franklin possessed. Beyond that, McClellanism had inculcated a risk-averse spirit in the Army of the Potomac.

Decision

"I consulted with my corps commanders about this order, as it was not what we expected," Franklin recounted.[19] The conference lasted only long enough for Franklin to decide that his role had changed, and Burnside now depended on him to conduct a reconnaissance in force rather than a sweeping full-scale assault. With the fog dissipating, Franklin "acted upon the order at once, as nearly according to its literal directions as was in my power."[20]

Because the First Corps was already in position, he ordered Reynolds to pick a division and make the attack. Reynolds chose Maj. Gen. George Gordon Meade's unit, "the strongest division I had"—some 4,500 men.[21] Meade initially balked, not out of insubordination but frustration. "The mistake of Antietam was in one corps attacking at a time, and here they were committing the same fault," Charles Wainwright recalled Meade arguing. "This is general Burnside's order," Franklin replied tersely.[22] Reflecting later, Meade realized Franklin "was hampered by his orders and a want of information as to Burnside's real views and plans. A *great* captain would have cast them aside and assumed responsibility."[23] But Franklin wasn't that man. Meade excused himself to begin preparations for the attack.

Burnside's order said Franklin had to keep the attacking force "well supported" while keeping "its line of retreat open." To Franklin, that meant reinforcing the division enough to ensure it "might not be utterly destroyed."[24] Reynolds assigned John Gibbon's division to advance as support on Meade's right and Abner Doubleday's division to strengthen Meade's left.

Curiously, though, when it came to keeping the troops' "line of retreat open," Franklin took a much more expansive view. Rather than just clearing the way for Meade's division, he interpreted the directive to mean he should do so for the entire grand division. Perhaps the three pontoon bridges suddenly felt like a tenuous connection to safety if things went poorly. Franklin's dispro-

While it would be reasonable for all commanders to keep an eye on their line of retreat, Franklin seemed inordinately concerned for his, thereby crippling his ability to devote resources to the fight. Library of Congress.

portionate concern meant Smith's Sixth Corps would sit almost entirely unengaged for the day, held in readiness in case of a Confederate counterattack.

"I put in all the troops that I thought it proper and prudent to put in," Franklin said. "I fought the whole strength of my command as far as I could, and at the same time keep my connexion [*sic*] with the river open. The reason that we failed was, that we had not troops enough to carry the points where the attack was made under the orders that were given."[25]

Results

Unknown to the Federals, Jackson's entire corps had concentrated on Franklin's front thanks to Burnside's delay of the previous day. Meade would advance, break through, and be repulsed because of a lack of reinforcements to counter Jackson's greater numbers. Franklin's decision to withhold Smith's Sixth Corps from the main action would undercut any chance of success. Franklin was right insofar as there were not enough troops to carry the position, but it was because of his own lack of initiative, not because of the orders.

Other factors would play into Meade's repulse, as well (see the next two critical decisions).

Impact

"The orders issued to Franklin have formed the subject of an extended controversy," Second Corps historian Francis Walker aptly understated years later.[26]

Burnside bore a considerable degree of culpability for sending a poorly worded order and sending it so late. He could have made his intentions clearer, and he could have written the commands more plainly. Also, had the order arrived earlier, Franklin might have felt like he had more time to ask for clarification instead of preparing "to move at once." Burnside should also have better prepped Hardie about his intentions. After all, why send a brigadier general unless he had some authority, expertise, and insight that uniquely qualified him for a job a regular courier could have otherwise done?

That said, if Franklin didn't understand his orders, he should have sought clarification. It was this decision to go ahead with the attack anyway, even though he didn't properly comprehend his role or his expectations, that doomed Burnside's entire plan. The close proximity of the telegraph office made his dereliction even more stunning. In fact, at 7:40 a.m., once Meade's division got underway, Franklin had Hardie send a message to Burnside with an update—a fact Franklin later broadcast widely and loudly.[27] "By eight o'clock of that morning General Burnside was informed . . . of the fact that I had sent General Meade's Division to make the movement directed by him,"

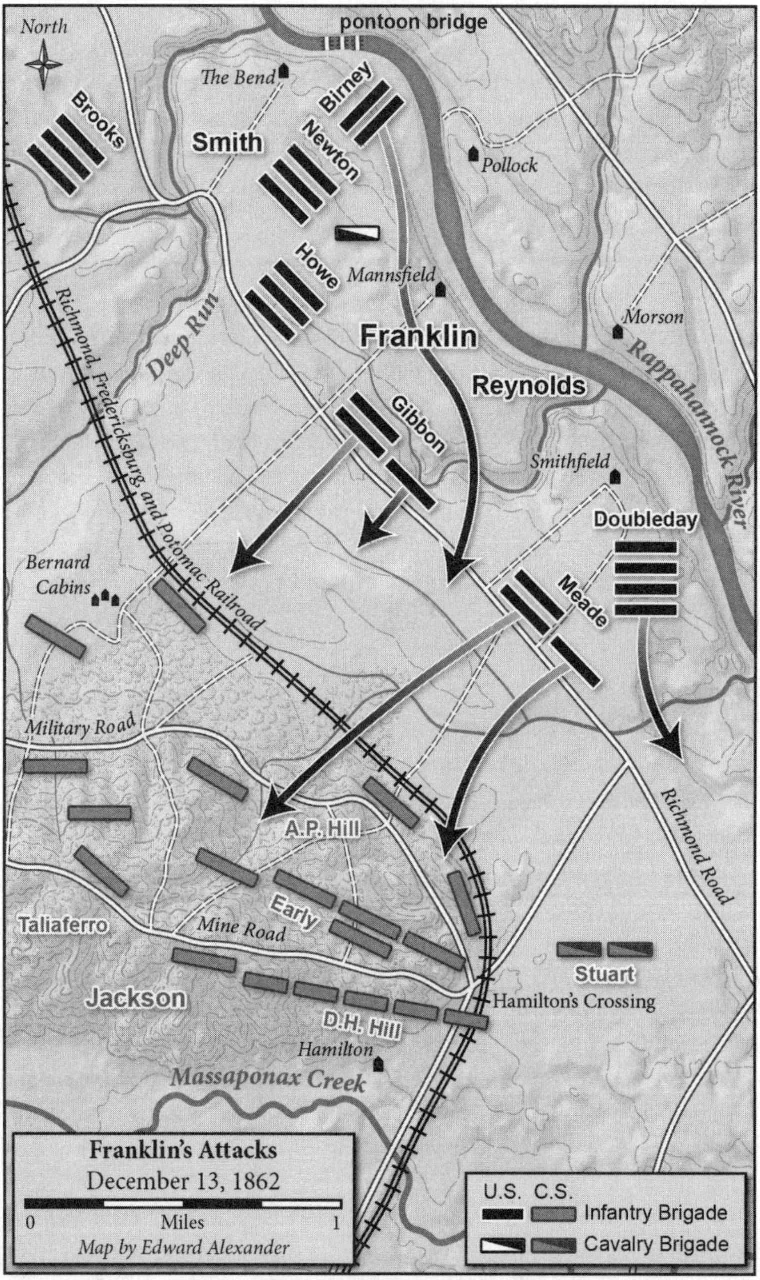

Reynolds sent the divisions of Brig. Gen. John Gibbon, Maj. Gen. George G. Meade, and Brig. Gen. Abner Doubleday forward, but Doubleday, tasked with guarding the entire army's left flank, was drawn off. When Meade broke through and called for reinforcements, Brig. Gen. David Birney's undersized division had to come forward all the way from the pontoon bridges before it could enter the fight. This was one of several factors that cost the Federals irreplaceable time. Edward Alexander.

Franklin crowed. "Had General Burnside, on the receipt of General Hardie's first dispatch, discovered that I had either misapprehended his order or was sending too small a force to its execution, he would at the moment have corrected my misapprehension."[28]

In fact, though, Burnside did send one of his staff officers to get a better sense of what was going on. A short time after that, he sent a follow-up order, carried by another staff officer, for Franklin to "advance his right and front." The Left Grand Division commander demurred.

Burnside and Franklin would spill considerable ink over the years explaining their respective sides of the misunderstanding. Ironically, Burnside articulated his defense with great clarity:

> General Franklin was directed to seize, if possible, the heights near Captain Hamilton's, and to send at once a column of attack for that purpose, composed of a division at least, in the lead, well supported, and to keep his whole command in readiness to move down the old Richmond road [to the Confederate flank]. . . . He was ordered to seize these heights, if possible, and to do it at once.[29]

"I wanted to obtain possession of that new [military] road," Burnside later explained, "and that was my reason for making an attack on the extreme left. I did not intend to make the attack on the right until that position had been taken, which I supposed would stagger the enemy, cutting their line in two."[30] Elsewhere, Burnside said, "I directed General Sumner's column not to move until he received orders from me, while [General Franklin] was ordered to move at once. The movements were not intended to be simultaneous; in fact, I did not intend to move General Sumner until I learned that Franklin was about to gain the heights."[31]

Franklin, for his part, went so far as to publish a pamphlet laying out his side of the story and refuting testimony given to the Joint Committee on the Conduct of the War. "General Burnside's order, though incongruous and contradictory on its face, admitted of but one interpretation, viz., that he intended to make an armed observation from the left, to ascertain the strength of the enemy," Franklin argued.[32] He also claimed Burnside "never told me, or gave me to understand, that I had either misconstrued or disobeyed his orders, or was in any way responsible for the disaster of the 13th."[33]

Burnside's response, written from Cincinnati in May 1863, essentially said Franklin's explanation didn't pass the commonsense test. "He understood my plan very well, and knew that I did not cross more than 100,000 men over the river to make a reconnaissance," Burnside wrote, "and he also knows that I did not place him there in command of half the men of the Army, with the idea that he would make the attack with so small force, after he was ordered to seize a point if possible."[34]

In his official report, written in November 1865, Burnside stated, "The object of this order is clear."[35] Obviously it was not. The general's ongoing exhaustion, his short night of sleep, the pressure of imminent battle, and the rush to issue overdue orders all combined in a perfect storm of muddy prose. But in Burnside's defense, looking at the directive through his expectations and intentions, it's possible to see how his commands were clear *to him*. Writers know what they mean to say when they write something. The challenge is to ensure that what ends up on paper *actually says* what the writers mean, not just what they *think* it says. Knowing what Burnside *meant* to say, one can look at his order to Franklin and see that it can, indeed, be interpreted exactly as Burnside intended.

"The whole affair turned on a misapprehension," Meade later wrote to his wife, "[with] Burnside thinking he was saying and ordering one thing and Franklin understanding another. I know that Franklin did not, nor did any of those around him, believe or understand that Burnside intended our attack for the main attack, which Burnside now avers was always his intention."[36] The

Maj. Gen. George Gordon Meade would find the most success of any Federal officer at Fredericksburg, but he also found the army ill prepared to support him. Library of Congress.

mismatched maps account for this misunderstanding, but unfortunately, no one knew about them. The only way the discrepancy might possibly have come to light would have been if Hardie had sought clarification from Burnside in person. In the course of his discussions, he would have gotten a good look at Franklin's and Burnside's maps and then made the connection—a string of happenstances that begins to stretch the bounds of credulity, even if it doesn't break them.

Meade felt bad about getting dragged into the controversy between the two men. "I feel very sorry for Franklin, because I like him, and because he has always been consistently friendly to me," he said, later adding, "In all this war he has shown more real regard for me and appreciation for me than any other man."[37] He felt that Burnside and the Joint Committee were making a mistake in holding Franklin responsible for the disaster at Fredericksburg. "Franklin may be chargeable with a want of energy, with failing, without reference to orders, to take advantage of a grand opportunity for distinction, with, in fact, not doing *more* than he was strictly required to do," Meade conceded, "but it is absurd to say he failed to obey, or in any way obstructed the prompt executions of his orders; that is, so far as I know them."[38]

Meade biographer Isaac Pennypacker is less gracious than his biographee. "This part of the story of Fredericksburg reads as if [Franklin] had made up his mind that the assault would fail," Pennypacker said in 1901, "and could not change his trend of thought quickly enough to rise to the occasion." Burnside's orders "could have been interpreted as readily in favor of doing much as in favor of doing little, and a vigorous lieutenant would not have missed the opportunity to win a victory."[39]

9. John Pelham Harasses the Union Left Flank

Situation

Twenty-four-year-old Maj. John Pelham began December 13 with a farewell. He and other members of Maj. Gen. Jeb Stuart's staff, headquartered along the Telegraph Road just south of Fredericksburg at a bivouac they called "Camp No-Camp," arose early to make their preparations for battle.[40] "The darkness of night was just giving way to the doubtful light of morning," recalled Heros von Borcke, Stuart's chief of staff.[41] Sharing their company for the previous few days had been a Captain Phillips of the British Grenadier Guard. Phillips had been enjoying a short leave of absence from his battalion, then stationed in Canada, by serving as an observer with the Army of Northern Virginia.[42] For the day's battle, Phillips decided to watch alongside Lee, perched atop a

Maj. John Pelham left West Point just weeks before his graduation so he could join the Alabama militia. Library of Congress.

hill closer to the northern end of the Confederate line. Before he left, though, Phillips asked Pelham for a favor.

Pelham, an Alabamian, had withdrawn from West Point weeks before graduation in order to join the Confederate military at the start of the war. He eventually found himself serving as the lieutenant of an artillery battery on the Virginia Peninsula, where his skill caught the eye of Stuart, who transferred the major to command of the cavalry's horse artillery. Although one of Stuart's officers called him "a mere beardless boy," Pelham handled the assignment "with a genius and obstinacy combined which excited the admiration of the whole army."[43]

During his visit, Phillips enjoyed Pelham's company just as Pelham apparently enjoyed that of the "portly grenadier, whose engaging manners had endeared him to us all," as von Borcke described him.[44] The Englishman wore a red-and-blue striped necktie that included a bit of the ribbon from his Grenadier regiment. He asked Pelham to wear the ribbon as a talisman during the battle and return it afterward to be preserved as a relic. "The boy-hero," said von Borcke, "with the blush of modesty and pride suffusing his fair cheek, readily accepted the compliment, and, tying the ribbon around his cap, galloped off with us to the front, where we hastened to take our position on the extreme right."[45]

Along the way, the party stopped atop Prospect Hill, where Stuart conferred with Stonewall Jackson and division commander A. P. Hill. To their northeast, the open plain that stretched to the river was bathed in fog, but the conference of officers could hear the Army of the Potomac stirring. "Through the white mists of the morning," said von Borcke, "arose an indistinct murmur, like the distant hum of myriads of bees, vaguely announcing to us its hostile occupation by thousands of human beings."[46]

Jackson had packed four infantry divisions into his section of the Confederate line and arrayed an impressive number of artillery pieces—fifty-four in all—to support them. Pelham's horse artillery, positioned on the extreme right flank, on the far side of Hamilton's Crossing, added another eighteen. "The position was a commanding one," said Jackson's chief of artillery, Stapleton Crutchfield, "and [it] afforded admirable advantages against a direct assault from infantry."[47]

An artillerist himself, Jackson itched to go on the offensive with his formidable array.[48] However, after consulting both with Lee and Crutchfield, the Second Corps commander decided to reserve fire until the Federal infantry made its assault. This would be particularly important "should they endeavor to move down the river to threaten or turn our right," Crutchfield said. In anticipation, the artillery chief ordered Lieut. Col. Reuben Lindsay Walker, commanding the fourteen cannon on Prospect Hill, "to keep his guns concealed as well as he could, and not to allow himself to be drawn into an artillery duel." Then, when the infantry got within effective range, the artillery could open with everything it had.[49]

The cavalrymen bid Jackson adieu and continued on, descending the southeast slope of the hill. They passed over the tracks of the Richmond,

A granite monument erected in 1903 by James Power Smith, a member of Jackson's staff, announces the location of "Jackson on the Field" at Prospect Hill. Chris Mackowski.

Fredericksburg, & Potomac at Hamilton's Crossing, then crossed a road that led to the Richmond / Bowling Green Road two-thirds of a mile to the northeast. (This was the road Burnside's map mistakenly identified as the Richmond Road.) There, the soldiers took up their position on the far right of the army, where Stuart had posted two full brigades of cavalry. It would fall to them to protect the flank if the Federals tried to get around Prospect Hill—exactly what Burnside intended to do, despite Franklin's misinterpretation of his orders. Lee appeared shortly thereafter as part of an inspection of the full line, and he approved Stuart's dispositions.

Pelham, with Phillips's ribbon still hanging from his cap, took his place with the eighteen guns of his horse artillery, and together they waited—"the young leader longing for the combat," von Borcke noted, "and anxious to open the ball."[50]

Options

Option 1: Maintain the Defensive

Following Jackson's lead atop Prospect Hill, Pelham could let the situation play out. If the Federals went straight at Jackson's line, they would remain out of Pelham's effective range; an expenditure of ammunition in that case might be satisfying but also wasteful. However, if the Federals tried to outflank the Confederate position, their course would bring them straight at the horse artillery's position. In that case, Pelham would want all the ammunition he could get. Spending ammunition now, while Federals were out of effective range, would only diminish his supply for later, when he might really need it.

Option 2: Create an Offensive Opportunity as the Federals Prepare to Attack

Horse artillery was mobile in a way most other artillery was not. Its guns were equipped for speed and light travel, an advantage Pelham could use. While Federals might be out of range from Pelham's position, Pelham could alter that distance by moving some or all of his artillery closer to them. Stuart's skirmishers that morning had pushed all the way to the Federal picket line, which took them beyond the Richmond / Bowling Green Road. Coming up behind these men, Pelham could potentially get within a few hundred yards of any advancing Federal force. The fog could provide enough cover to mask his movement out there.[51]

If he moved to this location without finding any suitable place to deploy, though, Pelham would leave his artillery exposed and vulnerable. He also risked getting caught out of position. If the major moved forward and Federals cut him off, this result could not only spell capture or death for him and his men, but also diminish Confederate firepower on the vulnerable flank.

Option 3: Create a Counteroffensive Opportunity as the Federals Attack

Rather than act alone, Pelham could work in concert with the rest of the Confederate artillery placed along Prospect Hill. That would mean allowing the Federals to advance within effective range of Crutchfield's guns. With Pelham situated somewhere on the Federals' flank, he and Crutchfield could open fire simultaneously, catching Federals in a cross fire that would make their position untenable. That could potentially break up the entire Federal assault.

Waiting for the Federals to get into position, though, would allow more fog to burn away. As a result, Pelham would not enjoy as much of its protective cover as he would if he advanced sooner. Pelham might also find himself in the direct path of any Federal units sent in to support the left flank of the main assault. Indeed, although he didn't know it, he would sit somewhere astride the very path Reynolds had laid out for Doubleday.

Decision

Further recon revealed a good location where the road from Hamilton's Crossing intersected with the Richmond / Bowling Green Road. A Northern artillerist, Charles Wainwright, eyed the Richmond Road for many of the same reasons Pelham did. "This road along our front is very nearly straight" Wainwright wrote. "The fence on either side is made . . . by throwing up an earthen bank about two feet high. . . . All along on this bank are growing numerous cedars, and that on the north side is farther raised by a wattle fence of a couple feet affording a most complete screen though no other protection."[52] Pelham, by contrast, did find additional protection: a depression in the ground that would help keep his men out of sight.

With a suitable place to deploy and Stuart's subsequent approval, Pelham gathered up Capt. Mathis Henry's crew and its 12-pounder Napoleon and set out through the fog.[53] At the intersection, the crew unlimbered and took aim in the direction of the Federal left flank a mere four hundred yards away. "In a few minutes, his solid shot were ploughing at short range with fearful effect through the dense columns of Federals," recalled von Borcke, who further claimed, "[The] boldness of the enterprise and the fatal accuracy of the firing seemed to paralyse for a time and then to stampede the whole of the extreme left of the Yankee army, and terror and confusion reigned there during some

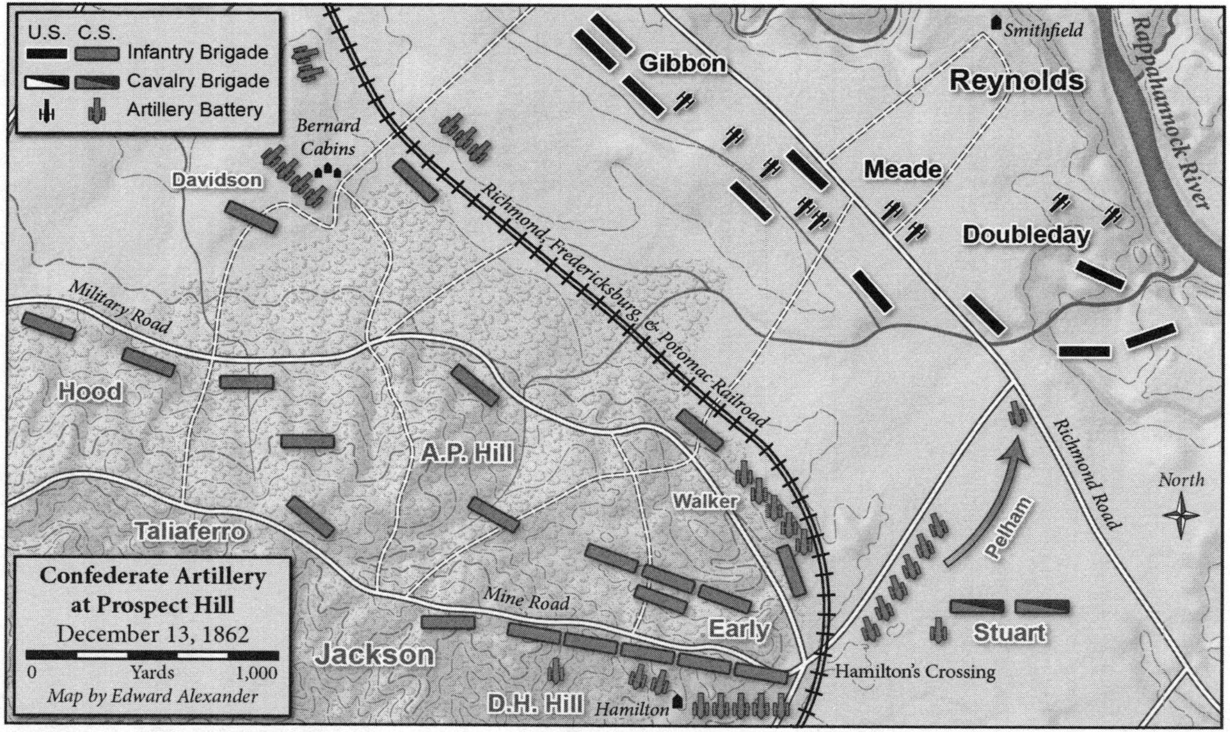

The southern end of the Confederate line did not enjoy the same topographical dominance as the northern end along Marye's Heights. Jackson compensated by loading his right flank with artillery, anticipating an attack that would try to get around him there. Stuart's horse artillery would provide extra mobility to defend against any such assault. Pelham took advantage of that mobility by taking a gun to a forward position to harass the Federal advance. Edward Alexander.

minutes."[54] In fact, Pelham managed to get off but two or three shots before Federals responded.

And thus began "one of the most remarkable 'artillery duels' of the war," wrote artillerist John Esten Cooke.[55] The time was 10:00 a.m.

Results

Because of the way Reynolds had deployed the First Corps after it initially crossed the Rappahannock River, George Gordon Meade had to march his division parallel to the Richmond / Bowling Green Road in order to get out from behind John Gibbon's division, which fronted the road. Once past, Meade would swing around and advance toward the Confederate line, with Gibbon advancing on his right as support. Meanwhile, Abner Doubleday's division would advance behind Meade as support and protection for his left.

As Meade made his turn, he exposed his left flank to Pelham's gun. "This disposition had scarcely been made when the enemy opened a brisk fire," Meade wrote. He redeployed so one of his brigades faced southeast while the rest stayed facing southwest, "thus forming . . . two sides of a square," he said.[56] Lee, watching from Prospect Hill, noted the effect of Pelham's "rapid and well-directed enfilade fire, which arrested their progress."[57]

Meade brought forward his own batteries to try and silence the threat on his flank, and big guns from the far side of the Rappahannock added their weight. Everyone seemed to miss. Federal artillerist Charles Wainwright, tasked with ferreting out Pelham's position, complained, "This section was so well sheltered by the cedar trees and hedge that it was difficult to meet its fire effectually."[58] The fog and low ground helped Pelham too.

Pelham also had more targets to shoot at, so the fog hampered him less than his opponents. Battery A of the First Pennsylvania Light Artillery came to immediate grief. "Shortly after entering action had the axle of my third piece broken by a shot from the enemy," said Lieut. John G. Simpson, "at the same time destroying the sponge bucket, sponge staff and rammer, and lunette strap."[59]

Stuart's skirmishers noted additional movement on the Federal flank: Doubleday's division moving up behind Meade. Using the cover of the hedges and trees on the roadside, Stuart's men advanced up the Bowling Green Road to delay them.[60] Doubleday responded by going all in. This drove Stuart's skirmishers back into a patch of pine woods to Pelham's right. The woods "proved to be a very strong position," Doubleday discovered, "intersected with ravines and covered with a thick undergrowth."[61] It took some time for his men to drive the Confederates out.

During the fight between the Confederate skirmishers and Federal infantry, Pelham let his guns go quiet so as not to fire on his fellow cavalrymen, but once they began to clear out of the way, he opened up again—on Meade's men and, with cannister, on Doubleday's. "It was obvious, however, that the piece would soon be disabled unless assistance came," observed John Esten Cooke.[62] Stuart sent Cooke forward with an additional gun, a British Blakely with impressive firepower, but Cooke never got it into the fight. "The first shell thrown by them struck the gun. and dismounted it, killing two of the men," he said.[63]

The concentrated fire against Pelham "did great execution among his cannoneers," and after nearly an hour, his crew had suffered enough casualties that Pelham was reduced to helping serve the cannon himself.[64] Stuart gave him as many as three opportunities to withdraw. One courier found Pelham "calmly sitting on his horse with one leg thrown over the [pommel] of his saddle giving orders." The messenger further described the encounter: "I rode up and delivered General Stuart's message, which was to ask him how he was getting on. His reply was, 'Go back and tell General Stuart I am doing first rate; that I have only lost one man so far.'"[65] Pelham was "too obstinate a fighter to retire," Cooke later said.[66] Von Borcke chimed in, too: "[T]he young hero could not be moved. 'Tell the General I can hold my ground.'"[67]

However, Doubleday's deployment allowed the First Maryland Battery to change its position, allowing it to take aim at Pelham from the rear, from a position near Smithfield.[68] Running low on ammunition, with several wounded men knocked out of action, Pelham finally withdrew. "He sustained their heavy fire," Lee noted, "with the unflinching courage that ever distinguished him."[69]

Impact

In his official report of the battle, Lee made mention of "the gallant Pelham," a phrase that would attach itself to the young artillerist for the rest of his short life. Pelham would be killed just three months later—on St. Patrick's Day 1863—opposing a Federal cavalry raid at Kelly's Ford, upriver on the Rappahannock. In death, the Gallant Pelham would be enshrined as a Confederate martyr whose memory would live on.

Although Lee lauded Pelham's work on the morning of December 13, he did see a missed opportunity. Had Meade advanced a bit farther before Pelham opened, Meade's division would have made an excellent target for the artillery Crutchfield had placed along Prospect Hill (as Meade would soon find out, anyway). The resultant cross fire from Pelham and Crutchfield could have proven very hot, indeed. Lee apparently considered Stuart, not Pelham, responsible for the early trigger pull.[70]

Brig. Gen. Abner Doubleday made a reasonable decision at Fredericksburg to play it safe—but he did so at a time when bolder thinking would have allowed Federals to exploit a breakthrough in the Confederate position. Library of Congress.

As it was, Pelham tied down Abner Doubleday's division for the entire day. Doubleday later defended his decision by contending that he could not simultaneously advance in support of Meade's left flank and protect the whole Union army's left flank from any Confederate force returning to Pelham's corner. Because of Doubleday's decision, Meade would hold a festering grudge that would come back to bite both men following action on July 1, 1863, at Gettysburg. Following John Reynolds's death during that battle, Meade would deny Doubleday command of the First Corps. Doubleday would in turn exact revenge by offering inflammatory testimony against Meade to the Joint Committee on the Conduct of the War.

Despite Doubleday's decision to defend the army's left flank on December 13, Meade's division went on to pierce the Confederate line. Without reinforcements, though, the division was unable to hold its ground. Had Doubleday made the turn to the southwest as Meade had, and then advanced as Meade's support, the presence of his division would have given Meade much-needed help exactly when and where Meade needed it. Instead, Doubleday's approximately four thousand men remained effectively out of the fight, waiting for an attack from phantoms who had vanished with the morning fog.

"Pelham has for all time illustrated the power of guns in the hands of a dashing and energetic horse artilleryman, associated with a bold cavalry leader," wrote an adoring Jennings Cropper Wise in his 1915 history of the Army of Northern Virginia's artillery, *The Long Arm of Lee*. "Almost unaided and with a single piece he entirely neutralized Doubleday's whole infantry division," Wise further said of the officer.[71] Adoring tone or not, as the old expression goes, it's not bragging if it's true.

On the east bank of the Rappahannock River, Ambrose Burnside heard the lone cannon blasts fired by Pelham and the artillery duel that erupted as a result. He took it as a sign that Franklin had started his attack. Burnside also thought of the military road that connected the two ends of the Confederate army and the reinforcements Lee could send from the north end of the line to bolster the soon-to-be-beleaguered south end. To hold those reinforcements in place, the Union general set into motion his plans to pin them down. Word soon went down the chain of command from Burnside to Sumner to Darius Couch to begin the assault against Marye's Heights.

10. Jubal Early Marches to the Sound of the Guns

Situation

The sun rose red and fiery that morning, said one Confederate staff officer, and soon it began to burn away the fog.[72] Watching from Prospect Hill, Lee saw that "the partial rising of the mist disclosed a large force moving in line of battle against Jackson." In addition, "dense masses appeared in front of A. P. Hill, stretching far up the river in the direction of Fredericksburg."[73] Jackson, A. P. Hill, and their assembled staffs noticed the dense crowds too. Stuart's chief of staff, Heros von Borcke, described the sight as "a moving forest of steel, their [the Federals'] bayonets glistening in the bright sunlight."[74]

George Gordon Meade's 4,500-man division had begun its approach.

Confederate artillery fire finally opened, pinning Meade's men in the field for a couple hours. There they sought shelter behind a ridge so low no one had even noticed it at the start of their advance. By 1:00, Meade's men were up again, advancing in strength, and they pierced the middle of A. P. Hill's line. Federals swept to the right and left, widening their breakthrough, and they flooded forward, moving deeper into the breach. "Thunder soon rolled all along our lines," von Borcke said.[75]

With only two miles of front to cover, Jackson had stacked his four divisions deep. Maj. Gen. Ambrose Powell Hill held the front along Prospect Hill, extending northward to link up with Maj. Gen. John Bell Hood's First Corps division. Behind Little Powell, Brig. Gen. Jubal Early held the back of Prospect Hill, with Brig. Gen. William Taliaferro positioned on his left, extending the second line behind Hill's men. Maj. Gen. Daniel Harvey Hill waited as a reserve behind Early.

When A. P. Hill positioned his troops, however, he discovered part of

Maj. Gen. A. P. Hill predicted the trouble that would come his way at Fredericksburg. "The almighty will get tired of helping Jackson after a while, and then he'll get the damndest thrashing," he complained to Jeb Stuart earlier in December, adding, "[though] I shall get my share and probably all the blame, for the people never blame Stonewall for any disaster." Library of Congress.

his line ran through a swamp. Believing no organized body of men could advance through such a morass, he posted his troops on either side of it and behind it. But he left the swamp itself undefended, creating a gap of some six hundred yards. Lee and Jackson, on their inspections of Hill's line, agreed with the division commander's reasoning and let his disposition stand.[76]

As Meade's men advanced, they took terrible fire from Hill's soldiers. Naturally, the Federals gravitated to the area where the least amount of fire came from—right into the undefended swamp. The swarm of men, barely holding together as cohesive units amid the confusing terrain and fire of battle, knew enough to push their advantage. By 1:30, Meade's troops found purchase on the northern and eastern slopes of Prospect Hill, where Lee, Jackson, and the others had first glimpsed the moving forest of steel that morning.

Brig. Gen. James Archer, holding that portion of the hill, watched his regiments fall one by one. Federals "succeeded in passing round my flank, and attacked the Nineteenth Georgia and Fourteenth Tennessee in rear and flank," he said. "The greater part of the Seventh Tennessee, also seeing the regiments on their left give way and hearing the cry that the enemy was in their rear, left the trenches in disorder."[77] The diminutive Archer, known as the Little Gamecock because of his fierce fighting spirit, understood the serious trouble he faced, so he sent aides to Brig. Gen. Maxcy Gregg and Brig. Gen. Jubal Early to ask for support.

Gregg, however, was buried in trouble himself—deeply enough that he'd be mortally wounded trying to rally his men from the thick of the fight. Posted

The irascible Brig. Gen. Jubal Early was the only man known to swear in front of Robert E. Lee, but his cool head and bold decision-making at Fredericksburg flagged him in Lee's eyes as someone worthy of greater responsibilities. Library of Congress.

behind the swamp and caught off guard, his brigade took the full momentum of Meade's breakthrough when Federals pushed into the breach. Early, meanwhile, had arrived on the battlefield just that morning after marching nearly fifteen miles the previous evening. He had come from the lower Rappahannock River, where Jackson had posted him to contest any possible river crossings in the direction of Port Royal. At midnight, Early's men had camped two miles from Hamilton's Crossing, then finished the march in the morning. They took up their position behind A. P. Hill just as Pelham was starting out on his fog-shrouded poke against the Federal left flank.

From his position on the lee side of the hill, Early heard the sounds of battle and noticed the fighting "becoming quite animated" as it seemed to get closer. Just then, the messenger from Archer appeared, "stating that General Archer was pressed, and wished re-enforcements." As Early considered the urgent request, a second messenger appeared. "I received an order from the lieutenant-general commanding the corps [Jackson's] . . . to hold my division in readiness to move to the right of the railroad, as the enemy was making a demonstration in that direction."[78]

Options

Option 1: Ignore Archer's Request and Obey Jackson's Order

By December 1862, Jackson's rigidity when it came to following orders was not just legendary but gospel.[79] Col. James A. Walker, commanding one of

Early's brigades, once summed it up well. Years earlier, as a student of Jackson's at the Virginia Military Institute, a classroom dispute with Jackson led to a court-martial. During his defense, Walker spoke of Jackson's disciplinary expectations. "With a rigidity of adherence to the letter of his instructions known only to the veteran, he unites a mind suspicious by nature, a temper made irritable by sickness and suffering; and a tone imperative by long habit of commanding," the colonel testified.[80] Walker, who was dismissed, challenged Jackson to a duel over the matter. (By the war, all would apparently be forgiven between them, and by mid-1863, Walker would command the Stonewall Brigade, where he would earn the nickname "Stonewall Jim" for bravery in combat.)

Jackson brought the same attitude to war that he'd once brought to bear on Walker. In the earliest days of the conflict, while assigned to Harpers Ferry, "some willful young officers made experiment of resisting [Jackson's] authority." According to onetime chief of staff Robert Lewis Dabney, "his [Jackson's] penalties were so prompt and inexorable, that no one desired to adventure another act of disobedience."[81]

Most notoriously, Jackson court-martialed Richard Garnett for withdrawing his outnumbered and out-of-ammunition brigade against orders during the Battle of Kernstown in March 1862. Later in the Valley Campaign, after the Twelfth Georgia abandoned Front Royal, Jackson arrested both the unit's colonel, Z. T. Conner, and Conner's second-in-command, Maj. Willis Hawkins. In August, Jackson apprehended all five of Maxcy Gregg's regimental commanders for allowing their men to burn fence rails on a rainy night against orders. In September, he arrested Brig. Gen. William E. Starke for refusing to help clear up a disciplinary matter. That same week, Jackson jailed A. P. Hill for neglect of duty—a matter that still festered between them by the time of the fight in Fredericksburg.

In addition, Stonewall Jackson had deserters shot. He arrested artillerists for riding on cannon during river crossings. During the Romney Campaign in first days of 1862, in the midst of killing cold, he ordered his men to forego campfires so as to not reveal their positions; men froze to death in their obedience rather than risk his wrath.[82]

Early had his own reason for staying on Jackson's good side. On November 25, as the corps marched from the valley to join Lee, members of the Louisiana Brigade—part of Early's Division—opened some confiscated barrels of liquor. Early himself had apparently partaken of the spirits, too, and was "merry and a-grinning." Jackson later sent Early a note confronting him about it; Early replied irreverently. Jackson wanted him put under arrest, although a staff member talked him out of it. The issue had hung unresolved between the two men ever since.[83]

This is all to say that there was strong precedence for Early to follow his commander's orders, despite any pleas from Archer.

Option 2: Ignore Jackson's Order and Comply With Archer's Request

By the sound of it, the fighting might come to Early if he didn't go to it. Early could preempt the approaching combat by moving his division toward the sound of the guns. Rather than move to the road per Jackson's order, Early could hunker down in place and brace himself for the Federals' inevitable appearance. If he was not proactive, he could at least form up his men like a breakwall and let the Federals crash into him. However, he didn't know the extent of the fighting, the number of enemy troops approaching, or even from which direction they came. Finally, by passively waiting, Confederates would allow Federals to keep the initiative.

Option 3: Partially Comply With Both Orders

Early had placed the four brigades of his division in two lines, with two brigades in each. In front, closest to the fighting, he had Col. Edmund Atkinson's brigade on the right and Walker's Brigade on the left; Walker linked with two brigades from Taliaferro's Division. In the second row, Early had Trimble's Brigade, commanded by Col. Robert F. Hoke, behind Atkinson. The Louisiana Brigade under Brig. Gen. Harry T. Hays was stationed to Hoke's right.

Hoke and Hays were both positioned on Mine Road, which led directly to the right of the railroad—exactly where Jackson expected Early to move. Early could ready troops to march on Jackson's command, and using the road, they would be in position in minutes. Meanwhile, Early could send either Atkinson or Walker forward as support, depending on where reinforcements were needed. If Walker went forward, Atkinson could extend to the left to link with Taliaferro and prevent any additional gaps in the line. If Atkinson went forward, Walker could maintain connection with Hoke, just to his rear and right. If Jackson ordered a movement, Hays, Hoke, and either Atkinson or Walker could move while the fourth brigade still went in as support for Archer.

Regardless of the permutation, Early would also need to inform Jackson of what he'd done and why.

Decision

The conflicting messages "caused me to hesitate a moment," Early admitted. Quickly tabulating his troop deployments and his options, he ordered Atkinson's Brigade to ready itself for an advance into the maelstrom. "The

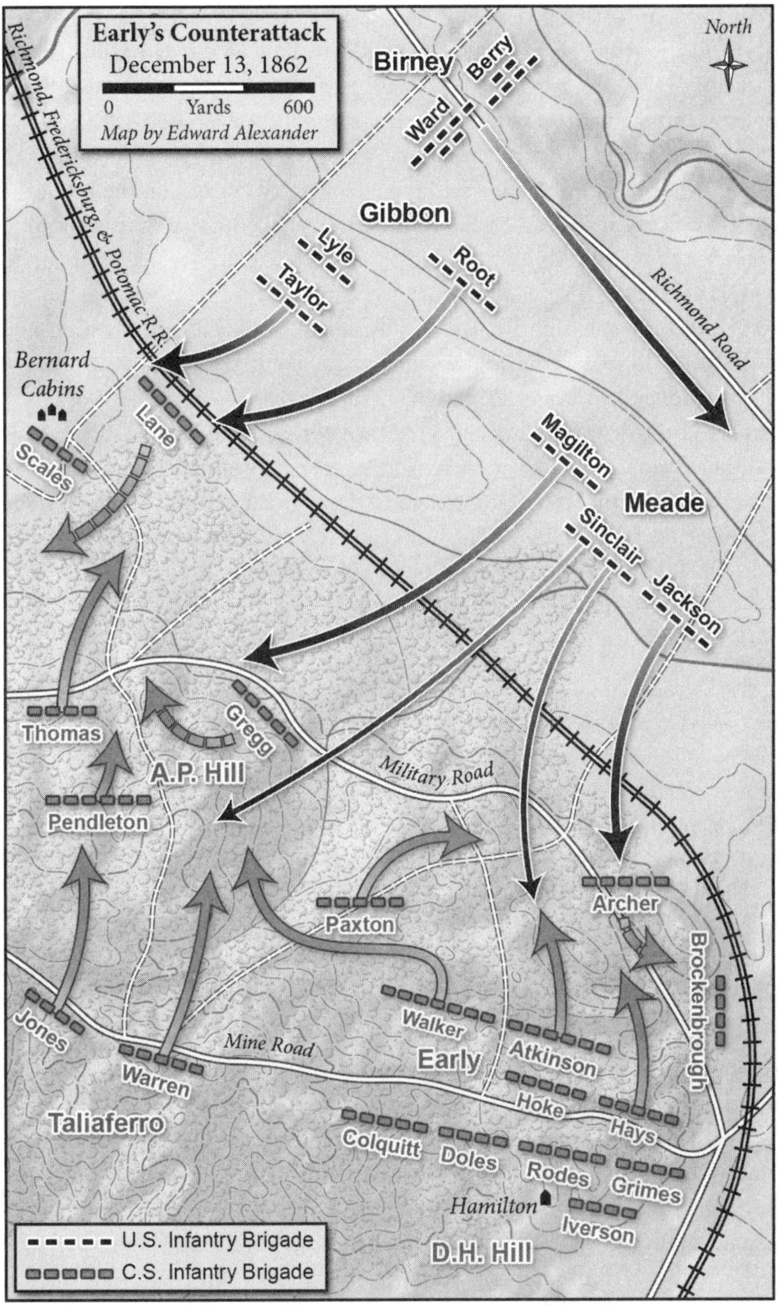

While Meade broke through, Gibbon bent the Confederate line backward. Early responded by sending his brigades to the sound of the guns. Edward Alexander.

order had hardly been given" Early said, when another messenger "came galloping to the rear." From this news, he learned about the gap Hill had left in the line—"an interval" and "an awful gulf," as Early wrote in his official report—and the heavy column of Federals that had penetrated it.[84]

Early ordered the brigade forward. It "moved in fine style," he observed, "and in a few minutes encountered the enemy in the woods on the hill." The general quickly realized how close the Federals had come to surrounding Archer and obtaining "a lodgment from which it would have been difficult to drive him."[85] Early also realized Atkinson's Brigade would not suffice for the job at hand, considering the size of the Federal breakthrough. He then sent in Walker's Brigade at the double-quick to help plug the gap.

No sooner had Early dispatched Walker than he received word that "Archer's brigade was giving way." He then commanded Hoke to advance as additional support. "Hoke attacked the enemy vigorously," Early said, "and drove him from the woods and trench to the railroad in front, in which there were reserves."[86] As Hoke went in, a courier arrived from Jackson with an order "to advance to the front with the whole division."[87] In response, Early sent Hays's Brigade in to reinforce Hoke.

Early was now all in.

Results/Impact

"This was so serious an emergency that I determined to act upon it at once, notwithstanding the previous directions from General Jackson to hold my division in readiness for another purpose," Early explained in his memoirs, "and I accordingly ordered Atkinson to advance with his brigade."[88]

"That gallant old warrior, General Early, to whom I had sent, came crashing through the woods at the double-quick," a thankful Hill later marveled. "The enemy, completely broken, fled in confusion."[89] Hill's glossy summation belied the intensity of the fight once Early swept in, though, as well as the stubborn stand Meade's men made once driven back to the railroad track, which swept around the base of the hill and offered them a strong defensive position.

Yet in the end, Meade's men did fall back across the open field. Without reinforcements to exploit their initial success or help them hold the ground they'd captured, they had no hope of resisting three brigades of reinforcements—even ones as footsore and tired as Early's were from their previous day's march and abbreviated night of sleep. It was not for a lack of trying on Meade's part, though (see the next critical decision).

To Meade's right, John Gibbon's division, sent forward as his support, also met with initial success. While they did not break through the Confederate line, the soldiers savaged Brig. Gen. James Lane's North Carolina brigade (a fight that, unbeknownst to Gibbon, placed him in direct conflict with three of his brothers, Tar Heels all).

In his official report, Early lavished praise on the Little Gamecock:

> I feel it incumbent on me to state that to Brigadier-General Archer . . . is due the credit of having held the enemy in check, with a small portion of his men, after his flank and rear had been gained, until re-enforcements arrived. . . . But for the gallant stand made by General Archer the enemy would have gained an advantage which it would have required a greater sacrifice of life to wrest from him than was made.[90]

In contrast, Early's own superior, Stonewall Jackson, made slim notice of Early's work on December 13, although Jackson did single out Atkinson and Hoke for their work in the counterattack, as well as Lane for his "brave and obstinate resistance."[91] If Jackson was upset by Early's independent judgment to advance into the fight instead of holding his position, no record of that fact exists. But even so, Early's success made it impossible to reprimand him.

Tellingly, when Lee wrote to Richmond on December 14, he described the incident thus: "During the attack, which was protracted and hotly contested, two of General Hill's brigades were driven back upon our second line. General Early, with part of his division, *being ordered to his support* [emphasis added], drove the enemy back."[92] Lee did not make reference to Early's independent decision to move to Archer's aid, which came well before any order from Jackson to do so. However, no documentation of why Lee made that omission exists. He might have been recounting the incident as Jackson and others relayed it to him.

But Lee certainly found out about Early's action at some point. Because of the incident, the commander of the Army of Northern Virginia marked Early as someone who could exercise quick, decisive judgment and who wasn't afraid of hard action. Lee began to entrust Early with greater and greater responsibilities. During the Chancellorsville Campaign in May 1863, the commander gave Early the job of protecting the army's rear in Fredericksburg while Lee and Jackson marched westward with the rest of the force to meet Joe Hooker head on. During the fall of 1863, Early would serve as temporary commander of the Second Corps, and in May 1864 at the Battle of Spotsylvania Court House, he would serve as temporary commander of the Third Corps. Later in the campaign, Lee would place Early back in command of the Second Corps. That summer and fall, Early would get semi-independent command in the Shenandoah Valley. That adventure would end poorly for Early, and Lee would recall most of his detachment back to the Army of Northern Virginia, by then in Petersburg. However, Early would remain in command of a brigade in the valley until a disastrous defeat at Waynesboro, Virginia, in March 1865.

In his gracious letter relieving Early, Lee cited his Bad Old Man's "zealous and patriotic services" as reason for taking the time to explain his rationale:

> I have reluctantly arrived at the conclusion that you cannot command the united and willing co-operation which is so essential to success. Your reverses in the Valley, of which the public and the army judge chiefly by the results, have, I fear, impaired your influence both with the people and the soldiers. . . . While my own confidence in your ability, zeal, and devotion to the cause is unimpaired, I have nevertheless felt that I could not oppose what seems to be the current of opinion, without injustice to your reputation and injury to the service. . . .
>
> Thanking you for the fidelity and energy with which you have always supported my efforts, and for the courage and devotion you have ever manifested in the service
>
> I am, very respectfully and truly,
> Your ob't servant,
>
> R. E. Lee.[93]

Early bore no ill will toward Lee for that final decision. Instead, in repayment his commander's ongoing trust in him, Early spent his postwar years as the staunchest of Lee's many defenders. His continued efforts to defend and praise Lee turned Early into a powerful voice of the rising "Lost Cause" movement, which would dominate historical interpretation of the Civil War for more than a century. In effect, Early became one of the most influential Confederates ever.

In contrast, his opponent on December 13, George Gordon Meade, would nearly fade into obscurity.

11. John Reynolds Directs His Artillery

Situation

Not until 1871 would Prussian field marshal Helmuth von Moltke the Elder coin a phrase that could have perfectly described John Reynolds's morning on December 13, 1862: "No plan survives contact with the enemy." Reynolds had rolled his First Corps forward with a clear plan to gain the high ground of Prospect Hill, and Pelham's unexpected single-cannon bombardment brought everything to a halt.

The decisions Reynolds would make in response to this first contact would test him in a way he had never been tested before. A Pennsylvania native and 1841 West Point graduate, Reynolds was a well-regarded career officer with experience at many levels of command in the Mexican-American War, the peacetime army, and the current war, where his combat record had earned the respect of his men and his peers. "Reynolds is a man who is very popular," wrote his admiring friend George Meade, "and always impresses those around him with a great idea of his superiority."[94] In September, Reynolds missed the Battle of Antietam while on special assignment commanding Pennsylvania's state militia, but in late September, he returned to the army and a promotion

Maj. Gen. John Reynolds did not lack for personal bravery, although his fighting instincts sometimes made him forget his proper role in the chain of command. Library of Congress.

to command of the First Corps. Two and a half months later, Fredericksburg was his first test as a corps commander under fire.

"The artillery combat here raged furiously for some time," Reynolds noted of the exchange with Pelham. When his own artillerists finally silenced the Confederate gun, they redirected their fire toward the far woodline, in the direction Meade's division was pointed, "where [Confederate] infantry was supposed to be posted."[95] There, Stonewall Jackson urged his troops to hunker down and ride it out. "The enemy directed his artillery on the heights . . . and upon the wood generally occupied by our troops," he wrote, "evidently with a view of causing us to disclose whatever troops or artillery were there. Not eliciting any response, the enemy was seemingly satisfied that he would experience but little resistance."[96] Jackson soon disabused Reynolds of that notion with an artillery bombardment against Meade's and Gibbon's advancing divisions. Again, Reynolds's plan suffered under contact with the enemy.

With Doubleday's division diverted to protect the Union left flank, Reynolds called for reinforcements from across the river: the Third Corps divisions of Brig. Gens. David Bell Birney and Dan Sickles, borrowed from Joe Hooker's Center Grand Division. As Birney's men arrived, Reynolds directed them into a reserve position behind the embankment of the Bowling Green Road. Birney's men would, for the time being, serve as an added safeguard for the batteries posted there. Reynolds, an old artillerist himself, liked to give his pieces as much protection as possible.

Out in the field, Meade's men suddenly lurched forward. Seated on his big black horse on the Bowling Green Road, Reynolds watched them "advancing in fine order and with gallant determination" toward the Confederate line—but then noticed John Gibbon's division was not advancing on Meade's right.[97] Reynolds spurred his mount in Gibbon's direction, intent on urging along his tardy brigadier. Gibbon, it turned out, hadn't been ready for Meade's advance and was taking the time to dress his ranks before moving forward in support. Annoyed by this latest glitch, Reynolds ordered the division forward.

All three of his divisions had encountered unforeseen difficulties, but now, *finally*, Reynolds had his First Corps all in. First contact with the enemy had derailed his plan in significant ways, but his vigorous battlefield management allowed him to adapt and continue. With the attack again moving forward, Reynolds needed to decide where to position himself so he could best serve his division commanders as they led their troops into the thick of the fray. The calculus of the choice, complex and intense—particularly with enemy artillery fire raining down—involved anticipating to some extent the sorts of decisions he might need to make. Reynolds would need to be able to see the battlefield, easily communicate with his division commanders and his superior, and react swiftly to changing conditions. He also had to balance his own hand directing the entire corps against the hands of his subordinates as they directed their divisions.

At its core, though, the choice Reynolds faced was familiar. Indeed, every general officer, from brigade level all the way up to army command level, faced it on every battlefield: whether (and when) his place would be at the front or in the rear.[98]

Options

Option 1: Return to the Bowling Green Road

Returning to the Bowling Green Road would put Reynolds back near the geographical center of his command. Not only would a position there give him the widest possible panoramic view of the battlefield, it would also make him easy to find. That circumstance would facilitate smooth and regular communication with his three division commanders and his superior, General Franklin. Reynolds could also balance the news he received from couriers with what he could see for himself, allowing him to better exercise his judgment in conducting the fight.

If his division commanders needed help, Reynolds's position along the road could be useful in two ways. First, the corps' artillery was posted along the road. Based on couriers' messages and his own observations, Reynolds could redirect artillery fire as necessary. Second, a more rearward position would give Reynolds ready access to reinforcements should he need to direct them into battle. He recognized the capable leadership of his division commanders. A position rearward would be a tacit endorsement of his trust in them, allowing them to handle things on the front while he held back in a location that would enable him to better support their frontline decisions.

Option 2: Stay In the Thick of the Fight

With his three divisions committed, Reynolds might have chafed at his relative impotence. He loved to be in the thick of the action (something that would eventually lead him to grief on the first day of the Battle of Gettysburg). Staying close to the front would allow him to stay busy, make split decisions more readily, and keep closer to the pulse of the action. He could also inspire his men through his personal example.

Furthermore, a position closer to the front would allow the First Corps commander to keep a closer eye on his division commanders. This was Gibbon's first battle at the helm of a division; for Meade and Doubleday, this was only their second time each. With Reynolds likewise being new at the job, tighter lines of communication would only help.

Decision

Reynolds had two reasonable options, yet he selected neither of them. In fact, at this most critical juncture of the battle, Reynolds seemed to vanish from the battlefield. We know he did not return to the Bowling Green Road—at least not for any length of time or in any way that made him conspicuous.

According to historian Frank O'Reilly, "A close search of the records reveals that Reynolds spent most of his time worrying the artillery about ephemeral details rather than monitoring the overall situation. At one time or another, every battery in the First Corps encountered, received advice from, or took orders from Reynolds."[99] For instance, Captain James H. Cooper of Battery B, First Pennsylvania Light Artillery, noted that it was "by order of General Reynolds" that the battery was redirected from the fight against Pelham to join the general bombardment of the Confederate line. Later in the fight, Capt. Frank P. Amsden of Battery G, First Pennsylvania Light Artil-

Federal artillery advanced from the Bowling Green Road into the field in this area, where Meade had crossed shortly before. Doing so kept the road itself clear for the movement of men and supplies. "Being no breeze to carry the smoke of our guns, the gunners on firing would quickly run to either flank to clear the great volume of smoke hanging in front of their muzzles that they might see where their shells were going," said Pvt. Bates Alexander of the Seventh Pennsylvania Reserves. With that kind of smoke surrounding the artillery pieces, it's little wonder Reynolds was hard to spot. Chris Mackowski.

lery, unable to find Wainwright, received orders from Reynolds instead, who told him, "Fill my chests with ammunition, and report to General Meade."[100]

In his official report of the battle, written December 21, Reynolds outlined the detailed deployments of specific batteries without the benefit of artillery chief Col. Charles Wainwright's report, not written until December 22. Reynolds also singled out eight battery commanders "for the intrepidity with which they maintained their positions, and the coolness and judgment with which they managed their commands under . . . severe fire."[101] His familiarity with these details suggests firsthand knowledge, although it might also have resulted from Reynolds's natural inclination to pay attention to the performance of his artillery.

When Reynolds first assumed command of the corps in late September, Wainwright wrote of him—presciently, as it turned out—"He is an old light-battery captain, and ought to know how to take care of his artillery."[102] How hands-on that care turned out to be. Wainwright noted during the battle that Reynolds "exposed himself in the most reckless manner," suggesting the artillerist saw plenty of him, even if the infantry officers did not.[103] As a former artillerist himself, it's likely Reynolds felt he had expertise to offer, and with eighteen guns along his front, he certainly had much to attend to. Unfortunately, by acting as a major instead of a major general, Reynolds lost sight of the larger battle at its most crucial juncture.

Results

George Gordon Meade had considered it an honor to lead the attack on December 13.[104] "My men went in *beautifully*," he later told his wife, pleased that they "carried everything before them, and drove the enemy for nearly half a mile."[105] Meade waited along the railroad tracks while his soldiers pushed through the swamp and into the forest beyond and the gap in the Confederate line. He remained far enough back to continue directing the fighting as best he could, but close enough that a bullet passed through his hat—so close, he wrote, that he was nearly "a goner."[106]

As Meade's assault began to lose its momentum and his units began to lose their cohesion, he rode along the tracks, doing his best to continue managing the action. He knew he needed help, though: his men would not be able to hold what they'd gained without support. Perceiving what he called "the danger of the too great penetration of my line," Meade dispatched staff officers to both John Gibbon on his right and David Bell Birney in his rear "urging an advance to my support."[107]

A Federal infantryman once said of the puritanical Birney that the army

Brig. Gen. John Gibbon was a North Carolinian who remained loyal to the US Army when his home state seceded. Library of Congress.

"A more dignified individual never mounted a charger," one of Brig. Gen. David Bell Birney's men once said of him. "He reminds me of a graven image and could act as a bust for his own tomb, being utter destitute of color." Library of Congress.

"had few men who could command 10,000 men as well as he," but on this day, Birney's leadership skills failed him. Twice, frantic messengers arrived from Meade, asking the officer to advance his division in support; twice, Birney demurred. Reynolds himself had dictated his position, Birney argued, and he would not accept contradictory orders from one of Reynolds's subordinates. Isaac Pennypacker, an early Meade biographer, later described these events as "a situation to arouse in Meade all that vigorous indignation of which he was fully capable, over a breach of soldierly duty."[108]

And so it was that Meade himself thundered on to the scene, "almost wild with rage," said a witness, as his golden opportunity slipped away and his men were being slaughtered for naught.[109] The general's tattered and confused division, trying to rally along the railroad tracks, desperately needed his leadership. Yet he'd been forced to leave the troops in order to personally seek reinforcements from a man who should have understood the situation and reacted with urgency, not officiousness. In language so ablaze it was enough to "almost make the stones creep," Meade laid into Birney.[110]

Birney protested, claiming he'd been trying for an hour to find Franklin in an effort to get permission to move forward, yet Franklin, it seemed, was nowhere to be found. Nor was Reynolds, for that matter. In the meantime, his orders from Reynolds were preemptory, Birney said.[111] Meade pulled rank.

As the army's newest major general, he claimed responsibility for ordering Birney's division forward. In his official report, Birney rather disingenuously claimed that he "immediately" responded.[112] However, Pennypacker later corrected that characterization: "Birney's action was tardy and feeble."[113]

Birney began to advance just in time to cover the retreat of Meade's men as they tumbled back from the railroad. "The best troops would be justified in withdrawing without loss of honor," Meade later said.[114] A wave of Confederates drove after the Federals. Birney met them head on with a stout defense along the Bowling Green Road that blunted the counterattack and drove the rebels back to their original position.

Meanwhile, Gibbon's men had likewise spent their momentum. The Confederate line in their front hadn't broken but, instead, bowed in like an elastic band. When it snapped back into shape with reinforcements, Gibbon's division retreated back to the safety of the Bowling Green Road and the awaiting Sixth Corps.

Impact

"My God, General Reynolds, did they think my division could whip Lee's whole army?" Meade later groused, bitter at his lost opportunity.[115] As he wrote to his wife, Margaretta, "Had we held the position gained till our reinforcements came up—I should have been the great hero of the fight."[116]

But his reinforcements didn't come up. In direct contrast to Confederate Jubal Early, who disobeyed a direct order and marched to the sound of the guns at the moment of crisis, Federal David Bell Birney stuck stubbornly to protocol. By that parallel, Birney's decision not to march to Meade's aid might be classified as the critical decision of this moment, but the fault rested squarely at the corps level. "If, instead of repeated requests and a final emphatic order from Meade, there had been an order from Reynolds to Birney to support Meade actively," mused Pennypacker, "there would have been no room for hesitation on Birney's part."[117] Reynolds, he added, "was just the soldier to infuse these supports with the necessary spirit."[118]

Reynolds's misplaced priorities were part of a larger pattern of behavior, argues historian Kris White, who says Reynolds consistently "demoted" himself by acting in roles better suited to subordinates. "It took Reynolds from a Division, Corps, and Wing commander down to a regimental commander at the greatest moment of crisis—a tendency he repeated time and again," White says.[119] Fredericksburg was a clear example of this behavior. Instead of directing the fight at Fredericksburg, Reynolds was directing artillery, a job Charles Wainwright already had well in hand. At Gettysburg, this tendency would get Reynolds into fatal trouble.

The command vacuum can't fully be blamed on Reynolds, although his absence was the one most keenly felt. Burnside received a string of telegrams throughout the day from General Hardie but never sent any in return. Franklin bunkered in his Mannsfield headquarters as though waiting for preordained bad news. Third Corps commander George Stoneman, who'd had several of his divisions stripped from him for various assignments, stalked the area around Franklin's headquarters like a commander without a command—which he literally was for most of the day.

Later, Burnside reflected on Meade's breakthrough with stoicism. "The supports which the order had contemplated were not with him," he wrote.[120] Meade, for his part, stewed on it. "The more I think of that battle, the more annoyed I am that such a great chance should have failed me," he told his wife. "The slightest straw almost would have kept the tide in our favor."[121]

12. Franklin Calls Off the Attack Without Telling Burnside

Situation

When Burnside heard the first booms of John Pelham's guns echoing up out of the fog from the extreme left of the battlefield, he mistook them for the opening salvos of Franklin's assault against Prospect Hill. With action there underway, he turned to his Left Grand Division commander, Maj. Gen. Edwin "Bull" Sumner. Burnside had ordered Sumner to prep an attack against the Confederate position atop the heights west of the city—Marye's Heights—but he had also told Sumner, "[Do] not move until the general commanding communicates with you."[122] With the fight occurring to the south, Burnside sent word to Sumner to start his men forward in support of Franklin.

Sumner led with Maj. Gen. Darius Couch's Second Corps, with Brig. Gen. William H. French's division marching in the lead. At about 11:00 a.m., French's three brigades advanced from the relative safety of the city onto an open plain that gently inclined nine hundred yards to the base of the heights. There, Confederate infantry waited in a sunken road behind a stone wall. "How beautifully they came on!" said Confederate artillerist William Owen while watching the advance from atop the heights. "Their bright bayonets glistening in the sunlight made the line look like a huge serpent of blue and steel."[123]

Owen and his comrades quickly opened on the advancing force, tearing holes in blue lines. "The shells fell thick and fast, exploding with deafening roar right in our midst," recalled William Landon of the Fourteenth Indiana. "Shattered, torn and bleeding, our column still pushed on—gained the open

Confederates began the battle with about two thousand infantrymen behind the Stone Wall. As the fighting continued and soldiers began to run out of bullets, the only way to resupply them was by sending in reinforcements with additional ammunition. By the end of the battle, some six thousand Confederates would occupy the Sunken Road. *Battles and Leaders of the Civil War.*

ground—drew up in line of battle, and with bayonets fixed, rushed forward to the charge. And such a charge may I never witness again!"[124]

"We could see our shells bursting in their ranks, making great gaps," Owen said, "but on they came, as though they would go straight through and over us. Now we gave them canister, and that staggered them. A few more paces onward and the Georgians in the road below us rose up, and, glancing an instant along their rifle barrels, let loose a storm of lead into the faces of the advance brigade."[125] This, he said, was too much, and the first Federal brigade faltered and fell back. French's second and third brigades likewise withered under the intense artillery and infantry fire.

Couch then sent forward Brig. Gen. Winfield Scott Hancock's division. "Pandemonium at once broke loose," wrote Lieut. Josiah Favill of the Fifty-Seventh New York. "The whizzing, bursting shells made one's hair stand on end."[126] Co. John Brooke of the Fifty-Third Pennsylvania stated, "The fire was so heavy, and the shells were bursting in such numbers that I involuntarily turned my head as you would in a rain storm."[127]

Hancock's assault, too, melted, so Brig. Gen. Oliver Otis Howard went forward with his division. Then Brig. Gen. Samuel Sturgis, Brig. Gen. Charles Griffin, and Brig. Gen. Andrew Humphreys.

"What chance had flesh and blood to carry by storm such a position, garrisoned too as it was with veteran soldiers? Not one chance in a million," attested a rueful member of the Seventh Virginia. "All that day we watched the fruitless charges, with their fearful slaughter, until we were sick at heart. As I witnessed one line swept away by one fearful blast from Kershaw's men behind the stone wall, I forgot they were enemies and only remembered that they were men, and it is hard to see in cold blood brave men die."[128]

At sunset, Brig. Gen. George Getty finished the fighting when part of his division charged with fixed bayonets against the right end of the stone wall. A railroad cut and the cover of darkness let them get within fifty yards of the Confederate position before the men let out a whoop with their final charge, alerting the enemy to their advance. Confederate artillery mowed the Federals down. A member of the Second Michigan, watching the final fight from afar, said, "I could not hear the guns but could see the flash and the wavering of the lines. Sometimes there was a solid sheet of flame but for the most part, twinkle, twinkle, twinkle, like sparks when a fire is stirred—rapid as thought."[129] Getty's survivors finally fell back to the railroad cut.

"Finding that I had lost as many men as my orders required me to lose," Joe Hooker later said contemptuously, "I suspended the attack, and directed that the men should hold."[130]

The day, said one Federal, had been "a mad sacrifice of men."[131]

Even as the initial attack order trickled down from Burnside to Sumner to Couch to French, the general commanding "was anxiously expecting to hear that the hill near Hamilton's had been carried."[132] At 10:30 a.m., eager for more news than the telegraph could bring, Burnside sent staff officer Capt. P. M. Lydig to get a firsthand update from Franklin. Lydig found Franklin in a grove of trees, watching Meade, who was "hotly engaged."[133] Franklin explained the situation to Lydig and sent him back to Burnside. Burnside, after debriefing Lydig, seemed "annoyed at the smallness of the force engaged, and expressed his surprised that none of General [Baldy] Smith's troops had been put into the fight."[134]

As Lydig returned to headquarters with his update, he passed fellow staff officer Capt. James M. Cutts. Cutts carried an order from Burnside to Franklin "to advance his right and front immediately."[135] Franklin balked. Then he sent Cutts back to Burnside. "There was no advance," Cutts reported, then shared Franklin's own explanation as to why he couldn't move forward.

"But he must advance," Burnside replied.[136]

By now, it was after 2:00 p.m. Howard's attack had sputtered out in front of the stone wall, and Sturgis's division was grimly advancing. Burnside directed Cutts to return to Franklin with an order to resume the offensive,

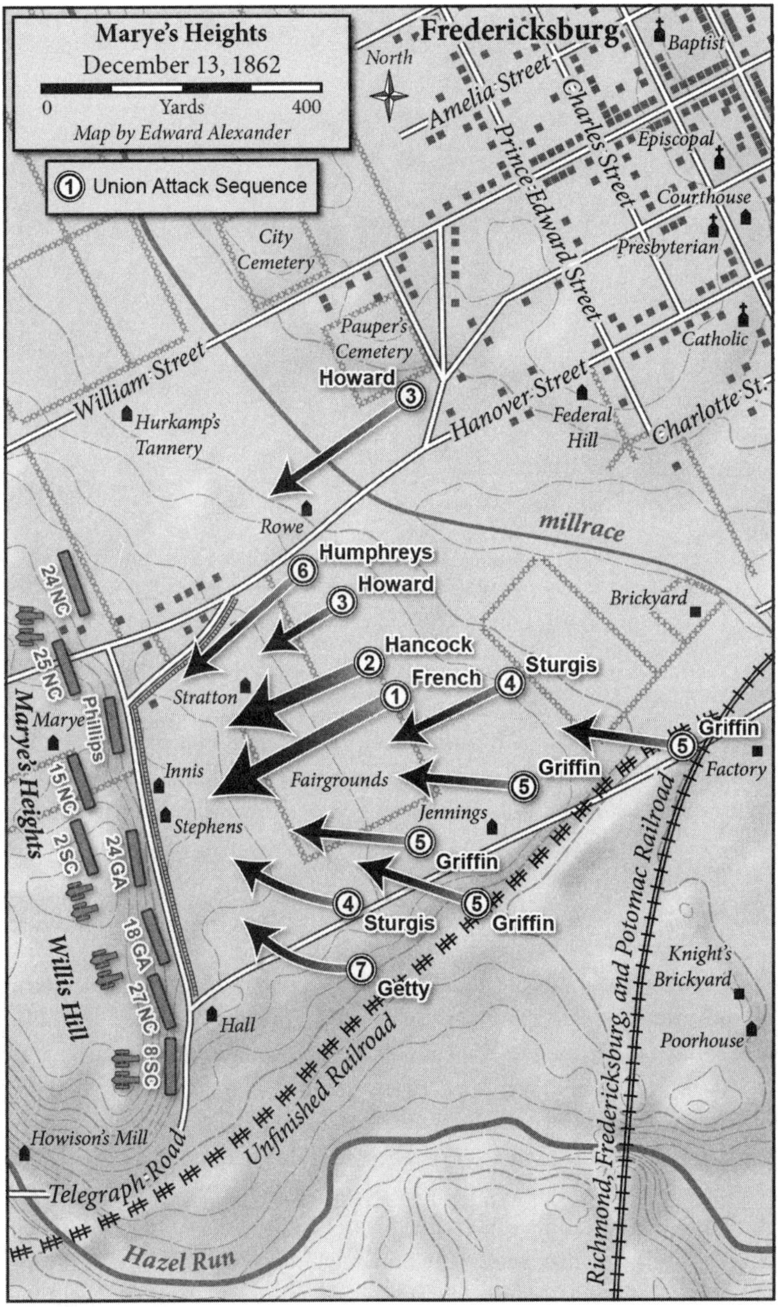

Seven major waves of attacks swept toward Marye's Heights on December 13. Burnside kept up the pressure in the hope of supporting a late-day renewed assault by Franklin on the south end of the field—an assault that never materialized. Edward Alexander.

Maj. Gen. William "Baldy" Smith had talent as a battlefield leader, but his tendency to scheme against his commanders would lead him into trouble time after time—as it would eventually do with Burnside. Library of Congress.

then stopped him. "Wait," Burnside said, "I will send someone else."[137] The commanding general called on a third captain, R. H. I. Goddard, to carry an explicit order for Franklin to "make a vigorous attack with his whole force; our right is hard pressed."[138]

All the while—starting at 7:40 a.m. and continuing through 2:15 p.m.—Burnside's ersatz man on the scene, Brig. Gen. James Hardie, sent a string of telegrams to army headquarters with updates on the fighting. Burnside replied to them only through his couriers. "Dispatch received," Hardie telegraphed at 2:25 p.m. after Goddard's arrival with Burnside's preemptory order. "Franklin will do his best. New troops gone in. Will report soon again."[139]

However, those "new troops" were just a few regiments from Baldy Smith's Sixth Corps, sent to better secure the grand division's right flank anchored on Deep Run. Their sortie triggered a Confederate counterattack that spooked Franklin even worse than he already was, but the arrival of a Federal division under Brig. Gen. Daniel Sickles defused the situation. By then, things had fully stabilized along the Bowling Green Road—"Reynolds seems to be holding his own," Hardie reported. "Things look better, somewhat." But Franklin worried about additional pressure from the rebels.[140]

Goddard observed all this for the report he planned to give Burnside upon his return to headquarters. Just before leaving, he reminded Franklin, "Burnside was very explicit in giving this order to make a vigorous attack."[141]

Options

Option 1: Make a Vigorous Attack

Although Meade's and Gibbon's divisions had, in Hardie's words, "suffered severely," Doubleday's division had remained essentially unengaged.[142] Birney's division saw heated action in its repulse of the Confederate counterattack, but it maintained a strong position along the Bowling Green Road and still boasted strong regimental and brigade cohesion. Sickles's division—like Birney's, on loan from Stoneman's Third Corps—was fresh to the field. And, of course, nearly the entirety of Smith's Sixth Corps had remained unengaged. Burnside described the corps, at twenty-four thousand strong, as "the strongest and one of the most reliable in the army."[143] Bolstering its strength even more, Smith had a four-thousand-man division from the Ninth Corps to call on, as well.

Franklin could still send for powerful artillery support from the far side of the river, as well as 3,500 cavalrymen at his disposal. Considering he'd made the day's first attack with his two smallest divisions, Franklin certainly had more than enough power left to throw another strong punch. In fact, if he wanted to, he could throw a stronger punch than his first, with enough men left over to still guard his route back across the river.

Option 2: Prepare to Defend Against a Possible Attack

The Bowling Green Road, with its embankments, offered a strong, straight defensible position. Topographical features on both ends of Franklin's line offered good anchors. Defended by fresh troops, the commander could hold out against any additional Confederate attacks. He had already pushed back two, and he knew he faced Stonewall Jackson across the way. Legendary even then for springing nasty surprises on his opponents, Jackson might make an incautious Franklin his next victim.

Decision

Franklin sent forward skirmishers from Smith's corps to explore the situation, but "the position of the enemy in this part of the field being exceedingly strong, the attempt to advance here was abandoned."[144] Franklin subsequently tried to make much of the engagement, but Burnside recognized it as "unimportant fighting . . . going on in front of Howe's and Brooks' divisions."[145] Franklin finally made his ambivalence known in a 3:40 p.m. telegram to Burnside: "Gibbon's and Meade's Divisions are badly used up,

The embankment along Bowling Green Road can still be seen in places, such as along this stretch adjacent to the Slaughter Pen Farm. Chris Mackowski.

and I fear another advance on the enemy on our left cannot be made this afternoon. Doubleday's Division will replace Meade's as soon as it can be collected, and if it can be done in time, of course another attack will be made."[146] But Franklin continued to dither, maintaining his defensive position. At 4:30 p.m. he informed Burnside, "It is too late to advance."[147]

Results

"General Franklin . . . had been positively ordered to attack with his whole force, and I hoped before sundown to have broken through the enemy's lines," Burnside wrote. "This order was not carried out" in the end.[148] However, Burnside continued his attacks against the stone wall on the northern end of the battlefield under the assumption that his directive *was* being executed.

Without the accompanying attack by Franklin, though, the assaults against Marye's Heights took on a fruitless life of their own. "I had never before seen fighting like that," recalled Second Corps commander Darius

Couch, "nothing approaching it in terrible uproar and destruction. There was no cheering on the part of the men, but a stubborn determination to obey orders and do their duty. I don't think there was much feeling of success."[149]

Whether Franklin would have spared any of that bloodshed by following Burnside's order, or even by reiterating to Burnside his reasons for *not* attacking, it's impossible to say. He had already told Burnside that he found it impossible to attack, so perhaps Franklin felt saying so again would do no good. For all his subsequent self-defense, he remained silent on that point. But by dithering instead, and not saying anything to Burnside, Franklin allowed Burnside to think he was attacking—an act of omission with grim consequences.

"When Birney's and Sickles' divisions were placed in position it had become too late to organize another attack before dark," Franklin later tried to explain.[150] By coupling the two divisions, though, he was trying to fudge his timetable. Birney had been situated in time for offensive action (as Meade had frustratingly noted), and Sickles had moved into position early enough that Goddard watched the division arrive, then returned to Burnside sometime between 2:30–3:00 p.m.

After Sickles's arrival, Franklin shifted John Newton's division in Doubleday's direction as support. By the time Newton finally got into position, Reynolds agreed with Franklin's assessment: "I judged it then too nearly night to make another attempt to carry the enemy's position."[151]

The normally affable Burnside later scoffed at these justifications. "Meade and Gibbon badly used up. No wonder," he wrote. "It is not surprising that these dispatches should indicate that Gen. Franklin thought it too late to remedy the delay of the first part of the day."[152] In Burnside's eyes, Franklin had stumbled at the outset and, through a lack of initiative, had never gotten himself back on track. But also true to form, Burnside took ultimate responsibility. "General Franklin speaks of our relations being good," he said, referring to one of Franklin's public attempts at self-exoneration. "They were in reality so good that I trusted largely to his discretion believing that he would use all his effort . . . , and I confess I probably did not think of that part of the field as much as I should have done."[153]

CHAPTER 5

THE BATTLE NOT FOUGHT, DECEMBER 14–15, 1862

13. Burnside Does Not Renew the Offensive

Situation

"Our force had been repulsed at all points, and it was necessary to look upon the day's work as a failure," Ambrose Burnside admitted in his official report of the battle, written in November 1865. "It is not pleasant to dwell upon these results, even at this distance of time."[1]

It's little wonder, faced with the day's failure, that the Army of the Potomac's commander searched desperately for some way to salvage the situation. "Burnside remained shocked and bewildered at the disaster which had befallen his army," wrote Army of the Potomac historian Francis Walker, "at one time telegraphing to Washington that though his assault had not been successful, he had gained ground and was holding it; at another time scheming to transfer all the troops to the left; at another time declaring that he would form a column of the Ninth Corps and lead it in person up Marye's Heights; at another time plunged in the deepest distress."[2]

Frantically, Burnside cast about for options, answers, solutions—some kind of plan to carry him and his army forward. "That night, I went all over the field on our right," he recalled a few days after the battle; "in fact, I was with the officers and men until nearly daylight. I found the feeling to be rather against an attack the next morning; in fact, it was decidedly against it."[3]

Darius Couch, who awoke from sleep at 2:00 a.m. for an hour-long conversation with Burnside, said his commander "was cheerful in his tone and did not seem greatly oppressed." Yet Couch also said of Burnside, "It was plain that he felt he had led us to a great disaster." The commander left Couch with the impression that "he wished his body was also lying in front of Marye's Heights."[4]

As Burnside rode about, one of the brigade commanders from his old Ninth Corps, Col. Rush Hawkins, was on a similar parallel mission. Hawkins was a thirty-two-year-old Vermont native who had resettled in Manhattan, where he raised a regiment, the Ninth New York, at the outbreak of the war. The regiment wore flashy Zouave uniforms patterned after a style worn by some units in the French army and bearing their leader's name: Hawkins's Zouaves. Late on December 13, Hawkins, in Getty's division, had led the final assault against the stone wall.

"The attack of our division closed a battle which was one of the most disastrous defeats to the Union forces during the war," Hawkins wrote. "The sadness which prevailed through the whole army on that night can neither be described nor imagined. The surgeons were the happiest of all, for they were so busy that they had no time to think of our terrible defeat."[5]

Col. Rush Hawkins, photographed in his Zouave uniform. Library of Congress.

Hawkins had been searching for his commander, George Getty, when he found the division commander in consultation with a clutch of other senior officers. "They were seriously discussing the proposed renewal of the attack the next day as though it had been decided upon," Hawkins recounted incredulously. "I listened until I was thoroughly irritated because of the ignorance displayed in regard to our situation, and then uttered a solemn, earnest, and emphatic protest against even the consideration of another attack."[6]

Slashing pencil marks across the soldiers' map to indicate the troops' position on the front, Hawkins argued vehemently against any resumption of offensive action in front of the stone wall. "It did not take long to convince these officers that a second attack would probably end more disastrously than the first," he recalled.[7] In response, the officers unanimously "requested" that Hawkins ride directly to Burnside and make the case against a renewed attack.

And so Hawkins found himself on his mission, "a cheerless ride in the wet and cold, and through the deep mud of an army-traveled road that dark night."[8] Weary from the day's action and a lack of sleep, he felt depressed by his position. "An officer of very inferior rank was bent upon an ungrateful errand," Hawkins wrote, further describing himself as a man powered only by "a solemn sense of duty, and a humane desire to save further useless slaughter."[9]

Somewhere in the night, Hawkins passed Burnside, still apparently on the city side of the river after conferring with the same clutch of officers Hawkins had just spoken to. Hawkins crossed to the Stafford side of the river, ascended the heights, and made his way to the Phillips House. Soon thereafter, the brigade commander found himself making his pitch to the three grand division commanders while awaiting Burnside's return.

"Well, it's all arranged," the army commander told them all when he arrived. "We attack at early dawn, the Ninth Corps in the center, which I shall lead in person." Burnside directed Sumner to form the corps into a column of attack by regiments for "a direct attack upon the enemy's works" at Marye's Heights. He believed the column could come up quickly enough to drive Confederate pickets back into the main line, and he stated, "By going in with them they would not be able to fire upon us to any great extent." Thus the column would be able to carry the stone wall and the batteries in front.[10] At this point, Burnside seemed to notice Hawkins. "Your brigade shall lead," Burnside told him; "we'll make up for the bad work of today."[11]

Burnside was met by perfect silence. Astonished, he looked to Sumner for affirmation. With "hesitation and great delicacy," Sumner explained the reason for Hawkins's presence. As the men clustered around a table covered with maps and charts, Hawkins again felt the weight of his charge. Once more, he began to clarify the situation.

Options

Option 1: Resume the Offensive Against Marye's Heights

Burnside's choice to resume the attack using the Ninth Corps had been inspired by the late-day success of George Getty's division, which had come tantalizingly close to the stone wall in its last assault—only fifty yards away. Burnside seems to have attributed that achievement to Hawkins and his men, not the topography or darkness.

Burnside knew the Ninth Corps well. He had led those men to success along the Carolina coast and again during the Maryland Campaign; he felt confident they would follow him once more into battle. With the exception of Getty's division, much of the Ninth Corps had sat out the day's action, so they would be fresh to spearhead a new assault. And if Burnside had delegated field command to his grand division commanders and they had failed, perhaps taking personal command would do the trick, particularly in the lead of men who felt personal loyalty to him.

Burnside also seemed to either discount or ignore any additional preparations by the Confederates—and, as Lee later wrote in his battle report, the Confederates were indeed making such arrangements. "During the night," Lee stated, "our lines were strengthened by the construction of earthworks at exposed points, and preparations made to receive the enemy the next day."[12] Stuart's chief of staff later overheard Lee express great confidence about the preparatory measures. "My army is as much stronger for their new intrenchments as if I had received reinforcements of 20,000 men," the Confederate commander supposedly said.[13]

Option 2: Resume the Offensive on Franklin's Front

On the afternoon of December 13, Burnside had ordered Franklin to resume his attack—and Franklin dithered. So, when the Left Grand Division commander arrived at Burnside's headquarters after dark and proposed an attack for the next day, Burnside unsurprisingly showed little inclination to listen. "I urged upon him that if the attack was to be renewed to renew it from the left," Franklin said, "but with such force and preparations as would command success."[14] Franklin certainly had plenty of troops not yet committed to battle and so could conceivably assemble the kind of force he proposed. However, his lackluster leadership might have soured Burnside, who had trusted Franklin implicitly only to be disappointed. Burnside had little reason to put his faith in Franklin again.

Option 3: Call Off the Offensive and Try Elsewhere

Hawkins "explained the enemy's positions, called attention to several pertinent circumstances, and made something of an argument."[15] Seven major waves had crashed against the formidable Confederate defenses on Marye's Heights already, and with a full night to further strengthen their position, the rebels would certainly be more difficult to dislodge than they'd been on December 13. Continued assaults looked all but hopeless.

If Burnside decided against renewing his attacks on December 14, he could look at the options before him and formulate a new plan. Potentially, he could maintain his hold on the city with part of his force as a decoy while recrossing the rest of his men back to the east bank. Through a fast march, Burnside could then outflank Lee at a different location.

Option 4: Call Off the Offensive Entirely

Burnside might consider calling off the offensive entirely and settling in to winter camps, even if temporarily. With Christmas just ten days away, a break for the holiday might buoy the men's spirits. However, just a week after that, the first of the year would roll around, thereby enacting the final Emancipation Proclamation. Lincoln still needed a military victory to help legitimize the proclamation, so political pressure would prevent Burnside from occupying winter camps for long.

Sumner articulated what Burnside's entire senior staff well knew: "Neither our government nor our people would be satisfied to have our army retire from this position, or go into winter quarters."[16]

Decision

While accounts of the council of war differ, Burnside seemed resolute in his decision to attack. At 4:00 a.m., he sent a wire to Lincoln that said, in part, "We hold the first ridge outside the town, and 3 miles below. We hope to carry the crest today."[17]

Sumner assembled the Ninth Corps as ordered. Brig. Gen. William W. Burns marched his division from Deep Run, where it connected with Franklin's grand division, to take up a position along Hazel Run. There, at 10:00 a.m., the unit would follow in the footsteps laid down by Hawkins's brigade the evening before. Hawkins and Getty both sent urgent pleas for Burnside to reconsider: "It would be a perfect slaughter of men," Getty predicted.[18] Hooker, who had acted almost insubordinate in his opposition to the plan, continued to radiate defiance. Officers crammed the Phillips House, waiting for Burnside to give the order to mobilize—an order that would send Burnside himself across the river to lead the attack.

In the midst of the fraught moment, Bull Sumner somehow found an opportunity to take Burnside aside. "General, I hope you will desist from this attack," the old veteran told his commander; "I do not know of any general officer who approves of it, and I think it will prove disastrous to the army."[19] Burnside, so resolute just hours earlier, finally blinked. "Advice of that kind from General Sumner, who has always been in favor of an advance whenever it was possible, caused me to hesitate," he explained. A council of war with his available corps and division commanders resulted in a unanimous vote against the attack. Consultation with other officers in the command revealed that they agreed. Franklin, too, "was of exactly the same opinion."[20] "This caused me to decide that I ought not to make the attack I had contemplated," Burnside said.[21]

Results/Impact

Burnside biographer William Marvel notes the significance of Sumner's quiet conversation with Burnside on the morning of December 14. "With that reluctant admission Sumner did the country—and Burnside—the greatest service of his long career," Marvel writes.[22] So deeply loyal that some of his critics have labeled him a "yes-man," Sumner was ever supportive of Burnside, so his dissent made a significant impression.

The hindsight of a couple of days would convince Burnside that he'd made the right call. It "could not have been done, owing to the great strength of the enemy, the time given them for reenforcing, and the belief also of our officers that it could not be done," he told congressional investigators just days after the battle. "And besides," Burnside added, contorting the political pressure on him to his military advantage, "inasmuch as the President of the United States had told me not to be in haste in making this attack; that he would give me all the support that he could, but he did not want the army of the Potomac destroyed, I felt that I could not take the responsibility of ordering the attack, notwithstanding my own belief at the time that the works of the enemy could be carried."[23]

So, with no Ninth Corps column making a desperate charge against the stone wall, December 14 passed instead with acrimonious sniping between the two sides. Federal survivors from the previous day's assaults, pinned in place by Confederate fire, hunkered behind the bodies of fallen comrades or flattened themselves as prostrate as possible in small dips and swales. "There, prone on the ground, the living mingled with the dead," wrote Francis Walker. The casualties totaled "three or four thousand men, the remains of twenty regiments." Walker elaborated on the sight before him: "The line zigzags as the fortunes of the several charges have left it, at some points fifty, at others one hundred or two hundred, yards from the stone wall. Except for those who cluster for shelter at the rear of the few huts or houses on the line, not a man is erect."[24]

Occasionally, Federals would take potshots at any Confederate who showed his head. "Something was done in the way of intrenching, and some angry skirmishing and annoying artillery firing was indulged in in the meantime," Burnside reported.[25]

As the army commander pondered his other options, the first question seemed whether to leave an occupying force to hold the city and the bridgeheads for future operations. "If we held the town," argued Second Corps commander Darius Couch, "we should have a little something to show for the sacrifice of the day before; that the people would feel we had not failed utterly."[26] Sumner agreed. "I did not wish to relinquish Fredericksburg," he testified. "I thought we could have held it with a single division by posting our batteries right." In doing so, the army could reposition itself for another offensive. As Sumner asserted, "It would not have been giving up an expedition, but simply a change of tactics. That is the way in which I viewed it; that we would just be drawing back a little in order to try it again."[27]

Hooker opposed occupation, arguing that the concentration of troops in the city would make them easy pickings for Confederate artillery. "If the enemy should throw a shell into the city, it could not fall amiss with all those troops there," he said. He need not have worried. "It has been said that General Lee might have inflicted tremendous damage upon the enemy by forcing hot shot and shell into Fredericksburg while the enemy's troops were massed there," wrote Jubal Early after the war. Early said that "it was not in the heart of the noble commander of the Army of Northern Virginia" to bombard the city—and its remaining residents—"for the sake of killing and wounding a few thousand of the enemy, and causing dismay among the remainder."[28]

Aside from the danger of artillery, Hooker groused about the poor shape his men were in. "Many of the troops were in such a condition that they gave me no additional strength," he said.[29] Oddly, Second Corps commander Darius Couch recalled a combative Hooker on that day. "We must fight those people," Hooker supposedly said. "We are over there [in the city] and we must fight them."[30] However, the general had gladly discontinued the futile offensives the night before and had argued almost insubordinately against a morning attack for December 14. Couch's recollections of Hooker in these discussions—written well after the war—seem to contradict the latter's own actions. That he suddenly changed his tune might have been due to animosity

The quiet after the storm. Library of Congress.

that developed between the men during and after the Chancellorsville Campaign, which shaded Couch's account of Hooker.

In any case, Burnside ultimately heeded Hooker's worries and chose to fully evacuate Federal forces. On the evening of December 15, when darkness descended over the battlefield, orders went forward for the Army of the Potomac to withdraw back across the Rappahannock. "We have had too much to do," said Robert McCallister, the colonel of the Eleventh New Jersey, articulating the thoughts of many. "To go take those hights [*sic*] would be to sacrifice too much life. I am satisfied that it would cost us 50,000 lives. . . . I made up my mind that, to take it, many of us would have to bite the dust. I am not prepared to praise or condemn those in command. Time will tell us all."[31]

14. Lee Does Not Launch a Counteroffensive

Situation

When Confederate artillerist John Esten Cooke crossed paths with Stonewall Jackson late on the afternoon of December 13, Jackson's "face was on fire." With flushed cheeks and eyes that blazed from beneath his low-pulled hat, Jackson seemed restive.[32] Daylight was fast draining from the sky, and he wanted to take a swing at the Federal left flank while he still had time. Franklin had thrown the first punch of the day, and Jubal Early had effectively counterpunched. Surprisingly, Franklin hadn't taken a second swing—so Jackson would take it upon himself to launch a roundhouse of his own, thirty-five thousand men strong. He planned to "leave his intrenchments without further delay, fall upon the enemy, and render the victory complete."[33]

With intense purpose, Jackson rode from one part of his command to another—with his staff likewise fanning out with orders—trying to prepare his entire corps for an assault. He intended to form up along the railroad bed and, after an artillery bombardment to soften up the Federals, send his full corps forward. "The artillery of the enemy was so judiciously posted as to make an advance of our troops across the plain very hazardous," Jackson wrote, "yet it was so promising of good results, if successfully executed, as to induce me to make preparations for the attempt."[34]

His preemptive artillery bombardment would "guard against disaster." Then his infantry would march out of the setting sun, whose glare would blind the Federals as the Confederates advanced. The long shadows of the gloaming would help mask the rebels' movements.[35] "If compelled to retire," Jackson added, "it would be under the cover of night."[36]

From this area, "Stonewall" Jackson planned to launch a night attack on December 13. He ordered his men to tie white cloths around their arms so they would be able to tell friend from foe in the dark. Chris Mackowski.

Jackson called on John Bell Hood from Longstreet's Corps to provide support on his left; on his right, he asked Stuart to cover. Jackson asked Cooke, who was Stuart's ordnance officer, to deliver the request. Cooke cast one last look over his shoulder as he left and noticed "the sun just sinking like a large ball of fire on the summit of the woods."[37] Time was growing short. "Minute by minute passed by," wrote another cavalry staff officer, Heros von Borcke, "and the dark veil of night began to envelop the valley."[38]

Despite Jackson's best efforts, he could only assemble about half of his force in time, but he opted to try the attack anyway, with errant forces to come in as reserves if necessary. "We would have had to advance nearly a mile, over an entirely bare plain swept by all this artillery, as well as cannonaded by the heavy guns on Stafford Heights," observed Jubal Early, one of the errant commanders.[39] Early, so proactive earlier in the day, received late word of Jackson's newest plan because the staff officer delivering the order had gotten lost.[40]

No sooner had Jackson sent his first artillery pieces out to begin their barrage than their Federal counterparts responded. "The first gun had hardly moved forward," Jackson noted, "when the enemy's artillery reopened, and so completely swept our front as to satisfy me that the proposed movement should be abandoned."[41] Early thought that was just as well. "Nothing could have lived while passing over that plain under such circumstances," he wrote, adding, "and . . . while we were all ready to obey the orders of our heroic commander, there was not a man . . . who did not breathe freer when he heard the orders countermanding the movement."[42]

Jackson continued to have trouble communicating with subordinates, and not everyone got timely word of his countermanded order. Some units briefly advanced beyond the railroad cut before turning back under fire. On the far right, Stuart didn't get word for more than twenty minutes. He spent the time harassing Doubleday's strongly fortified flank as "the fire of the enemy's infantry began to be more and more destructive, and other fresh batteries opened upon us," von Borcke said.[43] Recalled, the cavalry withdrew. "The golden moment had now passed," von Borcke lamented.

December 14 offered another foggy morning. "General Lee confidently expected that there would be a renewal of the attack," said his aide Col. Walter Taylor.[44] The Federal offensives on the thirteenth "had been so easily repulsed, and by so small a part of our army," Lee told Richmond, that he did not believe Burnside was yet ready to quit. He knew the Army of the Potomac had more to throw at him, and he expected it.

Confederates had reinforced that expectation late the previous evening. Sometime in the late hours of December 13, the rebels captured a Union courier

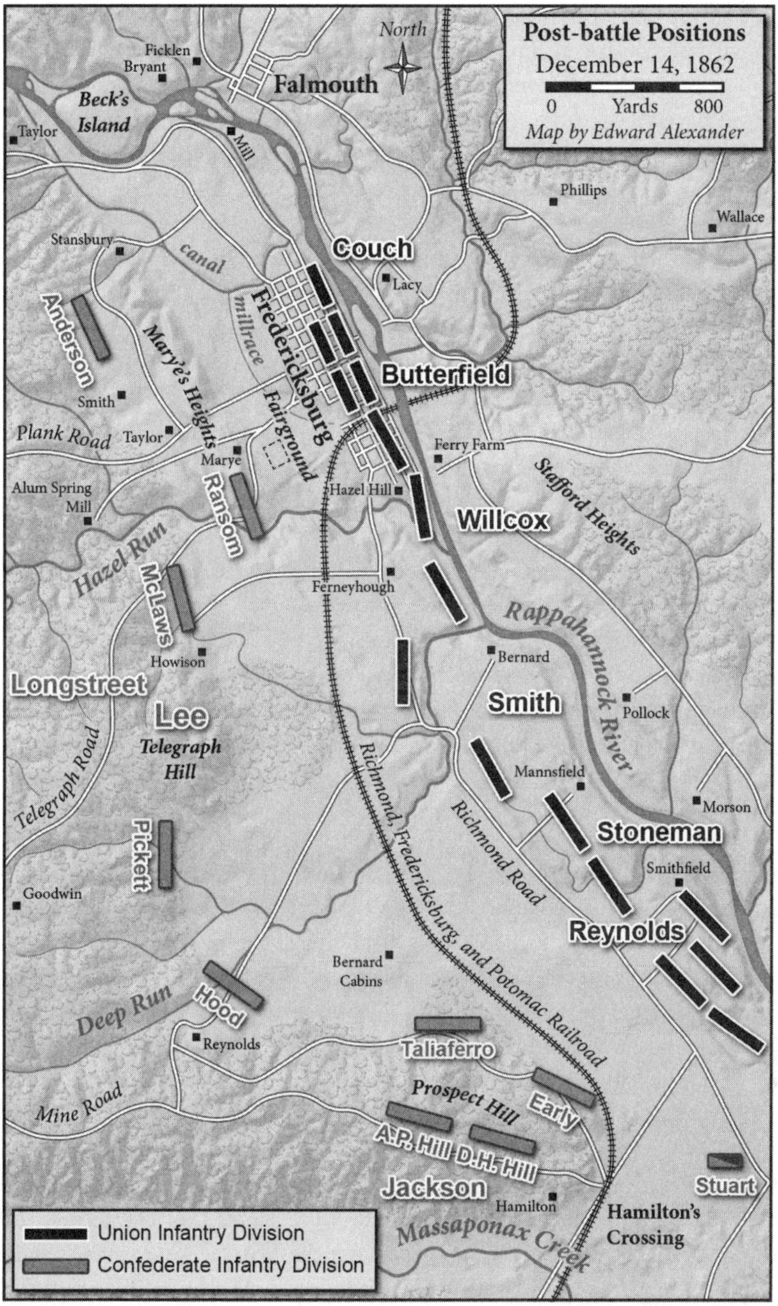

After being repulsed all along the line on December 13, Federals felt hemmed in along the river with nowhere to go but back. Lee, occupying strong ground all along his front and with a newly fortified position at Prospect Hill, waited for Burnside to take the offense again, but he dared not make an attack himself. Edward Alexander.

gone astray who, according to James Longstreet, carried "a memorandum of the purpose of General Burnside for renewing the battle against Marye's Hill in the morning." This development reinforced Lee's expectations about more fighting, and Lee, in high spirits, seemed happy to oblige. "Orders were sent... to improve defences and prepare for the next day," Longstreet said, "under conviction that the battle of the next day, if made as ordered, would be the last of the Army of the Potomac."[45]

But as the fog burned away and the blue host remained in place, Lee began to wonder what they were up to. "The enemy today has been apparently engaged in caring for his wounded and burying his dead," he telegraphed Richmond.[46] However, no attack materialized.

"So we waited & waited," said Confederate artillerist E. P. Alexander, "but the whole day passed without anything serious, anywhere along the line. But I remember the day as a very disagreeable one, for I had to move about a great deal, having guns at so many different places; & the sharpshooting & shelling everywhere made me quite unhappy."[47]

"Lee had every reason to be content with the issue of the hard day's fighting," artillerist John Esten Cooke argued.[48] But, ever aggressive and ever looking to seize the initiative, Lee looked at the Federal army and wondered how he might be able to best capitalize on the situation. "They suffered heavily as far as the battle went," he later wrote to his wife, Mary, "but it did not go far enough to satisfy me."[49]

Options

Option 1: Continue Waiting for Burnside to Make the Next Move

Lee assumed Burnside would attack on December 14 because the attacks on December 13 "seemed to be comparatively insignificant" compared to "the magnitude of [Burnside's] preparations and the extent of his force."[50] The captured dispatch from the previous night confirmed Lee's expectation that an assault was forthcoming. Just because it hadn't yet occurred didn't mean it wasn't going to. Alternatively, perhaps a different attack was in the works against a different part of the line.

In case of that very eventuality, Lee had fortified his entire line, not just his position at Marye's Heights. The safest option would be to let the Army of the Potomac come to the Confederates once more. Lee just needed the patience to wait out Burnside and see what the Federal commander would do. By default, Lee had had to adopt this approach for the entire campaign, anyway.

Option 2: Launch an Offensive

Unsatisfied with the results of the battle so far, Lee could "render the victory complete," in Jackson's words, by taking the offense and hitting the Federals while they still reeled from their defeat the day before.

But Jackson's unsuccessful attempt at a late-day attack on December 13 encapsulated all the challenges Lee would face: Confederates would have to assault over the same open ground that had proved to be such a devastating killing field for the Federals, all the while taking heat from enemy artillery without effective opportunity for counter–battery fire. Secure attachments to the river on both ends of the Federal line offered no opportunities for a flanking maneuver. And, of course, the defending Federals would outnumber the attacking Confederates—arithmetic that hardly recommended itself.

Forces attacking from Marye's Heights would not only face these same obstacles but also have to contend with the city itself. Federals concentrated there would have their backs to the river, yes, but they could also use the city to shield them. In effect, the December 11 fighting could happen but in reverse, with Confederates forced to ferret out defending Federals. But whereas Federals seemingly had not hesitated to lob shells into the city during their attack, Lee would be more reluctant to shell his own citizens as part of an attempt to drive out the Federals.

Longstreet's chief of staff, Moxley Sorrel, summed the situation up well: the risks of an offensive seemed to heavily outweigh the chances of success. "It is impossible to describe the confusion of such an attempt or to anticipate what might happen," he wrote.[51]

Decision

"Believing . . . that he would attack us," Lee wrote of Burnside, "it was not deemed expedient to lose the advantages of our position and expose the troops to the fire of his inaccessible batteries beyond the river, by advancing against him."[52]

Artillerist E. P. Alexander, from his perch atop Marye's Heights, saw the situation as clearly as anyone. "We could not attack [Burnside]," he declared, "for our advance would have been swept by his artillery on the north side, beside which the ground he occupied near the river was also very strong & favorable for defense."[53]

Result

Why no counterattack? asked Moxley Sorrel years later. After all, he wrote, "It is generally thought it would have been fatal to the Federals and it is

Under the cover of the northern lights, Federals recrossed the river, abandoning the battlefield. Library of Congress.

indisputable that they were in hourly dread of it."[54] Sorrel dodged his own question, though. "Not my part to attempt this explanation," he stated, "but it looks much as if we were 'building a bridge of gold for the flying enemy.'"[55] On the night of December 15, the enemy did, indeed, fly—not on bridges of gold, but ones of pontoons—right back over to the far side of the Rappahannock.

Confederates were jubilant. "Who could have imagined that Burnside with his immense army would turn back so easily!" marveled Alexander.[56] Lee, however, was crestfallen. "I had my suspicions that they might retire during the night," he admitted to his wife, "but could not believe they would relinquish their purpose after all their boasting & preparations, & when I say that the latter is equal to the former, you will have some idea of its magnitude."[57]

During the war and after, armchair generals criticized Lee for letting Burnside give him the slip. Heros von Borcke, though, was sympathetic to the army commander, whose readings of his enemies were normally pitch-perfect. "It surely cannot be censured as a fault to have speculated upon the incapacity of the adversary," the Prussian wrote.[58]

Von Borcke looked at the arithmetic of the situation, giving it a romanticized spin even while somehow being coolly pragmatic. "Everyone who knows how exceedingly difficult it had become, already at that time, to fill the ranks of the Confederate army, and how valuable each individual life in that army must have been considered," he remarked. "I say that every one who bears in mind these facts will agree with me in thinking that our commander-in-chief acted with great consideration and wisdom."[59]

As Lee's chief postwar apologist, Jubal Early, unsurprisingly offered the most spirited—but also the most rational—defense:

> The failure of General Lee to attempt to destroy the enemy's army after its repulse has been much criticised, and many speculations about the probable result of an attempt to drive the enemy into the river have been indulged in by a number of writers. In the first place, it must be recollected that no man was more anxious to inflict a decisive blow on the enemy than General Lee himself, and none understood better the exact condition of things, and the likelihood of success in any attempt to press the enemy after his defeat on the 13th. That defeat was a repulse with very heavy loss it is true, but it was not a rout of the enemy's army; and candid persons ought to presume that General Lee knew what he was about and had very good and sufficient reasons for not sallying from his line of defence, upon the exposed plains below, to make the attempt to convert the repulse into a rout.[60]

"General Lee," Early concluded with flourish, "accomplished all that was possible with the means under his control."[61]

CONCLUSION

For a brief hour on the evening of December 14, the agony and horror of the battle became especially sublime. Above the battlefield, still strewn with the dead and wounded, the northern lights began to shine—"a grand auroral display," said Confederate mapmaker Jed Hotchkiss, "one of the finest I have ever seen."[1] The display "surpassed in splendor any like exhibition I ever saw," wrote Confederate Robert Stiles. "The heavens were hanging out banners and streamers and setting off fireworks in honor of our victory."[2] In their defeat, Federals saw the heavenly colors in more somber tones.

The next night, December 15, the sky better reflected their mood. The starlit night gave way to heavy clouds blown in by an even heavier wind, then thunderstorms and torrents of rain. In the midst of the fen weather, the Army of the Potomac retreated across the Rappahannock. "A dense mass of men, horses, Artillery & the various impedimenta of an Army poured over until daylight," wrote engineer Wesley Brainerd, who was tasked with dismantling his pontoon bridge when the evacuation finished. "Casting loose the end towards the foe," he added, "the bridges were allowed to swing around by the force of the current, one end being held fast until they touched on our side."[3]

Burnside—defeated, frustrated, exhausted—had no idea what to do next.

"I presume he is meditating a passage at some other point," Lee told Secretary of War Seddon on December 16.[4] But, in truth, Lee was as clueless of Burnside's next move as Burnside was himself. "There is nothing to indicate his future purpose," Lee told Seddon.[5] The army commander later added a cautionary note: "I hope that there will be no relaxation in making every preparation for the contest which will have to be renewed, but at what point I cannot now state."[6]

Jubal Early later said the moment was pregnant with anxiety for the Confederates and possibility for the Federals. "Had Burnside moved down the river to the Massaponix [*sic*], after crossing, or had thrown other bridges across at or near the mouth of that stream, and crossed one of his grand divisions there, he would inevitably have forced us to abandon our line of defence, and fight him on other ground," Jubal Early later hypothesized.[7]

As a safeguard, Lee defaulted to his prebattle deployment, sending a brigade of cavalry down the Rappahannock and putting Jackson's Corps in motion in the same direction. "I think it probable an attempt will be made to cross at Port Royal," Lee reported. "Should the enemy cross at Port Royal in force before I can get this army in position to meet him, I think it more advantageous to retire to the Annas & give battle than on the banks of the Rappahannock. My design was to have done so in the first instance."[8] Even with a victory under his belt, he could not pass up the opportunity to remind Richmond of a defensive position he considered even stronger.

Aside from the downriver cavalry, Lee also sent a brigade of horsemen to cross upriver and try to get in the Federal rear in an attempt to ascertain Burnside's intentions. Burnside, Lee worried, could cross "at almost any point without molestation." In essence, the Confederate commander faced the same situation he'd faced in November and early December. For this reason, Lee felt especially frustrated by December's battle. His victory had neither decided anything nor changed the overall military picture in Virginia. If Burnside hadn't backed up Lincoln's Emancipation Proclamation with battlefield victory, he had nonetheless, from a strictly practical perspective, secured the Rappahannock River as the front line of emancipation. By some accounts, as many as ten thousand enslaved people had self-emancipated by fleeing bondage and crossing the river to the safety of Union lines during the spring and summer of 1862. The presence of the Union army in Fredericksburg for months subsequent to the Emancipation Proclamation sustained the north bank of the Rappahannock as a sanctuary for freedom.[9]

Despite their commander's disappointment, the men of the Army of Northern Virginia seemed jubilant over the battle's results. "Fredericksburg was the simplest and easiest won battle of the war," Robert Stiles proclaimed.[10] Lee's aide Col. Walter Taylor echoed a similar sentiment. "It was certainly the most easily won of all the grand battles of the war," he contended, "and it was, indeed, the most exhilarating and inspiring to look upon."[11] Lee himself had said as much. As the contest on the south end of the field unfolded, the martial splendor of it stirred the career soldier, who put his hand on the arm of his "Old Warhorse," James Longstreet, and declared, "It is well that war is so terrible, or we would grow too fond of it."[12]

Fredericksburg demonstrated to the Federals just how terrible war was. The 122,000-man Army of the Potomac suffered 12,653 casualties, including 1,284 killed, 9,600 wounded, and 1,769 captured or missing—a 10.3 percent casualty rate. In contrast, the 78,500-man Army of Northern Virginia suffered 5,377 casualties, including 608 killed, 4,116 wounded, and 653 captured or missing—a 6.8 percent casualty rate. Of the Federal casualties, some 8,000 of them fell in front of Marye's Heights, compared to fewer than 1,000 Confederate casualties there. In contrast, at Prospect Hill, where the fighting was more even, Federals and Confederates each lost about 4,000 men.

"Condoling with the mourners for the dead, and sympathizing with the severely wounded, I congratulate you that the number of both is comparatively so small," Lincoln wrote to his army on December 22. As the president was deep in a depression of his own, his attempt to buck up his men was halfhearted at best. "Although you were not successful, the attempt was not an error, nor the failure other than an accident," he added unconvincingly.[13]

Fredericksburg National Cemetery, which now occupies Marye's Heights, provides a dramatic reminder of the cost of battle. Fredericksburg and Spotsylvania National Military Park.

The Northern public was no more assuaged than the army. "The great loss of life appalls the people at home," wrote artillerist Charles Wainwright. "In the army the effect has been, so far as I can see, to take all life out if it."[14] While he couldn't quite put his finger on how to articulate the army's demoralization, Wainwright specifically noted "a universal distaste to talk about the future."[15]

Writing after the war, Confederate James Longstreet thought the whole thing unnecessary. "The battle of Fredericksburg was a great and unprofitable sacrifice of human life made, through pressure from the rear, upon a general who should have known better and who doubtless acted against his judgment," the Old Warhorse argued. "If I had been in General Burnside's place, I would have asked the President to allow me to resign rather than execute his order to force the passage of the river and march the army against Lee in his stronghold."[16] Longstreet seemed to contradict his own armchair generaling, though, in suggesting that a different deployment might have done the trick. "Had [Burnside] thus placed Hooker and Sumner, his sturdiest fighters, and made resolute assault with them in his attack on our right, he would in all probability have given us trouble," the Old Warhorse speculated. "The partial success he had at that point might have been pushed vigorously by such a force and might have thrown our right entirely from position."[17]

Burnside biographer William Marvel offers a similarly tantalizing, if apologetic, take on Burnside's effort. "He contrived a plan that should have worked, and modified it serially as circumstances rendered elements of it obsolete," Marvel writes. "On the brink of exhaustion he [Burnside] conducted a battle he ought to have won, despite the mistakes he made: a battle he would have won, but for the hesitation of his colleagues."[18]

That last sentiment, at least, reflected the contemporaneous thinking of Charles Wainwright. The more the artillerist thought about it, the more inclined he was to blame William Franklin for the loss. In Wainwright's words, Franklin had been considered "one of the most able me we have," and the general had also been spoken of "both in the army and in the papers as likely at some time to have command of this army." Wainwright was baffled as to why such an able man would squander such a clear opportunity as he'd had on December 13, and the artillerist wondered whether Franklin's "natural laziness has become too strong to conquer."[19]

Franklin soon became the focus of great official scrutiny. The Joint Committee on the Conduct of the War began to look for causes—scapegoats—almost immediately, first during an investigative trip to Stafford, then by calling witnesses to Washington. Increasingly, the group's members honed in on Franklin, as well as the initial debacle with the pontoons. "Burnside proved that the crossing of the river had been peremptorily ordered from Washington, in the face of his opinion and of the majority of his principal officers," Meade wrote.[20] The committee held no love for Lincoln, so finding the War Department even partially responsible might have suited it just fine.

"What will be done next I cannot tell," Meade confided to his wife. "Burnside, I presume, is a dead cock in the pit, and your friend Joe Hooker . . . is next on the list."[21] He didn't think Old Burn would mind. "I think he would personally have no objection to their removing him," Meade wrote, "and that he is quite independent of them; willing to remain if they let him alone, but perfectly willing to retire if they desire him to."[22] The men of the Army of the Potomac seemed to exhibit a similar sort of ambivalence. "Very little is said of Burnside," Wainwright noted, "but neither officers nor men have the slightest confidence in him."[23]

Although downcast at times, Burnside tried to maintain his usual good cheer. "As a man he has behaved beautifully," Wainwright conceded, "clearly and unreservedly at once taking himself all the responsibility of the battle. I wish that I could feel that he did as well as a general before and during the fight."[24] And there was apt to be another fight on the horizon, the men realized. "General Burnside, smarting under a severe castigation and the criticism of his enemies, naturally has a strong desire to retrieve his late disaster," wrote Pvt. John Haley of the Seventh Maine, expecting a move at any minute.[25]

If Burnside was smarting, his commander in chief, Lincoln, was in downright depressive agony. "If there is a place worse than hell, I am in it," Lincoln said. And the woes only worsened. In the immediate aftermath of Fredericksburg, the president had to fend off a political crisis from Radical Republicans, deal with news of William T. Sherman's repulse at Chickasaw Bayou, and then wait anxiously for the dust to settle outside Murfreesboro, Tennessee, where the Army of the Cumberland ushered in the new year with a bruising battle against the Army of Tennessee. Even with that battle still in doubt on January 1, 1863, Lincoln signed the final Emancipation Proclamation.

By that point, Burnside had begun to look at options for another offensive. Confederate artillerist E. P. Alexander, writing after the war, gave the Federal army commander credit for not wanting to give up: "Whatever may be said of Burnside's strategy or tactics, he was not deficient in moral courage," he wrote.[26] The men and officers of the Army of the Potomac, though, had mixed feelings about their leader. Meade, by then promoted to command of the Union Fifth Corps, explained to his wife, Margaretta, that the most important opposition came from Burnside's principal subordinates—Franklin, Hooker, and Sumner. However, Meade said he favored a crossing under certain conditions: "[I would proceed] if a suitable place could be found above or below, where we could rapidly cross and attack them [Confederates] before they could get ready to receive us, and I believed we could whip them."[27] A victory gained, he said, would be of "immense advantage to us."[28]

Before Burnside could execute, though, Lincoln nixed the plan. A string of officers—Franklin, Baldy Smith, John Newton, and the politician-turned-brigadier John Cochrane—had been surreptitiously undermining Burnside's command. Newton and Cochrane even showed up at the White House. Lincoln sent them back to the army, but he also sent Burnside a telegram: "I have good reason for saying you must not make a general movement of the army without letting me know."[29] The order, said Burnside's chief of staff, "came upon him like a thunderbolt."[30]

And so it was that, for the next few weeks, Burnside had to contend not only with the pall of his loss at Fredericksburg, the new political context created by the Emancipation Proclamation, and pressure from Washington and the press, but also with significant dissent in his own officer corps. And all the while, the call "On to Richmond" continued. "It is understood Halleck says: 'This army shall go to Richmond, if it has to go on crutches,'" Meade wrote, "which (as over ten thousand cripples were made the other day) seems likely to occur before long. The army are willing enough to go to Richmond, if they could only see the way to get there."[31]

Across the river, Lee continued to watch for any sign that Burnside had finally "seen a way." Inactivity on his front had sparked talk in Richmond

Brig. Gen. John Newton engaged in political backbiting against Burnside. Library of Congress.

Brig. Gen. John Cochrane was among those in an anti-Burnside cabal, making it as far as the White House where they secured an audience with Lincoln. Lincoln broke up the conspiracy, but it nonetheless further undermined Burnside's standing as commander of the Army of the Potomac. National Archives and Records Administration.

of reassigning some of Lee's troops to other embattled areas. Lee strongly cautioned against this move. He still didn't believe Burnside was finished, although the Confederate commander remained flummoxed by the apparent lack of Federal energy. "Nor is there any indication of an embarkation or retrograde movement or going into winter quarters," Lee told Richmond. "I think it dangerous to diminish this army until something can be ascertained of the intentions of that opposed to it."[32]

On January 20, Burnside tried again, with an eye on the Rappahannock's upriver fords—a plan that would lay the foundation for Joe Hooker's Chancellorsville Campaign in the spring. Unfortunately, this endeavor was fated to become "Burnside's last wild effort to justify himself," said Second Corps staff officer Francis Walker.[33] A day into the movement, the skies opened in biblical fashion, bogging the Federals down so badly that their journey would ever after be known as the Mud March. "I never felt so disappointed and sorry for any one in my life as I did for Burnside," Meade wrote afterward. "He really seems to have even the elements against him."[34]

The failed maneuver sapped the last remaining vestiges of confidence the army had in Burnside. With the officers' malcontent worse than ever, with whisperings to bring back McClellan, with his Fredericksburg-tarnished reputation getting only worse, with "even the elements against him," Burnside traveled to Washington on January 23 and offered Lincoln his resignation. In what would become the first critical decision of the Chancellorsville Campaign, Lincoln accepted the general's notice and placed Maj. Gen. Joseph Hooker in command of the army.

"The privates in the ranks knew just as well as their officers that they had not a fair chance at Fredericksburg," wrote Francis Walker, "and in their minds they dismissed Burnside from the command long before the Administration was prepared to act."[35]

APPENDIX I

DRIVING TOUR OF THE FREDERICKSBURG BATTLEFIELD

The driving tour in this book is designed to highlight areas associated with the critical decisions made during the battle. As such, it skips over some parts of the battlefield and invites you to explore other areas on your own. Several optional stops are included for die-hard enthusiasts. However, they're optional either because there's little or nothing at the site to see anymore, or because they're ancillary to the main theme of the book.

The tour is laid out as conveniently as possible for hitting the key sites, although that means it follows a geographic rather than chronological route. The text accompanying each stop will specify which decision/chapter from the main text the site relates to.

Additionally, two sites associated with Burnside's ascension to command—as recounted in chapter 1—are too geographically distant from Fredericksburg to be included in the tour. However, the curious traveler may wish to visit them.

Rectortown: The Site of George McClellan's Headquarters

In Rectortown, Virginia, at the downtown intersection of Routes 713 and 710, follow Route 713 (Maidstone Road) for 0.5 mile to the intersection with Route 624 (Lost Corner Road). Cross the railroad tracks. Debate exists among local historians as to which of the several hills on the right side of the road played

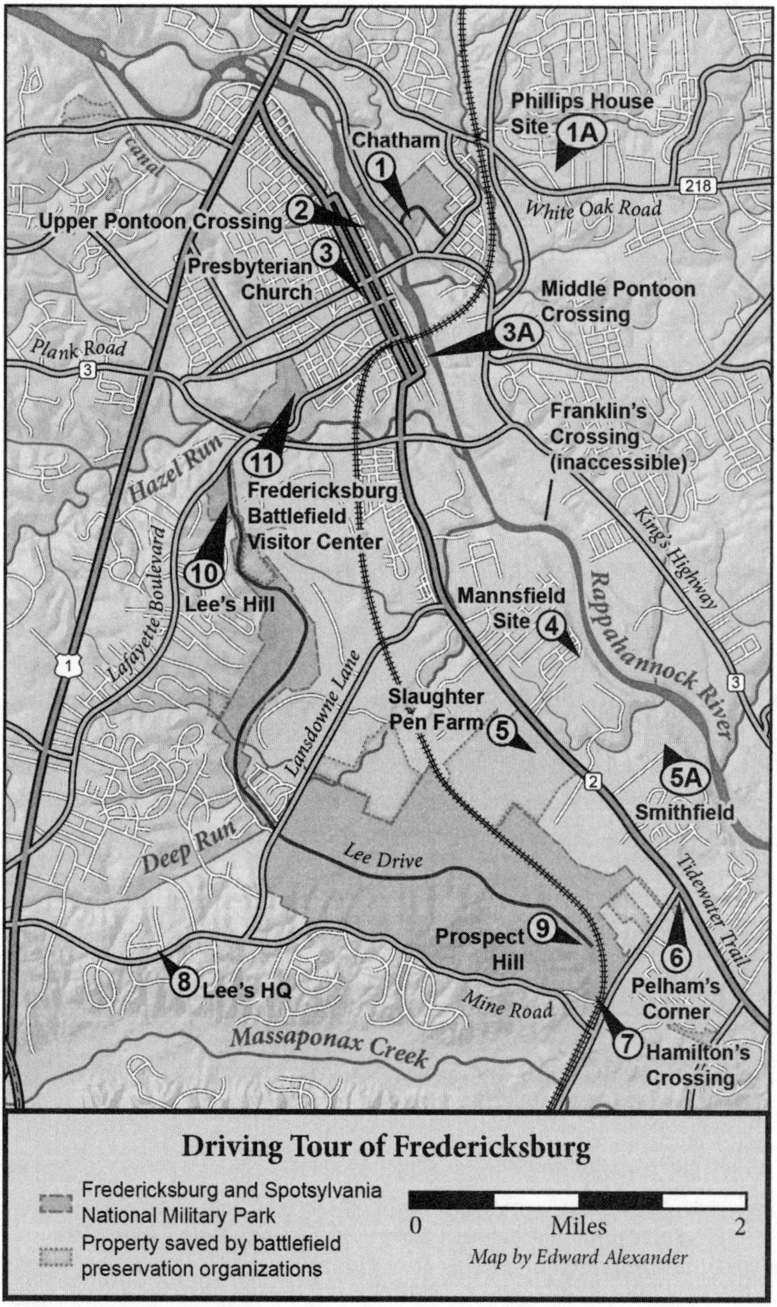

Driving tour of Fredericksburg.

host to McClellan's headquarters tent, but McClellan headquartered on one of them.

Warrenton: Warren Green Hotel

In Warrenton, Virginia, at the intersection of Court Street and Hotel Street, look for a Fauquier Historical Society marker for "the Warren Green / Norris Tavern." The nearby office complex for Fauquier County occupies a reconstructed version of the old Warren Green Hotel. Here, following a November 11 reception, McClellan stood on the second-story balcony and issued his final farewell to his army. Fire destroyed the original building in 1874.

The Fredericksburg Battlefield

Tour Stop 1: Chatham

This site relates primarily to critical decisions 2, 4, and 5.

Chatham Manor is the crown jewel of Fredericksburg and Spotsylvania National Military Park, particularly when the summer gardens are in full bloom or when the autumn leaves frame the grounds. Built in 1771, Chatham saw visits from Washington, Jefferson, and Lincoln, making it one of the most noteworthy historic homes in America. (James Monroe had a law office in Fredericksburg, so he likely he visited at some point, too, and William Henry Harrison was on the grounds as president-elect.)

Chatham has gone through many lives of its own, and today it serves as the park headquarters. It also makes an excellent place to begin any extended tour of the Fredericksburg battlefield. The two-story brick home represents a textbook example of Georgian architecture: the north and south wings of the house are laid out symmetrically, and the east and west faces of the house look almost identical. This symmetry has stimulated much debate over the years regarding which side of the house was the front and which was the back, and evidence suggests that various owners invited their guests to enter the home on either side over Chatham's long history.

The colonial-era property also included a laundry and kitchen, both of which survive. In the property's antebellum life, an icehouse, carriage house, and dairy were added, as were barns, stables, and a racetrack. Subsequent owners added a sun-room, greenhouse, and other buildings. A wall around the home's elaborate gardens enclosed a private back yard. The property also had a number of slave dependencies.

At the time of the war, 39-year-old James Horace Lacy and his 31-year-

Chatham's gardens make the grounds a must-see stop in the summer. Chris Mackowski.

old bride, Betty, owned the home and its surrounding 800 acres. Some 39 enslaved people worked 550 of these acres to produce wheat, corn, oats, and wool.[1] Lacy was an ardent secessionist, and with his wealth and connections, he made his anti-Union influence felt—so much so that Federal authorities considered him to be "the most dangerous Rebel in the county."[2] By the time Federals occupied the city in the spring of 1862, though, Lacy had taken a position as a staff officer in the Confederate army, serving at various times with Theophilus Holmes, Daniel Ruggles, and Gustavus Smith.[3]

During the Battle of Fredericksburg, Chatham took at least one hit from a Confederate artillery shell but otherwise made it through the fight unscathed. However, the Union presence was hard on the house—it was even used to stable horses—and after the war, the financially strapped Lacys did not have the money to fully restore it. In 1872, they sold the property, which ultimately allowed Chatham to rebloom again and again under a series of new owners.

When going inside the house today, you can find guides who will answer questions, provide a tour, and orient you to the battlefield. A museum explains the property's role before, during, and after the battle, including its use as a hospital. Clara Barton and Walt Whitman were among those who

Chatham now serves as the headquarters for Fredericksburg and Spotsylvania National Military Park. Exhibits can be viewed inside, and house tours are available. Chris Mackowski.

tended patients at Chatham. "Spent a good part of the day in a large brick mansion on the banks of the Rappahannock, immediately opposite Fredericksburg," Whitman wrote on December 21, 1862. "It is used as a hospital since the battle, and seems to have received only the worst cases."[4] Some 130 soldiers were buried on the manor's ground; most were moved to Fredericksburg National Cemetery, although three were overlooked and still remain on the property.

Chatham dominates the hillside that overlooks Fredericksburg, and from the river side of the house, visitors today get a clear panoramic view of the city thanks to landscape restoration by the National Park Service in 2014. Federal officers enjoyed a similar view in 1862. On the evening of December 13, though, a *New York Times* correspondent observed an "externally calm" but "agitated" Burnside in this area pacing "the garden gloomy as night."[5]

A two-thirds scale pontoon boat sits on one of the riverside terraces. Several artillery pieces point across the river (imagine the cacophonous roar of 183 of them at the height of the December 11 bombardment).

Back at the parking area, the large field beyond was once occupied by the camps of Second Corps. When Burnside's pontoons finally arrived, engineers parked them in this field; in preparation for battle, engineers manhandled

One of the most useful interpretive tools on the battlefield is the set of reproduction pontoons, built to two-thirds scale, that sit on the riverside of Chatham's grounds. Chris Mackowski.

the boats down ravines that led from either side of the house to the river. In March 1863, Abraham Lincoln reviewed part of the army in this field.

It's doubtful Lincoln realized it, but the Great Emancipator's presence at Chatham had a particular poetic justice. On January 2, 1805, a slave revolt at the manor left one White man and two Black men dead, a third Black man seriously injured, and two others sold away.[6] A wayside sign along the brick sidewalk leading from the parking lot to the house briefly recounts the story.

To the northwest, visitors can see a radio tower rising above the tree line. That tower marks the location of the Phillips House, Ambrose Burnside's headquarters during the battle. Unfortunately, there's nothing to see there today and no public property to access; however, this tour offers die-hard battlefield explorers who want to say, "I know where that is" the option to swing by. To do so, follow the directions to Tour Stop 1A; otherwise, follow the directions to Tour Stop 2.

<u>Walt Whitman on His Visit to Chatham</u>:

"Outdoors, at the foot of a tree, within ten yards of the front of the house, I noticed a heap of amputated feet, legs, arms, hands, etc.—about a load for a one-horse cart," Whitman recalled, referring to a catalpa tree that still stands on the riverside of the building. He continued,

Several dead bodies lie near, each covered with its brown woolen blanket. In the dooryard, toward the river, are fresh graves, mostly of officers, their names on pieces of barrel staves or broken board, stuck in the dirt. . . .

The house is quite crowded, everything impromtu, no system, all bad enough, but I have no doubt the best that can be done; all the wounds pretty bad, some frightful, the men in their old clothes, unclean and bloody.[7]

Chatham as Described in the Philadelphia *Sunday Dispatch*, January 18, 1863:

The floors are covered with dirt and rubbish. Pieces of broken glass ware and old rags are scattered around, and on the verandah is to be seen the wreck of a fine piano. . . . The arbors, trellis work and shrubbery have disappeared, and scarcely one of the many beautiful trees in the garden are left. Here and there the stump of a tree tells where the . . . branches of the beech and sycamore once afforded shade and beauty to the scene. The garden walks are a mud hole, trampled by men and horses.

A squad of soldiers in in the house, and outside a short distance some are cooking rations at a fire. The fine old stone barn is gone, and the neat-looking servants' houses are dirty and filthy, with a deposit of mud an inch thick upon the floors. 'Tis a perfect picture of desolation.[8]

To Tour Stop 1A / Tour Stop 2

Exit the Chatham parking lot by bearing to the right. Follow the driveway 0.35 mile. Along the way, you'll get an excellent view of Fredericksburg on the far side of the river.

At the end of the driveway, turn left onto River Road. Visibility exiting the park driveway is poor, so use caution. Travel 0.1 mile to the intersection with King's Highway. At the intersection, you can continue along the main tour route or take a short detour for an optional stop at the site of the Phillips House.

If you'd like to follow the main tour, turn right onto Kings Highway and cross the Rappahannock River, then pick up the directions after Tour Stop

1A. If you'd like to go to the optional tour stop, follow the directions immediately below.

To Optional Tour Stop 1A

At the stop sign, turn left onto Kings Highway. Travel 0.1 mile. At the traffic light, turn left onto Chatham Heights Road. Drive 0.85 mile, and turn right onto White Oak Road (Route 218) at the traffic light. Travel 0.35 mile, then left onto Northside Drive.

Travel 0.2 mile. Pull into the parking lot on the left, behind a senior living facility. Straight ahead, you'll see the radio tower visible from Chatham. However, if you pull into the spaces on the left, you will be facing the direction of the former location of the Phillips House. Please note, though, that this is private property. Please respect the rights of the property owners and do not trespass.

Tour Stop 1A: Phillips House Site

This site relates primarily to critical decisions 5, 7, and 13.

The Phillips House had a short, inglorious life, occupied as much by Federal officers as by the man who built it, fifty-eight-year-old Alexander Phillips. Phillips built the house in 1860 atop a knoll on a ridge that sat about a mile and a quarter back from the river. According to historian Noel Harrison, the house "was two stories tall and built of brick. It was an elaborate example of the Gothic Revival architectural style and featured vergeboarding, lancet windows, and an asymmetrical plan. An indoor tank supplied water to 'marble wash basins through silver faucets,' and other components of one of the area's few indoor plumbing systems."[9]

When the Union army first moved into the area in the spring of 1862, officers took up residence in the Phillips House because of the commanding view it offered. The elevation offered, "on the whole, the best post of observation," said staff officer George Noyes.[10] For that same reason, Burnside made it his headquarters during the battle, and aeronaut Thaddeus Lowe operated his scouting balloons nearby.

Railroad genius Herman Haupt, on special assignment with the army at the time of the battle, watched from a window in Burnside's room. "I could, with a field glass, see our columns move to the attack, then the smoke of battle would obscure everything," he wrote. "When it cleared away, our forces were found driven back and the ground strewn with dead and wounded."[11] As the battle continued, hospital tents sprung up in a glen to the right of the Phillips House, "safely out of range of the rebel batteries," said George

Noyes, who also noted, "Long streets of those temporary houses of refuge were quickly going up."[12] Two hundred and twenty-seven Union soldiers were buried on the property and eventually reinterred across the river in the national cemetery.[13]

After the battle, delegates from the Joint Committee on the Conduct of the War visited Burnside in the house and conducted some of their interviews there. In the weeks that followed, the Phillips House saw a carousel of Union officers occupy and leave. During one such turnover, as Brig. Gen. Gen. George Stoneman moved out to make way for a field hospital, a second-story stove ignited a fire on February 14. "There has been quite a sad affair in our neighborhood," wrote Provost Marshal Marsena Patrick. "The Phillips House was burned, & only the walls left standing tonight. . . . Not a bucket of water could be had to quench the fire–wells all dry."[14]

From the parking lot, a screen of trees hides the modern house that sits on the site of the Phillips House. A single outbuilding from the plantation—probably a slave house—still survives, but it's also tucked away in a far tree line.[15]

From the June 10, 1862, Diary of George F. Noyes, Staff Officer for Brig. Gen. Abner Doubleday:

A fine residence it was, overlooking the valley of the Rappahannock and the pretty city, with the Blue Ridge bounding the western horizon, and treating us occasionally to a sunset of wonderful beauty. The plantation once formed a part of the estate of Mary, the mother of Washington, who half-finished monument, just back of Fredericksburg, was visible from its balcony. It must have been a charming spot ere War, with its desolating footfall, had invaded this lovely valley; but now fences, trees, and waving grain had departed; the owner had deserted, leaving only an overseer with an immense wife and two babies, whose capacity for crying was equally extensive, with a superannuated negro or two in the outbuildings, too old to accompany their fellows on the Northern tour. If we were condemned to temporary inactivity, we could not have had a more delightful sport for our involuntary sojourn.[16]

To Tour Stop 2 from Phillips House Site:

Turn right out of the parking lot and travel 0.2 mile. At the stop sign, turn right onto White Oak Road (Route 218). Proceed 0.15 mile, and turn left onto

Cool Springs Road at the traffic light. Drive 1.0 mile. At the traffic light, turn right onto King's Highway and travel 0.6 mile. This will bring you back past the intersection with River Road and across the Rappahannock River. Resume the tour directions below.

To Tour Stop 2:

At the far end of the bridge, there will be a traffic light. Turn right onto Sophia Street.

Travel 0.2 mile to the intersection of Sophia and Hawke Street. Park along the street as you are able.

Tour Stop 2: The Upper Pontoon Crossing

This site relates primarily to critical decisions 5 and 6.

Two monuments mark the location of the upper pontoon crossing. The larger of the two, a boulder with a bas-relief plaque, commemorates the groundbreaking crossing of the Seventh Michigan. "Every eye was strained upon them," one witness of the crossing said, "& every heart wished them success in their courageous and self-sacrificing mission."[17] Dedicated in August 2003, the five-ton monument cost $10,000.[18]

The second memorial is a granite block dedicated in 1917 by the United Daughters of the Confederacy. The text on the block incorrectly identifies

A monument to the Seventh Michigan sits at the site of the upper pontoon crossing. Chris Mackowski.

December 12, rather than December 11, as the day of the crossing. The UDC installed a matching marker at the middle pontoon crossing, but in 1923, flood waters washed it away.[19]

The green area that extends from the street to the riverbank is National Park Service property. If you walk down to the river and look back up to the street, you can see how the topography of the riverbank served as a shield for Union soldiers as they rowed their pontoon boats closer to this side. Confederates could not shoot down past the crest of the hill. However, you can also see how open and exposed Federal engineers would have been as they tried to work on their bridges. "As there were no Troops in the Army that understood our duties or that could relieve us," engineer Wesley Brainerd said, "there was nothing left for us but to die."[20]

This location offers an excellent view of Chatham on the far shore, sitting high above the river.

On the opposite side of Sophia Street, Hawke Street stretches away from the river through a quaint neighborhood. Some of these houses were here at the time of the battle; many of these would have been filled with William Barksdale's men as they contested the Federal advance down Hawke. Imagine the Michiganders and Massachusetts men going room to room, house to house, as they slowly progressed under stubborn resistance.

Walking all the way to the end of the block brings you to the intersection of Hawke and Caroline Streets. Here, the Twentieth Massachusetts came under withering fire from Confederates posted in houses on all four corners. "Here we cleared the houses near us, but shot came from far and near," wrote Capt. George Macy of the Twentieth Massachusetts. "We could see no one and were simply murdered."[21]

From Wesley Brainerd of the Fiftieth New York Engineers:

The bulletts [*sic*] of the enemy *rained* upon my bridge. They went whizzing and spitting by and around me, pattering on the bridge, splashing into the water and thugging through the boats. . . . Every one [of my men] started for the shore end of the bridge. Some fell into boats, dead. Some fell into the Stream and some onto the bridge, dead. Some, wounded, crawled along on their hands and knees and in a few moments all of us were off the bridge, all except the dead. The storm of lead continued.[22]

From William McCarter of the 116th Pennsylvania:

The boats with their brave and daring crews dashed onward, but had scarce reached the middle of the river when at least 50 rifles were leveled and fired at them from the opposite shore by some of the enemy yet concealed below low banks of earthworks skirting the stream, and who, even the destructive fire of our artillery, had failed to dislodge. . . . When nearing the other side, several squads of the enemy's Infantry were seen, from our point of observation, hurrying down the streets of the town to the river, to assist their comrades in preventing the advance and landing of the Federal troops on the Confederate side of the water. They opened a galling fire on our men, who, without any, or the slightest indication of wavering from it, plyed their oars the quicker, and returned volley after volley of musketry with telling effect on their opponents. A few minutes later and the shore is touched, and then a furious hand-to-hand fight ensues. Sabres, Butt-ends of muskets and bayonets are freely and desparately used, together with powder and ball on both sides, tinting the beautiful Rappahannock with the blood of the Confederate and Federal slain alike. . . .

The surviving Western troops quickly form on the opposite bank, and with bayonets fixed, and wild demoniac yells, charge the now demoralized enemy up the streets of the ill-fated town.[23]

To Tour Stop 3

Travel 0.1 mile to the end of Sophia Street, and turn left onto Pitt Street.

Go to the stop sign at the end of the block; this is the intersection with Caroline Street. When the traffic allows, cross Caroline Street and continue straight on Pitt Street. Drive to the stop sign at the end of the block, which is the intersection with Princess Anne Street. Turn left.

Travel 0.3 mile. Along the way, 0.15 mile from Pitt Street, you'll pass a large white house on the right. This is the Gordon House, built in 1802 and used during the battle as a headquarters first by Brig. Gen. Alfred Sully—a Northern relative of the Gordons—and then by Sully's immediate commander, Brig. Gen. Oliver Otis Howard.

Continue along Princess Anne Street to the intersection with William Street, then go straight through the intersection. Park anywhere along the block between William Street and George Street.

Tour Stop 3: Market House and Fredericksburg Presbyterian Church

Market House relates to the decision recounted in chapter 6. The church relates (or, more accurately, does not relate) to the decision recounted in chapter 3.

For orientation purposes at this stop, keep in mind that Princess Anne Street is one-way. Facing in the direction that traffic drives is south; facing against traffic is north. If you walk to the north end of the block, on the east side of the street, you'll see Market House, now the Fredericksburg Area Museum. The museum, well worth a visit, does an excellent job of telling Fredericksburg's long, rich history.

If you walk to the south end of the block, on the west side of the street, and cross the intersection with George Street, you'll see the Fredericksburg Presbyterian Church. In one of the white pillars in front of the church, you'll see an embedded cannonball. This is a postwar decoration, not actual wartime damage, although the church did come under fire during the December 11 bombardment.

James Power Smith, a member of Stonewall Jackson's staff, returned to Fredericksburg after the war and served as the Presbyterian church's pastor. An influential member of the community, Smith played a key role in shaping the way the local battles were remembered, commemorated, and monumented. Of particular note are ten granite markers that he placed around the area's battlefields in 1903 to call attention to pivotal moments. Not coincidentally, those moments tended to focus on Lee and Jackson. (James Longstreet, meanwhile, would be virtually written out of local history because of his postwar feuds with Lost Cause writers.) You'll see all four Fredericksburg-related Smith markers on this tour.

Also of note at the church is a small stone plaque set into the front corner of the wall that surrounds the churchyard. The plaque faces Princess Anne Street on the corner of the intersection with George Street, and it reads, "Gen. Stonewall Jackson, by Gen. Lee's request, on this corner, planned the battle of Fredericksburg, Nov. 27, 1862." The information on the tablet, Dedicated in November 1924 at a cost of twenty-five dollars, is patently false. On November 27, Jackson was encamped somewhere between Gordonsville and Orange, still on his way to Fredericksburg, which was a couple days' march distant. That evening, word reached him that his wife had given birth to their baby girl. Thus, battle planning was far from his mind. In fact, it was James Longstreet who helped Lee plan the battle and lay out the Confederate line, but by 1924, Lee's "Old Warhorse" had fallen so far out of favor that his role at Fredericksburg was actively blotted out by a Lost Clause–flavored interpretation.

To Tour Stop 3A/4

Continue along Princess Anne Street to the intersection with George Street. Drive past the intersection for 0.25 mile to the intersection with Lafayette Boulevard. At the intersection with Lafayette Boulevard, you can continue along the main tour route or take a short detour for an optional tour stop at the middle pontoon crossing.

If you'd like to follow the main tour, proceed straight through the intersection, then pick up the directions after Tour Stop 3A. If you'd like to go to the middle crossing, follow the directions immediately below.

To Optional Tour Stop 3A

Turn left onto Lafayette Boulevard and follow it for two blocks until it dead-ends at a *T.* Turn right onto Sophia Street, and follow it to the parking lot at the city boat landing.

Tour Stop 3A: The Middle Pontoon Crossing

This site relates primarily to critical decisions 5 and 6.

Once upon a time, as legend has it, George Washington—whose boyhood home, Ferry Farm, sits on the far bank of the river—skipped a silver dollar across the Rappahannock River at this spot. In 1862, Federal engineers threw across a pontoon bridge here. A trio of wayside signs tells the history of the area.

Several monuments have been installed in this area over the years and then subsequently wiped out by high water. With that in mind, a monument to the Irish Brigade sits on the north end of the parking lot, flush with the ground to avoid being swept away .

The historical Rocky Lane, a wartime alleyway that Federal troops used to push into the city as they set up the initial cordon around their beachhead, is located on the west side of the parking lot at its southern end.

> From the Report of Lieut. Michael McGrath,
> Fiftieth New York Engineers:
>
> Arrived about 3 o'clock on the morning of the 11th of December, unloaded the bridge material, and proceeded to lay the bridge. All went on quietly until we got within about 80 feet of the dock in Fredericksburg, when we were opened upon by a body of infantry lying concealed on the opposite shore. We had 2 privates wounded this first fire.

> Our artillery on the left bank opened fire on the points where the enemy were concealed, which, in about thirty minutes, silenced their fire. We went on the bridge again, and commenced work, but, as soon as we were collected together, the enemy poured a very heavy fire on us, which wounded Captain McDonald, 1 sergeant, and 3 privates. The range being so short and the fire so heavy, it was impossible for the men to work; they accordingly went under cover. Captain McDonald being wounded, I assumed command. Our artillery gave them round shot and shell for another half hour, when their fire slackened, and finally entirely ceased. I then collected my men together, and made another attempt to finish the bridge, but, as soon as I got fairly at work, we were fired upon, the fire being much heavier than either of the others. We lost by this fire 2 men killed and 9 wounded.
>
> It was then determined to make another attempt to lay the bridge, and to throw a body of infantry across the river in boats, to dislodge the enemy, which was accordingly done.[24]

To Tour Stop 4 from Middle Pontoon Crossing

To return to the main tour, retrace your route to Lafayette Boulevard, then up two blocks to Princess Anne Street. At the intersection with Princess Anne Street, turn left. Resume the tour directions below.

To Tour Stop 4

Follow Princess Anne Street beyond the Lafayette Boulevard intersection for an additional 0.5 mile. Turn right onto Dixon Street. Travel one block to the traffic light, and turn left at the light. This remains Dixon Street, also designated as Route 2 / Business 17.

Go 2.0 miles. Along the way, after 1.5 miles, you'll cross Deep Run. This was the right flank of Franklin's Left Grand Division. Beyond Deep Run, 0.5 mile on the left, you will come up on the driveway for the Elks Lodge. Pull into the driveway and drive to the parking lot behind the building. You may turn around in the parking lot.

This property is owned by the Fraternal Order of the Elks. As it is not available for public access except for occasional special events, please respect private property and remain in your vehicle.

Today, the former site of Mannsfield sits empty, although archaeological excavation has been done on the location in the past. Chris Mackowski.

Tour Stop 4: Site of Mannsfield

This site relates primarily to critical decisions 7, 8, and 12.

Mannsfield, the stately plantation where William Franklin made his headquarters, was "one of Virginia's ancestral homes." One Federal occupant described it as having been "in former days the center of generous hospitality."[25] "It is a splendid establishment, far superior to anything I have seen elsewhere in Virginia," said artillerist Charles Wainwright. "The central building is some fifty feet square or more, with semi-circular wings running out on each side; the whole is of stone, and not only pretentious but realizing what it pretends to. The interior is handsomely finished, and has been well furnished, but most of the furniture has been removed."[26]

Dating back to 1766, Mannsfield sat at the heart of an 1,800-acre plantation. The land was worked by at least seventy-seven enslaved people who lived in a settlement of cabins on the far side of the railroad tracks.[27]

Baldy Smith, who also used the house for his Sixth Corps headquarters, could not resist a flourish of antebellum romance when describing the place. Outside, he said, waited "saddled horses, not for the use of fair ladies and gay cavaliers, as in the olden time, but for staff-officers and orderlies to carry orders into the fight and bring back reports from the field."[28]

Arthur Bernard, the fifty-year-old "testy owner," as Smith called him, was a bachelor who lived in the stone mansion with his mistress "in very considerable style: the mistress, though, has been sent away for safe keeping."[29] Bernard protested about the Federals occupying his house, so the soldiers arrested him. Bernard then appealed to Franklin, "representing himself . . . as a good Union man," and Franklin released him—but then John Reynolds appeared at headquarters. Reynolds had served as military governor in Fredericksburg in the late spring of 1862, and he knew Bernard *not* to be such a good Union man. "He clapped him under arrest again," a witness said.[30] Bernard rode out the battle as a prisoner on the far side of the river.

During and after the battle, surgeons converted the house into a hospital. "Ghastly and bloody wounds met the eye in every direction," said chaplain E. P. Roe of the Second New York Cavalry. "Some had their eyes shot out; the tongues of some were swollen out of their mouths; some had their bodies shot through; others were torn and mangled by shell and shot, and all were crowded wherever there was any space."[31] Amputated body parts were tossed out one of the windows into a large heap. Nearly 150 Union soldiers were buried on the property, later to be disinterred and moved to Fredericksburg National Cemetery.[32]

Mannsfield survived the battle, but in April 1863, Confederate soldiers burned the interior of the building. The crumbling exterior remained standing until 1891. Sometime in the early 1920s, the ruins finally collapsed.[33]

From Chaplain Edward P. Roe

The large house to which the wounded were brought was now filled with mutilated and dying men. Cries and groans resounded from every apartment. Ghastly and bloody wounds met the eye in every direction. . . . The surgeons were hacking off limbs and arms by the dozen. The odor of blood was oppressive. . . . Such is the horrid reality of war behind the painted scenes of honor, glory, and romance. . . . One wounded boy had his leg taken off just as he was entering the hospital, which building was under fire all day, and was repeatedly struck. The scene from the windows of the hospital was truly splendid as night came on. Innumerable camp-fires gleamed from the hillsides, and occasionally the darkness was lighted up by the flash of cannon. . . . The ground outside the hospital was so tramped up, muddy, and filled with horses, that it was impossible to sleep there. But there was a stone alley-way under the hospital, filled with tobacco in the lead, part of it lying on the ground, and part drying overhead. One end of this place was already filled with wounded men.[34]

To Tour Stop 5

Retrace your route back down the driveway to Route 2. Turn left, and travel 0.2 mile. The Slaughter Pen Farm battlefield will be on your right. Turn into the driveway and pull up to the parking area near the wayside markers.

This property is owned by the American Battlefield Trust. It is available for public access.

Tour Stop 5: Slaughter Pen Farm

This site relates primarily to critical decision 11.

For a century and a quarter, public attention on the Battle of Fredericksburg focused on the Sunken Road and Stone Wall along the base of Marye's Heights. When the National Park Service built its battlefield visitor center in 1935, it conspicuously did so on that portion of the field—"at key interest areas, near the significant park features," per NPS policy—thus cementing an interpretation of the battle that gave primacy to the assaults there. [35]

It's little wonder: southern-centric historians like Douglas Southall Freeman had a major impact on the park's interpretation in its earliest days. According to historian Joan Zenzen in the park's official administrative history, "Freeman devoted his career to perpetuating the Lost Cause tradition" and "in particular held mystic admiration Virginia's Confederate heroes."[36] Freeman reviewed all of the park's museum exhibits, ensuring "only certain

A walking trail at the Slaughter Pen Farm gives visitors a chance to see how changing topography affected soldiers' advance toward the Confederate position in the far trees. Chris Mackowski.

story lines" made the cut, with a particular emphasis "on the fighting and not slavery and the causes of the war."[37]

This carried on a tradition that began as early as the park's establishment. The October 1928 dedication ceremony featured speakers who "used language associated with . . . Lost Cause tradition." Even northerners on the bill spoke "from a decidedly southern perspective."[38] Initial sketches for the park by the War Department—originally charged with administering the battlefield—were so South-centric that they prompted one park commissioner, himself a Virginian, to lament, "Those who had originally drawn up the plans had apparently 'forgot[ten] that any other than the Confederate army'" had fought there."[39] After the National Park Service took over administration in 1933, it continued the battlefield's development "within a mindset of southern traditions and cultural norms."[40] Such influences played out particularly in regard to race but also gave special consideration to the so-called home team. This was the case even though, as Zenzen says, "the battlefield park was meant to memorialize both the Federal and Confederate soldiers who fought on this landscape."[41]

Those complicated dynamics were further influenced by the land acquisition strategy Congress finally laid out. "The Antietam Plan," as that tactic was called, focused on purchasing earthworks and other physical remains of a battlefield while leaving farm fields in private hands under the assumption that they would always remain farmland. The approach saved Congress a huge outlay of cash to buy up thousands of acres—which representatives and senators had done for the first four battlefield parks—but the method proved woefully shortsighted in light of later explosive development pressures.[42]

"For the 1862 Fredericksburg battle, the Federals did not build trenches, thus providing no physical reminders for the park to acquire," Zenzen writes. As a result, "lands owned by the park to tell the story of the 1862 Fredericksburg battle largely enveloped Confederate positions, not Federal ones."[43] Compounding the bias of the ground, further acquisitions "may have had a southern focus," Zenzen admits. When properties associated with the Union army became available, such as the Meade Pyramid, "the park did not jump at the opportunity to receive a donation of key land associated with a Federal position during the Fredericksburg battle."[44]

Because of the southern influence on interpretation and the preservation of Confederate positions, the Fredericksburg battlefield highlighted portions of the field that best enshrined Lee's supremacy: the lopsided fight in front of Marye's Heights. (When you visit this site at Stop 11, for instance, note that the Confederate positions were preserved but the Union positions were not.) Meanwhile, here on the southern end of the battlefield, where casualties were about equal, Stonewall Jackson's position on Prospect Hill was kept intact not only because it was site of the successful counterattack, but also because, as a Smith marker proclaims, it was the site of "Jackson on the Field." Yet the Union attack field was left unpreserved.

That changed in 2006 when the American Battlefield Trust—then the Civil War Trust—purchased the 216-acre Slaughter Pen Farm. The $12 million financial outlay was the largest one for Civil War battlefield preservation up to that time. The importance of the purchase cannot be overstated. It significantly redefined interpretation of the Battle of Fredericksburg by calling renewed attention to the role—or intended role, at least—of William B. Franklin's troops.

Much of the credit for that rediscovery goes to National Park Service historian Frank O'Reilly, who began to further investigate the apparent mismatch between Meade's single division and Jackson's entire corps. His inquiries led to two books, *Stonewall Jackson at Fredericksburg: The Battle of Prospect Hill* (H. E. Howard, 1993) and the more comprehensive and in-depth *The Fredericksburg Campaign: Winter War on the Rappahannock* (LSU, 2002), which has become the definitive microtactical study on the battle.

Using the parking area as orientation, facing westward toward the far tree line and with Route 2 to your back, John Gibbon's division lined up behind you and to the right, while George Gordon Meade's division assembled behind you and to the left. A 1.75-mile walking trail extends out into the field, which was stubbled with harvested cornstalks in December 1862. Nine wayside markers along the trail help tell the story of the fighting in the field, with a focus on Gibbon's assault because that's the primary piece of preserved land. Meade's attack plain, including the spit of trees where his men initially broke through, still remains in private hands. If you take the hike, be sure to take water, because there's no shade in the field. Also, be sure you check for ticks when you get back.

The walk is definitely worth it: the lay of the land changes dramatically and unexpectedly as you cross the field, offering an illuminating lesson in the nuances of topography. Watch for such things as the ditch fence, partially filled with frigid water at the time of the battle, which disrupted unit cohesion as the Federals advanced. Watch, too, for the ridgeline that bisects the ground, hard to see from the parking area, which hides another entire half of the field. You'll also be able to see why Jubal Early believed a full-scale Confederate counterattack across this clearing would have been a bad idea. "It must be seen," he wrote, "that an attempt to pass over the wide plain intervening between our line and the enemy's position . . . while exposed to the fire of 150 heavy guns on the Stafford Heights, and the numerous field pieces securely masked in the River road, would inevitably have resulted in disaster, unless the enemy's forces had become so paralyzed as to be incapable of an effort at defence."[45]

Five Union soldiers were awarded the Medal of Honor for deeds on the Slaughter Pen Farm, with a sixth serviceman earning the award just on the other side of the railroad tracks at the far corner of the field. (Nineteen medals were awarded at Fredericksburg in all.)[46]

Excerpt from Testimony by Maj. Gen. John F. Reynolds to the Joint Committee on the Conduct of the War[47]

Question. If [Burnside's] order contemplated that that point should be taken and held, was it not the duty of the general commanding there [Franklin] to use his whole force to take that point—reserving only such portion as might be necessary to hold the heads of the bridges—if the whole force was requisite for that purpose?

Answer. It is very difficult for me to answer that question positively. The commanding officer of the whole force there must judge for himself as to the manner in which he will carry out the orders he has received. We were fighting with the river to our backs, and in case of a serious reverse there, the army would have been destroyed. I suppose it would be necessary, under such circumstances, for a general to hold a pretty large force in reserve; at least to have a large body of this troops ready to resist any counter-attack that might be made by the enemy, should the part of the troops that were engaged in carrying out that order meet with a reverse. Had we gone in with all our force over there and failed, the army would have been destroyed. If a larger force had been up there in time, I would have put it into the attack at once. I was going to put General Doubleday's division in behind Meade, and carry the whole thing through as far as my corps was concerned. But the demonstration made by the enemy on our left was so strong that I had to turn Doubleday square off to the left to meet it; and he did not succeed in driving the enemy off until it was too late to move Doubleday up again to support Meade.

Question. Why was not the attacking force better supported?

Answer. I think it was due to several causes. The troops ordered up did not come up in time to the scene of Meade's attack. . . .

Question. Why were not more troops placed in position to give immediate support to the attacking force?

Answer. I considered that the attacking force was my corps. I attacked with the whole corps, and there were no other troops that I know of ordered to follow me.

Question. In your judgement, should there not have been other troops in a position to give prompt support to you?

Answer. Yes, sir; I think there should.

Question. Who is responsible for that not having been done?

Answer. I can hardly say who is responsible, for I am not acquainted with all the orders that were given. . . .

Question. Were any of General Franklin's troops actively engaged, except those commanded by you?

Answer. None that I know of. The batteries of General Smith's corps were engaged a part of the time, and there may be have been some movement on the right which I did not know of.

To Tour Stop 5A/6

Retrace your route back down the driveway to Route 2. Turn right.

If you'd like to follow the main tour, continue straight on Route 2 for 1.5 miles to the traffic light at the intersection with Benchmark Road, then pick up the directions after Tour Stop 5A. If you'd like to go to the optional tour stop, follow the directions immediately below.

To Optional Tour Stop 5A

Go 0.5 mile. The Fredericksburg Country Club will be on your left. Turn into the driveway and follow it to the country club. You may turn around in front of the clubhouse.

This property is owned by the Fredericksburg Country Club. It is open to the public during special events, but otherwise, please respect private property.

Tour Stop 5A: Smithfield

This site relates primarily to events connected to critical decision 9.

Built in 1820, Smithfield was a two-story, "handsomely furnished" brick house owned by Thomas Pratt that sat at the heart of a 1,750-acre property adjacent to Mannsfield. Operated by some 107 enslaved people, the plantation grew wheat, corn, and oats.[48]

Like Mannsfield, Smithfield became a field hospital during the battle.

"It was an awful sight to see the hosts of wounded men being brought there," wrote one Federal soldier, "the ghastly amputating tables, the surgeons at work and the piles of arms and limbs and the poor fellows layed [*sic*] in the rows in and around the house and outbuildings."[49] Seventy-eight men were buried on the property and later reinterred at Fredericksburg National Cemetery.

In 1928, Pres. Calvin Coolidge visited Smithfield—by then converted to a country club. In remarks on the east lawn of the house, he dedicated Fredericksburg and Spotsylvania National Military Park. Today, Smithfield continues to serve as the country club's main building.

To Tour Stop 6 from Smithfield

Retrace your route back down the driveway to Route 2. Turn left, and drive 1.0 mile to the traffic light at the intersection with Benchmark Road.

To Tour Stop 6

Go straight through the light, then turn right into the 7-Eleven. Double back through the parking lot toward Benchmark Road, and park in one of the spaces facing Benchmark Road.

This is property owned by the Central Virginia Battlefields Trust. It is available for public access. However, because of heavy traffic around the intersection, please exercise caution when visiting this site.

Tour Stop 6: Pelham's Corner

This site relates primarily to critical decision 9.

On the fog-shrouded morning of December 11, John Pelham rode out to this intersection with his single gun and its crew. The soldiers tucked themselves into a low swale on the north side of Benchmark Road, well obscured by cedar trees, and opened fire. In doing so, they disrupted the Federal First Corps' attack plans and changed the entire course of the battle as a result.

Today, the Central Virginia Battlefields Trust protects 4.5 acres at the intersection now known as Pelham's Corner. Most notably, a lone artillery piece, Pelhamesque in its isolation, points northward at this location. Nearby, one of James Power Smith's granite markers sits atop a concrete base (installed to protect the monument from lawnmower damage). A pair of state historical markers and a pair of interpretive wayside signs recount some of Pelham's story.

Pelham's Corner represents the far outpost of the Fredericksburg battlefield. Visitors will find a cannon, a granite marker, some state historical markers, and interpretive wayside signs. Chris Mackowski.

From Robert E. Lee's Official Report

On the morning of the 13th, the plain on which the Federal army lay was still enveloped in fog, making it impossible to discern its operations. . . . Shortly after 9 a.m. the partial rising of the mist disclosed a large force moving in line of battle against Jackson. Dense masses appeared in front of A. P. Hill, stretching far up the river in the direction of Fredericksburg. As they advanced, Major Pelham, of Stuart's Horse Artillery, who was stationed near the Port Royal road with one section, opened a rapid and well-directed enfilade fire, which arrested their progress. Four batteries immediately turned upon him, but he sustained their heavy fire with the unflinching courage that ever distinguished him. Upon his withdrawal, the enemy extended his left down the Port Royal road, and his numerous batteries opened with vigor upon Jackson's line.[50]

To Tour Stop 7

Exit out the back of the parking lot onto Benchmark Road, and turn left. Drive 0.9 mile. Turn right onto Mine Road, and use caution when crossing the railroad tracks.

Proceed another 0.25 mile. Turn right onto Lee Drive Extension. Note: Lee Drive Extension intersects with Mine Run as a Y. Use the first fork; when making the turn, the second fork is not readily accessible from Mine Road.

Go 0.3 mile to the dead end, turn around, then park in the small gravel lot.

Tour Stop 7: Hamilton's Crossing

This site relates primarily to critical decision 10.

This area represents the extreme right of the Confederate line. Jeb Stuart's cavalry provided additional protection on the far side of the tracks, but Lee anchored his infantry here. Riding down from the crest of Prospect Hill to rejoin the cavalry, Stuart's chief of staff, Heros von Borcke, came through this area and "found our sharpshooters all along the Port Royal road, well posted in rifle-pits or behind the high embankments of the turnpike, the regiments themselves a little farther back in reserve, and Pelham's eighteen pieces of horse-artillery in favourable position."[51]

For those interested in a short walk, a 0.3-mile trail leads from the parking area up to Prospect Hill (which is Tour Stop 9 on our driving tour).

From here, you'll return to Mine Road on your way to the next tour stop. For the first half mile or so, you'll be on the back side of Prospect Hill, also known as Dead Horse Hill due to the number of Confederate artillery horses killed on the back of the hill by the Federal bombardment preceding Meade's attack. This was also the area Jubal Early occupied prior to his decision to march to the sound of the guns. Hoke's and Hays's Brigades were both posted on Mine Road, and Early had intended to send them along the road—in the direction opposite that in which you'll be traveling—to support Stuart per Jackson's orders.

<u>From the Official Report of Brig. Gen. Jubal Early</u>

Having, in obedience to orders from the lieutenant-general commanding the Second Corps, marched the division, on the night of the 12th instant, to the vicinity of Hamilton's Crossing, on the Richmond, Fredericksburg and Potomac Railroad, and bivouacked for the night, early next morning, in accordance with like orders, I moved to the crossing, and posted the division nearly at right angles with the railroad, along the dirt road which here crosses the railroad, with my right resting on the latter, so as to support the right of Maj. Gen. A. P. Hill's division, which occupied the front line. . . .

> As the division moved into position, the artillery fire commenced from the enemy's batteries, though not at first directed toward the place occupied by the division. After a short interval, however, shell began to fall in the vicinity, and for two or three hours the division was exposed to quite a severe cannonade, and suffered to some extent from the shells and other missiles which passed through the woods in front.[52]

To Tour Stop 8

Follow Lee Drive Extension 0.3 mile to the intersection with Mine Road. Use the right-hand fork at the intersection.

Go 1.9 miles to the traffic light at the intersection with Lansdowne Road. Continue straight through the light at this intersection, travel 0.4 mile, and turn right onto Ironwood Lane.

Proceed one block to Tulip Poplar Lane, which branches off to the left. Turn around in the intersection, using caution. Pull back up to the stop sign where Tulip Poplar Lane meets Mine Road.

Tour Stop 8: Lee's Headquarters Marker

This site relates primarily to critical decision 14 and events discussed in the conclusion.

Although Lee watched the battle from Telegraph Hill, later known as Lee's Hill (Tour Stop 10), he made his headquarters farther back from the front line. He positioned himself thus so he could still maintain close contact with James Longstreet nearby. Lee also established the position to more readily communicate with Stonewall Jackson, whose Second Corps had been flung far away to Port Royal just before the battle and was stretched out again afterward.

In 1903, James Power Smith installed a granite marker to indicate the area of Lee's headquarters. However, according to former Park Service historian Don Pfanz, "The best available evidence indicates that Lee's headquarters was actually south of Mine Road, about 250 yards from the marker."[53]

> <u>From a Letter by Gen. Robert E. Lee to His Wife, Mary Custis Lee</u>
>
> Our army was never in such good health & condition since I have been attached to it & I believe they share with me my disappoint-

Out of ten such markers, the marker for Lee's headquarters during the winter of 1862–63 is one of two that sit on a base. Chris Mackowski.

ment that the enemy did not renew the combat of the 13th. I was holding back all that day, & husbanding our strength & ammunition for the great struggle for which I thought he was preparing. Had I devined that was to have been his only effort, he would have had more of it. But I am content. We might have gained more but we would have lost more, & perhaps our relative condition would not have improved. My heart bleeds at the death of every one of our gallant men.[54]

To Tour Stop 9 from Lee's Headquarters Marker

Turn left. Retrace your route for 0.4 mile to the traffic light at the intersection with Lansdowne Road, then turn left again.

Travel 0.6 mile to the intersection with Lee Drive. Turn right onto Lee Drive, and go 2.0 miles to the road's end. This area is popular for walkers, joggers, bikers, and other recreational users, so please use caution. As you go, you will see stops for the park's self-guided driving tour. Feel free to get out and explore on your own at the trail to Bernard's Cabins or the stop for the Union breakthrough. When you reach the end of Lee Drive, park in the lot.

Cannon and empty lunettes give visitors a sense of Prospect Hill's strength as an artillery platform. Chris Mackowski.

Tour Stop 9: Prospect Hill

This site relates primarily to critical decisions 9 and 10.

As a James Power Smith marker announces, Prospect Hill was the location of "Jackson on the Field." Here, with the blue host advancing on him, Jackson famously told Heros von Borcke, "Major, my men have sometimes failed *to take* a position, but *to defend* one, never!"[55]

As a topographical anchor, Prospect Hill rises a modest 110 feet above the plain below. In 1862, it offered an unobstructed view to the Bowling Green Road and beyond—a viewscape obscured today by trees that block an old automotive parts plant (the Park Service's rationale being that trees are more attractive to look at than an industrial area). Two rail lines hug the base of the hill and curve around to the southwest to Hamilton's Crossing and beyond.

The remains of an old trench line run along the military crest of the hill (that is, a few yards downhill of the actual crest). This site also features fourteen gun pits, with several Civil War–era artillery pieces placed among them. In addition, one can see a tall pyramid of stones in the field in front of Prospect Hill. Known today as the Meade Pyramid, this monument was actually constructed in 1898 by the Confederate Memorial Literary Society in partnership with the Richmond, Fredericksburg, & Potomac Railroad, which wanted something that would let train passengers know they were passing through the Fredericksburg battlefield.[56]

Designed as a smaller version of a Confederate pyramid in Richmond's

The Meade Pyramid originally sat outside the national park boundary. When it was offered to the park, park officials debated for years about whether to accept it. It took a change in leadership before the park finally accepted the pyramid. Chris Mackowski.

Hollywood Cemetery, the monument was built between January 3 and March 31, 1898. Though originally intended to mark the area near Stonewall Jackson's headquarters, it nonetheless sat closer to the location of the Federal breakthrough and so became better associated with Meade. "In this case," says NPS historian Donald C. Pfanz, "geography trumped history." In 1954, the Park Service accepted the Meade Pyramid, and in 1978, the organization added another sixty-five adjacent acres.[57]

As you walk around Prospect Hill, please stay off the earthworks in order to help preserve them. Also, you may walk down to the railroad tracks by the pyramid, but for safety's sake, it's best not to cross the tracks. The pyramid needs structural stabilization, and it is a popular place for snakes to bask.

From the parking lot, a walking trail extends 0.3 mile down to Hamilton's Crossing (Tour Stop 7). Another trail extends 2.3 miles to the intersection with Lansdowne Road. An extensive trench system, which Jackson's men dug as they tried to avoid artillery fire, is visible in the woods.

From here, you'll retrace your route along Lee Drive and go to Lee's Hill. Along the way, you can visit two sites. The first, on the right-hand side of the road, is a walking trail to the former location of Bernard's Cabins. The area belonged to the Mannsfield Plantation, and the enslaved workers made their homes in the cabins here, directly across the fields from Mannsfield itself and connected to it by a farm lane.

In the area around Bernard's Cabins, James Lane's North Carolinians and Capt. Greenlee Davidson's artillery staunched the northward flood of men from Meade's breakthrough and barely held back John Gibbon's supporting advance. In the words of historian A. Wilson Greene, the site "makes the perfect mirror image for the visitor experience at the Slaughter Pen farm."[58]

The second location, on the left-hand side of the road, is Howison Hill, a stop on the park's self-guided driving tour. Feel free to get out and explore the artillery display, including a 30-pounder Parrott gun.

To Tour Stop 10

Retrace your route, following Lee Drive 2.0 miles back to the intersection with Lansdowne Road. Along the way, 1.5 miles from Prospect Hill, you will see where to pull off for Bernard's Cabins.

Continue straight through the intersection, using caution as you cross Lansdowne Road. Go 2.3 miles. Along the way, about 2.0 miles from the intersection, you will see the stop for Howison Hill on the left. Continue along Lee Drive; Lee's Hill will be on the left.

Tour Stop 10: Lee's Hill

This site relates primarily to critical decision 14.

Lee and Longstreet watched most of the Battle of Fredericksburg from this spot. Obscured by trees today, the view once opened to the southeast and gave

From here atop Telegraph Hill, Lee watched the spectacle of battle unfold on the south end of the field and said, "It is a good thing war is so terrible, or we should grow too fond of it." Chris Mackowski.

the generals a perfect panorama of the southern end of the battlefield. The view northward toward Marye's Heights was blocked by the heights themselves, so Lee and Longstreet were unable to see the assaults against the stone wall.

Longstreet's chief of staff, Moxley Sorrel, described the hilltop, which "had a light trench in which was mounted a 30-pounder Parrott gun, made in Richmond." Sorrel called the gun "treacherous"—an apt description because it exploded in the heat of battle. "The immense breech just appeared to have split into a dozen pieces of various sizes and then fallen heavily to the ground," he wrote. "Happily it did not send fragments flying about, and no one was hurt."[59]

Lee and Longstreet had a second near miss on the hilltop, too. A Federal artillery shell screamed in and buried itself in the dirt at the feet of the two generals. Fortunately for them, it was a dud and did not explode, which would have decapitated the Army of Northern Virginia by killing or incapacitating its leader and second-in-command.

Hilltop visitors can see restored artillery pieces as well as a Smith marker denoting Lee's Hill as the commanders' headquarters during the battle. A small exhibit shelter also talks about the Second Battle of Fredericksburg in May 1863 as part of the Chancellorsville Campaign; Federal soldiers overran this position in their effort to drive Confederates from Marye's Heights.

From Lee's Aide Walter H. Taylor

It is rarely vouchsafed to any one to witness so grand a tableau as was presented to our gaze on that December morning when the curtain of fog was lifted and the sun lit up the scene with the bright effulgence of its rays. As if by magic, the hosts of the grand Federal army were disclosed in martial array extending from the city down the river as far as the eye could reach. All was bustle and animation in the ranks of the great blue lines. The bright muskets of the men glistened in the sunlight, and countless flags with the stars and stripes floated with the breeze and marked the direction as the troops were maneuvering into line-of-battle formation to the sound of soul-stirring music. No doubt every heart of that mighty host beat high with hope in anticipation of the impending struggle. . . .

And now the left of the Federal line advances at a quickstep, the troops rapidly traverse the space intervening between the two armies, the big guns belch forth their death-dealing missiles, and the incessant rattle of musketry proclaims the issue joined.[60]

To Tour Stop 11

Continue along Lee Drive for 0.1 mile to the intersection with Lafayette Boulevard. Turn right into the traffic circle, then take the first right to exit the circle onto Lafayette Boulevard. Drive 0.6 mile. Along the way, you will go through a major intersection, cross Hazel Run, and come around a blind curve next to Fredericksburg National Cemetery. The visitor center for Fredericksburg National Battlefield will then be on the left. The entrance to the parking lot is just past the building. Turn left into the driveway, and circle around to the back of the building to find the main parking lot.

Tour Stop 11: Fredericksburg Battlefield Visitor Center

This site relates primarily to critical decisions 12 and 13.

Built in 1936 as part of the Civilian Conservation Corps' efforts to restore the battlefield, the Fredericksburg Battlefield Visitor Center (FVC) stands on the spot the Hall House occupied at the time of the battle. Badly damaged during the fighting, the house was demolished afterward. A second home, the Jennings House, stood about a hundred yards farther down modern Lafayette Boulevard, closer to town. It survived but was later moved when the city began to fill the once-open attack plain. The home sits across the street from FVC's RV parking lot.

The area by the Fredericksburg Battlefield Visitor Center includes the most iconic of the battle's landmarks: the Sunken Road, the Stone Wall, and Marye's Heights, as well as the Innis House, the grave of Martha Stevens, the Richard Kirkland Memorial, and Brompton. Chris Mackowski.

FVC has a great museum dedicated to the battle and the experience of Fredericksburg civilians. An orientation film there can also help you visualize and contextualize some of the places you've visited and things you've seen in this tour. Seasonally, historians offer guided tours of the Sunken Road.

Outside FVC is the most famous portion of the Fredericksburg battlefield: the Sunken Road, Stone Wall, and Marye's Heights (pronounced muh-REE's, not MARE-ees). No visit to this battlefield is complete without a walk along the road.

Although the city of Fredericksburg has encroached almost to the base of the heights, thus abolishing what was once an open plain, it's still worth a walk to the top of the heights to look out across the former attack field. The view remains pretty, and the modern-day city's skyline, visible a mile to the east, is quite similar to its wartime appearance. Not only can you get a good sense of just how commanding the heights were, you can almost imagine the waves of blue sweeping forward in their forlorn hope and dauntless courage.

To be reminded that Fredericksburg was "war so terrible," you need look no farther than Fredericksburg National Cemetery, which occupies the southernmost portion of the heights. In 1867, the government purchased twelve acres for $3,000 and began reinterring bodies from not only Fredericksburg, but also Chancellorsville, Mine Run, Wilderness, Spotsylvania, and North Anna. In total, some 15,436 Civil War soldiers rest in the cemetery, 84 percent of whom are unidentified—the largest percentage in any national cemetery. Veterans from other wars and a few family members are also buried there. The cemetery was closed to additional burials in 1945, although dependents of people already interred in the cemetery are still allowed to be buried there.

"We owe a great debt to those who fought for our country," writes historian Don Pfanz in his definitive book about the cemetery. "Fredericksburg National Cemetery stands as a vivid reminder of the debt we owe them."[61]

Jubal Early on Lee's Decision Not to Order an Artillery Bombardment of Federal Troops in Fredericksburg on December 14–15

It has been said that General Lee might have inflicted tremendous damage upon the enemy by forcing hot shot and shell into Fredericksburg while the enemy's troops were massed there. . . . It was not in the heart of the noble commander of the Army of Northern Virginia to doom, by his own act, the remaining few of that devoted people and the homes of the absent to destruction, for the sake of

Fredericksburg National Cemetery sits along a portion of Marye's Heights near the park visitor center. Each year for Memorial Day, a luminaria ceremony honors the fallen. Chris Mackowski.

killing and wounding a few thousand of the enemy, and causing dismay among the remainder.

Is this forbearance one to be criticised with severity as a grievous military blunder?

It is probable that if General Lee had known that the enemy was evacuating the town, his artillery might have inflicted considerable damage, but the enemy had given no indication of such a purpose, and he took advantage of the darkness of the night and the prevalence of a storm and wind to make good his retreat, when the noise attending the movement could not be heard.[62]

This concludes the driving tour.

APPENDIX II

UNION ORDER OF BATTLE

THE ARMY OF THE POTOMAC
Maj. Gen. Ambrose E. Burnside

ESCORT, ETC.
Oneida (New York) Cavalry
1st U. S. Cavalry (detachment)
4th U.S. Cavalry, Companies A and E

PROVOST GUARD
Brig. Gen. Marsena R. Patrick
McClellan (Illinois) Dragoons, Company A
McClellan (Illinois) Dragoons, Company B
9th New York Infantry, Company G
93d New York Infantry
2d U.S. Cavalry
8th U. S. Infantry

VOLUNTEER ENGINEER BRIGADE
Brig. Gen. Daniel P. Woodbury
15th New York
50th New York
Battalion United States Engineers

Artillery

Brig. Gen. Henry J. Hunt

Artillery Reserve

Lieut. Col. William Hays
New York Light, 5th Battery
1st Battalion New York Light, Battery A
1st Battalion New York Light, Battery B
1st Battalion New York Light, Battery C
1st Battalion New York Light, Battery D
1st United States, Battery K
2d United States, Battery A
4th United States, Battery G
5th United States, Battery K
32d Massachusetts Infantry, Company C

Unattached Artillery

Maj. Thomas S. Trumbull
1st Connecticut Heavy, Battery B
1st Connecticut Heavy, Battery M

RIGHT GRAND DIVISION

Maj. Gen. Edwin V. Sumner

SECOND ARMY CORPS

Maj. Gen. Darius N. Couch

FIRST DIVISION

Brig. Gen. Winfield S. Hancock

First Brigade

Brig. Gen. John C. Caldwell; Col. George W. Von Schack
5th New Hampshire
7th New York
61st New York
64th New York
81st Pennsylvania
145th Pennsylvania

Second Brigade

Brig. Gen. Thomas F. Meagher
28th Massachusetts

63d New York
69th New York
88th New York
116th Pennsylvania

Third Brigade

Col. Samuel K Zook
27th Connecticut
2d Delaware
52d New York
57th New York
66th New York
53d Pennsylvania

Artillery

1st New York Light, Battery B
4th United States, Battery C

SECOND DIVISION

Brig. Gen. Oliver O. Howard

First Brigade

Brig. Gen. Alfred Sully
19th Maine
15th Massachusetts
Massachusetts Sharpshooters, 1st Company
1st Minnesota
Minnesota Sharpshooters, 2d Company
34th New York
82d New York (2d Militia)

Second Brigade

Col. Joshua T. Owen
69th Pennsylvania
71st Pennsylvania
72d Pennsylvania
106th Pennsylvania

Third Brigade

Col. Norman J. Hall; Col. William R. Lee
19th Massachusetts
20th Massachusetts
7th Michigan

42d New York
59th New York
127th Pennsylvania

Artillery
1st Rhode Island Light, Battery A
1st Rhode Island Light, Battery B

THIRD DIVISION
Brig. Gen. William H. French

First Brigade
Brig. Gen. Nathan Kimball; Col. John S. Mason
14th Indiana
24th New Jersey
28th New Jersey
4th Ohio
8th Ohio
7th West Virginia

Second Brigade
Col. Oliver H. Palmer
14th Connecticut
108th New York
130th Pennsylvania

Third Brigade
Col. John W. Andrews
Lieut. Col. William Jameson
Lieut. Col. John W. Marshall
1st Delaware
4th New York
10th New York
132d Pennsylvania

Artillery
1st New York Light, Battery G
1st Rhode Island Light, Battery G

Artillery Reserve
Capt. Charles Morgan
1st United States, Battery I
4th United States, Battery A

NINTH ARMY CORPS
Brig. Gen. Orlando B. Willcox

ESCORT
6th New York Cavalry, Company B
6th New York Cavalry, Company C

FIRST DIVISION
Brig. Gen. William W. Burns

First Brigade
Col. Orlando M. Poe
2d Michigan
17th Michigan
20th Michigan
79th New York

Second Brigade
Col. Benjamin C. Christ
29th Massachusetts
8th Michigan
27th New Jersey
46th New York
50th Pennsylvania

Third Brigade
Col. Daniel Leasure
36th Massachusetts
45th Pennsylvania
100th Pennsylvania

Artillery
1st New York Light, Battery D
3d United States, Batteries L and M

SECOND DIVISION
Brig. Gen. Samuel D. Sturgis

First Brigade
Brig. Gen. James Nagle
2d Maryland
6th New Hampshire

9th New Hampshire
48th Pennsylvania
7th Rhode Island
12th Rhode Island

Second Brigade

Brig. Gen. Edward Ferrero
21st Massachusetts
35th Massachusetts
11th New Hampshire
51st New York
51st Pennsylvania

Artillery

2d New York Light, Battery L
Pennsylvania Light, Battery D
1st Rhode Island Light, Battery D
4th United States, Battery E

THIRD DIVISION

Brig. Gen. George W. Getty

First Brigade

Col. Rush C. Hawkins
10th New Hampshire
13th New Hampshire
25th New Jersey
9th New York
89th New York
103d New York

Second Brigade

Col. Edward Harland
8th Connecticut
11th Connecticut
15th Connecticut
16th Connecticut
4th Rhode Island

Artillery

2d United States, Battery E
5th United States, Battery A

CAVALRY DIVISION
Brig. Gen. Alfred Pleasonton

First Brigade
Brig. Gen. John F. Farnsworth
8th Illinois
3d Indiana
8th New York

Second Brigade
Col. David McM. Gregg; Col. Thomas C. Devin
6th New York
8th Pennsylvania
6th United States

Artillery
2d United States, Battery M

CENTER GRAND DIVISION
Maj. Gen. Joseph Hooker

THIRD ARMY CORPS
Brig. Gen. George Stoneman

FIRST DIVISION
Brig. Gen. David B. Birney

First Brigade
Brig. Gen. John C. Robinson
20th Indiana
63d Pennsylvania
68th Pennsylvania
105th Pennsylvania
114th Pennsylvania
141st Pennsylvania

Second Brigade
Brig. Gen. J. H. Hobart Ward
3d Maine
4th Maine
38th New York
40th New York

55th New York
57th Pennsylvania
99th Pennsylvania

THIRD BRIGADE
Brig. Gen. Hiram G. Berry
17th Maine
3d Michigan
5th Michigan
1st New York
37th New York
101st New York

ARTILLERY
Capt. George Randolph
1st Rhode Island Light, Battery E
3d United States Batteries F and K

SECOND DIVISION
Brig. Gen. Daniel E. Sickles

FIRST BRIGADE
Brig. Gen. Joseph B. Carr
1st Massachusetts
11th Massachusetts
16th Massachusetts
2d New Hampshire
11th New Jersey
26th Pennsylvania

SECOND BRIGADE
Col. George B. Hall
70th New York
71st New York
72d New York
73d New York
74th New York
120th New York

THIRD BRIGADE
Brig. Gen. Joseph W. Revere
5th New Jersey
6th New Jersey

7th New Jersey
8th New Jersey
2d New York
115th Pennsylvania

Artillery
Capt. James E. Smith
New Jersey Light, 2d Battery
New York Light, 4th Battery
1st United States, Battery H
4th United States, Battery K

THIRD DIVISION
Brig. Gen. Amiel W. Whipple

First Brigade
Brig. Gen. A. Sanders Piatt; Col. Emlen Franklin
86th New York
124th New York
122d Pennsylvania

Second Brigade
Col. Samuel S. Carroll
12th New Hampshire
163d New York
84th Pennsylvania
110th Pennsylvania

Artillery
New York Light, 10th Battery
New York Light, 11th Battery.
1st Ohio Light. Battery H

FIFTH ARMY CORPS
Brig. Gen. Daniel Butterfield

FIRST DIVISION
Brig. Gen. Charles Griffin

First Brigade
Col. James Barnes
2d Maine

Massachusetts Sharpshooters, 2d Company
18th Massachusetts
22d Massachusetts
1st Michigan
13th New York
25th New York
118th Pennsylvania

Second Brigade
Col. Jacob B. Swkitzer
9th Massachusetts
32d Massachusetts
4th Michigan
14th New York
62d Pennsylvania

Third Brigade
Col. T. B. W. Stockton
20th Maine
Michigan Sharpshooters, Brady's Company
16th Michigan
12th New York
17th New York
44th New York
83d Pennsylvania

Artillery
Massachusetts Light, 3d Battery (C)
Massachusetts Light, 5th Battery (E)
1st Rhode Island-Light, Battery C
5th United States, Battery D

Sharpshooters
1st United States

SECOND DIVISION
Brig. Gen. George Sykes

First Brigade
Lieut. Col. Robert C. Buchanan
3d United States
4th United States
12th United States

12th United States, 2d Battalion
14th United States, 1st Battalion
14th United States, 2d Battalion

Second Brigade

Maj. George L. Andrews; Maj. Charles S. Lovell
1st and 2d United States (battalion)
6th United States
7th United States (battalion)
10th United States
11th United States
17th and 19th United States (battalion)

Third Brigade

Brig. Gen. Gouverneur K. Warren
5th New York
140th New York

Artillery

1st Ohio Light, Battery L
5th United States, Battery I

THIRD DIVISION

Brig. Gen. Andrew A. Humphreys

First Brigade

Brig. Gen. Erastus B. Tyler
91st Pennsylvania
126th Pennsylvania
129th Pennsylvania
134th Pennsylvania

Second Brigade

Col. Peter H. Allabach
123d Pennsylvania
131st Pennsylvania
133d Pennsylvania
155th Pennsylvania

Artillery

1st New York Light, Battery C
1st United States, Batteries E and G

Cavalry Brigade

Brig. Gen. William W. Averell
1st Massachusetts
3d Pennsylvania
4th Pennsylvania
5th United States

Artillery

2d United States, Batteries B and L

LEFT GRAND DIVISION

Maj. Gen. William B. Franklin

ESCORT

6th Pennsylvania Cavalry

FIRST ARMY CORPS

Maj. Gen. John F. Reynolds

ESCORT

1st Maine Cavalry, Company L

FIRST DIVISION

Brig. Gen. Abner Doubleday

First Brigade

Col. Walter Phelps, Jr.
22d New York
24th New York
30th New York
84th New York (14th Militia)
2d U. S. Sharpshooters

Second Brigade

Col. James Gavin
7th Indiana
76th New York
95th New York
56th Pennsylvania

Third Brigade

Col. William F. Rogers

21st New York
23d New York
35th New York
80th New York (20th Militia)

Fourth Brigade
Brig. Gen. Solomon Meredith
Col. Lysander Cutler
19th Indiana
24th Michigan
2d Wisconsin
6th Wisconsin
7th Wisconsin

Artillery
Capt. George A. Gerrish; Capt. John A. Reynolds
New Hampshire Light, 1st Battery
1st New York Light, Battery L
4th United States, Battery B

SECOND DIVISION
Brig. Gen. John Gibbon
Brig. Gen. Nelson Taylor

First Brigade
Col. Adrian R. Root
16th Maine
94th New York
104th New York
105th New York
107th Pennsylvania

Second Brigade
Col. Peter Lyle
12th Massachusetts
26th New York
90th Pennsylvania
136th Pennsylvania

Third Brigade
Brig. Gen. Nelson Taylor
Col. Samuel H. Leonard
13th Massachusetts

83d New York (9th Militia)
97th New York
11th Pennsylvania
88th Pennsylvania

Artillery

Capt. George F. Leppien
Maine Light, 2d Battery
Maine Light, 5th Battery
Pennsylvania Light, Battery C
1st Pennsylvania Light, Battery F

THIRD DIVISION

Maj. Gen. George G. Meade

First Brigade

Col. William Sinclair; Col. William McCandless
1st Pennsylvania Reserves
2d Pennsylvania Reserves
6th Pennsylvania Reserves
13th Pennsylvania Reserves (1st Rifles)
121st Pennsylvania

Second Brigade

Col. Albert L. Magilton
3d Pennsylvania Reserves
4th Pennsylvania Reserves
7th Pennsylvania Reserves
8th Pennsylvania Reserves
142d Pennsylvania

Third Brigade

Brig. Gen. Conrad Feger Jackson
Col. Joseph W. Fisher
Lieut. Col. Robert Anderson
5th Pennsylvania Reserves
9th Pennsylvania Reserves
10th Pennsylvania Reserves
11th Pennsylvania Reserves
12th Pennsylvania Reserves

Artillery

1st Pennsylvania Light, Battery A

1st Pennsylvania Light, Battery B
1st Pennsylvania Light, Battery G
5th United States, Battery C

SIXTH ARMY CORPS
Maj. Gen. William F. Smith

ESCORT
10th New York Cavalry, Company L
6th Pennsylvania Cavalry, Company I
6th Pennsylvania Cavalry, Company K

FIRST DIVISION
Brig. Gen. William T. H. Brooks

FIRST BRIGADE
Col. Alfred T. A. Torbert
1st New Jersey
2d New Jersey
3d New Jersey
4th New Jersey
15th New Jersey
23d New Jersey

SECOND BRIGADE
Col. Henry L. Cake
5th Maine
16th New York
27th New York
121st New York
96th Pennsylvania

THIRD BRIGADE
Brig. Gen. David A. Russell
18th New York
31st New York.
32d New York
95th Pennsylvania

ARTILLERY
Maryland Light, Battery A
Massachusetts Light, 1st Battery (A)

New Jersey Light, 1st Battery
2d United States, Battery D

SECOND DIVISION

Brig. Gen. Albion P. Howe

First Brigade

Brig. Gen. Calvin E. Pratt
6th Maine
43d New York
49th Pennsylvania
119th Pennsylvania
5th Wisconsin

Second Brigade

Col. Henry Whiting
26th Ncw Jcrscy
2d Vermont
3d Vermont
4th Vermont
5th Vermont
6th Vermont

Third Brigade

Brig. Gen. Francis L. Vinton
Col. Robert F. Taylor
Brig. Gen. Thomas H. Neill
21st New Jersey
20th New York
33d New York
49th New York
77th New York

Artillery

Maryland Light, Battery B
New York Light, 1st Battery
New York Light, 3d Battery
5th United 8tates, Battery F

THIRD DIVISION

Brig. Gen. John Newton

First Brigade
- Brig. Gen. John Cochrane
- 65th New York
- 67th New York
- 122d New York
- 23d Pennsylvania
- 61st Pennsylvania
- 82d Pennsylvania

Second Brigade
- Brig. Gen. Charles Devens, Jr.
- 7th Massachusetts
- 10th Massachusetts
- 37th Massachusetts
- 36th New York
- 2d Rhode Island

Third Brigade
- Col Thomas A. Rowley
- Brig. Gen. Frank Wheaton
- 62d New York
- 93d Pennsylvania
- 98th Pennsylvania
- 102d Pennsylvania
- 139th Pennsylvania

Artillery
- 1st Pennsylvania Light, Battery C
- 1st Pennsylvania Light, Battery D
- 2d United States, Battery G

Cavalry Brigade
- Brig. Gen. George D. Bayard
- Col. David McM. Gregg
- District of Columbia, Independent Company
- 1st Maine
- 1st New Jersey
- 2d New York
- 10th New York
- 1st Pennsylvania

Artillery
- 3d United States Battery C

APPENDIX III

CONFEDERATE ORDER OF BATTLE

THE ARMY OF NORTHERN VIRGINIA
General Robert E. Lee

FIRST CORPS
Lieutenant General James Longstreet

MCLAWS'S DIVISION
Major General Lafayette McLaws

KERSHAW'S BRIGADE
Brigadier General Joseph B. Kershaw
2nd South Carolina
3rd South Carolina
7th South Carolina
8th South Carolina
15th South Carolina
3rd South Carolina Battalion

BARKSDALES BRIGADE
Brig. Gen. William Barksdale
13th Mississippi
17th Mississippi
18th Mississippi
21st Mississippi

Cobb's Brigade

Brig. Gen. T. R. R. Cobb
Col. Robert McMillan
16th Georgia
18th Georgia
24th Georgia
Cobb's (Georgia) Legion
Phillips's (Georgia) Legion

Semmes' Brigade

Brig. Gen. Paul J. Semmes
10th Georgia
50th Georgia
51st Georgia
53rd Georgia

Artillery

Col. Henry C. Cabell
Manly's (North Carolina) Battery
1st Richmond Howitzers
Troup (Georgia) Artillery
Pulaski (Georgia) Artillery
Richmond (Fayette) Artillery

ANDERSON'S DIVISION

Maj. Gen. Richard H. Anderson

Wilcox's Brigade

Brig. Gen. Cadmus M. Wilcox
8th Alabama
9th Alabama
10th Alabama
11th Alabama
14th Alabama

Featherston's Brigade

Brig. Gen. W. S. Featherston
12th Mississippi
16th Mississippi
19th Mississippi
48th Mississippi

Mahone's Brigade

Brig. Gen. William Mahone

6th Virginia
12th Virginia
16th Virginia
41st Virginia
61st Virginia

Wright's Brigade
Brig. Gen. Ambrose R. Wright
3rd Georgia
22nd Georgia
48th Georgia
2nd Georgia Battalion

Perry's Brigade
Brig. Gen. E. A. Perry
2nd Florida
5th Florida
8th Florida

Artillery
Donaldsonville (Louisiana) Artillery
Huger's (Virginia) Battery
Lewis's (Virginia) Battery
Norfolk (Virginia) Light Artillery Blues

PICKETT'S DIVISION
Maj. Gen. George E. Pickett

Garnett's Brigade
Brig. Gen. Richard B. Garnett
8th Virginia
18th Virginia
19th Virginia
28th Virginia
56th Virginia

Kemper's Brigade
Brig. Gen. James L. Kemper
1st Virginia
3rd Virginia
7th Virginia
11th Virginia
24th Virginia

Armistead's Brigade
- Brig. Gen. Lewis A. Armistead
- 9th Virginia
- 14th Virginia
- 38th Virginia
- 53rd Virginia
- 57th Virginia

Jenkins' Brigade
- Brig. Gen. Micah Jenkins
- 1st South Carolina
- 2nd South Carolina (Rifles)
- 5th South Carolina
- 6th South Carolina
- Hampton Legion
- Palmetto Sharpshooters

Corse's Brigade
- Brig. Gen. Montgomery D. Corse
- 15th Virginia
- 17th Virginia
- 30th Virginia
- 32nd Virginia

Artillery
- Dearing's (Virginia) Battery
- Fauquier (Virginia) Artillery
- Richmond Fayette Artillery

HOOD'S DIVISION
- Maj. Gen. John B. Hood

Law's Brigade
- Brig. Gen. Evander M. Law
- 4th Alabama
- 44th Alabama
- 6th North Carolina
- 54th North Carolina
- 57th North Carolina

Anderson's Brigade
- Brig. Gen. George T. Anderson
- 1st Georgia (Regulars)

7th Georgia
8th Georgia
9th Georgia
11th Georgia

Robertson's Brigade
Brig. Gen. J. B. Robertson
3rd Arkansas
1st Texas
4th Texas
5th Texas

Toombs' Brigade
Col. Henry L. Benning
2nd Georgia
15th Georgia
17th Georgia
20th Georgia

Artillery
German (South Carolina) Artillery
Palmetto (South Carolina) Light Artillery
Rowan (North Carolina) Artillery

RANSOM'S DIVISION
Brig. Gen. Robert Ransom, Jr.

Ransom's Brigade
Brig. Gen. Robert Ransom, Jr.
24th North Carolina
25th North Carolina
35th North Carolina
49th North Carolina
Branch's (Virginia) Battery

Cooke's Brigade
Brig. Gen. J. R. Cooke
Col. E. D. Hall
15th North Carolina
27th North Carolina
46th North Carolina
48th North Carolina
Cooper's (Virginia) Battery

FIRST CORPS ARTILLERY

Washington (Louisiana) Artillery

1st Company

2nd Company

3rd Company

4th Company

ALEXANDER'S BATTALION

Lieut. Col. E. Porter Alexander

Bedford (Virginia) Artillery

Eubank's (Virginia) Battery

Madison Light Artillery (Louisiana)

Parker's (Virginia) Battery

Rhett's (South Carolina) Battery

Woolfolk's (Virginia) Battery

SECOND CORPS

Lieut. Gen. Thomas J. Jackson

D. H. HILL'S DIVISION

Maj. Gen. Daniel H. Hill

FIRST BRIGADE

Brig. Gen. Robert E. Rodes

3rd Alabama

5th Alabama

6th Alabama

12th Alabama

26th Alabama

SECOND (RIPLEY'S) BRIGADE

Brig. Gen. George Doles

4th Georgia

44th Georgia

1st North Carolina

3rd North Carolina

THIRD BRIGADE

Brig. Gen. Alfred H. Colquitt

13th Alabama

6th Georgia

23rd Georgia

27th Georgia
28th Georgia

Fourth Brigade
Brig. Gen. Alfred Iverson
5th North Carolina
12th North Carolina
20th North Carolina
23rd North Carolina

Fifth (Ramseur's) Brigade
Col. Bryan Grimes
2nd North Carolina
4th North Carolina
14th North Carolina
30th North Carolina

Artillery
Maj. H. P. Jones
King William (Virginia) Artillery
Hardaway's (Alabama) Battery
Jeff. Davis (Alabama) Artillery
Morris (Virginia) Artillery
Orange (Virginia) Artillery

A. P. HILL'S DIVISION
Maj. Gen. Ambrose P. Hill

First (Field's) Brigade
Col. J. M. Brockenbrough
40th Virginia
47th Virginia
55th Virginia
22nd Virginia Battalion

Second Brigade
Brig. Gen. Maxcy Gregg
Col. D. H. Hamilton
1st South Carolina Provisional Army
1st South Carolina Rifles
12th South Carolina
13th South Carolina
14th South Carolina

Third Brigade

Brig. Gen. E. L. Thomas
14th Georgia
35th Georgia
45th Georgia
49th Georgia

Fourth Brigade

Brig. Gen. J. H. Lane
7th North Carolina
18th North Carolina
28th North Carolina
33rd North Carolina
37th North Carolina

Fifth Brigade

Brig. Gen. James J. Archer
5th Alabama Battalion
19th Georgia
1st Tennessee (Provisional Army)
7th Tennessee
14th Tennessee

Sixth Brigade

Brig. Gen. William D. Pender; Col. Alfred M. Scales
13th North Carolina
16th North Carolina
22nd North Carolina
34th North Carolina
38th North Carolina

Artillery

Lieut. Col. R. L. Walker
Branch (North Carolina) Artillery
Crenshaw (Virginia) Battery
Fredericksburg (Virginia) Artillery
Johnson's (Virginia) Battery
Letcher (Virginia) Artillery
Pee Dee (South Carolina) Artillery
Purcell (Virginia) Artillery

EWELL'S DIVISION

Brig. Gen. Jubal A. Early

Lawton's Brigade
- Col. Edmund N. Atkinson; Col. Clement A. Evans
- 13th Georgia
- 26th Georgia
- 31st Georgia
- 38th Georgia
- 60th Georgia
- 61st Georgia

Early's Brigade
- Col. James A. Walker
- 13th Virginia
- 25th Virginia
- 31st Virginia
- 44th Virginia
- 49th Virginia
- 52nd Virginia
- 58th Virginia

Trimble's Brigade
- Col. Robert F. Hoke
- 15th Alabama
- 12th Georgia
- 21st Georgia
- 21st North Carolina
- 1st North Carolina Battalion

Hays' (First Louisiana) Brigade
- Brig. Gen. Harry T. Hays
- 5th Louisiana
- 6th Louisiana
- 7th Louisiana
- 8th Louisiana
- 9th Louisiana

Artillery
- Capt. J. W. Latimer
- Charlottesville (Virginia)
- Chesapeake (Maryland)
- Courtney (Virginia)
- 1st Maryland Battery
- Louisiana Guard Artillery
- Staunton (Virginia) Artillery

JACKSON'S DIVISION

Brig. Gen. William B. Taliaferro

First Brigade

Brig. Gen. E. F. Paxton
2nd Virginia
4th Virginia
5th Virginia
27th Virginia
33rd Virginia

Second Brigade

Brig. Gen. J. R. Jones
21st Virginia
42nd Virginia
48th Virginia
1st Virginia Battalion

Third (Taliaferro's) Brigade

Col. E. T. H. Warren
47th Alabama
48th Alabama
10th Virginia
23rd Virginia
37th Virginia

Fourth (Starke's) Brigade

Col. Edmund Pendleton
1st Louisiana (Volunteers)
2nd Louisiana
10th Louisiana
14th Louisiana
15th Louisiana
Coppen's (Louisiana) Battalion

Artillery

Capt. J. B. Brockenbrough
Carpenter's (Virginia) Battery
Danville (Virginia) Artillery
Hampden (Virginia) Artillery
Lee (Virginia) Artillery
Lusk's (Virginia) Battery

Reserve Artillery

Brig. Gen. William N. Pendleton

BROWN'S BATTALION

Col. J. Thompson Brown
Salem Artillery, Hupp's Battery
Rockbridge Artillery
Brooke's (Virginia) Battery
2nd Richmond (Virginia) Howitzers
3rd Richmond (Virginia) Howitzers
Powhatan (Virginia) Artillery

SUMTER (GEORGIA) BATTALION

Lieut. Col. Allen S. Cutts
Company A
Company B
Company C

NELSON'S BATTALION

Maj. William Nelson
Amherst (Virginia) Artillery
Fluvanna (Virginia) Artillery
Georgia Battery

MISCELLANEOUS BATTERIES

Ells's (Georgia) Battery
Hanover Artillery

CAVALRY

Maj. Gen. James E. B. Stuart

First Brigade

Brig. Gen. Wade Hampton
1st North Carolina
1st South Carolina
2nd South Carolina
Cobb (Georgia) Legion
Phillips' (Georgia) Legion

Second Brigade

Brig. Gen. Fitzhugh Lee
1st Virginia
2nd Virginia

3rd Virginia
4th Virginia
5th Virginia

Third Brigade

Brig. Gen. W. H. F. Lee
2nd North Carolina
9th Virginia
10th Virginia
13th Virginia
15th Virginia

Artillery

Maj. John Pelham
Breathed's (Virginia) Battery
Chew's (Virginia) Battery
Hart's (South Carolina) Battery
Henry's (Virginia) Battery
Moorman's (Virginia) Battery

NOTES

Preface

1. James Longstreet, "The Battle of Fredericksburg," *Battles and Leaders of the Civil War*, vol. 3, Robert Underwood Johnson, et. al., eds. (New York: The Century Co., 1884), 79. Hereafter, *Battles and Leaders* shall be referred to as *B&L* and shall refer to volume three unless otherwise noted.
2. Matt Spruill III and Matt Spruill IV, *Decisions at Second Manassas: The Fourteen Critical Decisions That Defined the Battle* (Knoxville: University of Tennessee Press, 2018).
3. Harold Holzer, *Emancipating Lincoln: The Proclamation in Text, Context, and Memory* (Cambridge, MA: Harvard, 2012), 3.

Introduction

1. Abraham Lincoln, "Preliminary Emancipation Proclamation," in *Lincoln: Speeches and Writings, 1859–1865*, ed. Don E. Fehrenbacher (New York: Library of America, 1898), 368.
2. Lincoln, "Preliminary Emancipation Proclamation," 368.
3. Gideon Welles quoting Lincoln, in *Recollected Words of Abraham Lincoln*, ed. Don E. Fehrenbacher and Virginia Fehrenbacher (Stanford, CA: Stanford University Press, 1996), 471.

4. Gideon Welles, *Diary of Gideon Welles, Secretary of the Navy Under Lincoln and Johnson* (New York: Houghton Mifflin, 1911), 1:70.
5. Welles, *Diary*, 1:70.
6. Gideon Welles, "The History of Emancipation" (1872), 851.
7. Welles, *Diary*, 1:71.
8. George McClellan to Abraham Lincoln, July 7, 1862, in *The Civil War Papers of George B. McClellan: Selected Correspondence, 1860–1865*, ed. Stephen Sears (New York: Da Capo, 1992), 345.
9. Welles, *Diary*, 1:70–71.
10. Welles, "History of Emancipation," 842.
11. F. B. Carpenter, *Six Months at the White House with Abraham Lincoln* (New York: Hurd and Houghton, 1866), 19–22.
12. Carpenter, *Six Months at the White House*, 22.
13. "Letter to Horace Greeley," Abraham Lincoln Online, http://www.abrahamlincolnonline.org/lincoln/speeches/greeley.htm.
14. James McPherson, *Tried by War: Abraham Lincoln as Commander in Chief* (New York: Penguin, 2008), 130.
15. See Daniel J. Vermilya, *That Field of Blood: The Battle of Antietam, September 17, 1862* (El Dorado Hills, CA; Savas Beatie, 2018).
16. McClellan to Ellen McClellan, September 19, 1862, in *Civil War Papers*, 469.
17. John Hay, *Inside Lincoln's White House: The Complete Civil War Diary of John Hay*, ed. Michael Burlingame and John R. Turner Ettlinger (Carbondale: Southern Illinois University Press, 1997), 40.
18. Welles, *Diary*, 1:142.
19. Welles, *Diary*, 1:142.
20. Adam Gurowski quoted in Harold Holzer, *Emancipating Lincoln: The Proclamation in Text, Context, and Memory* (Cambridge, MA.: Harvard University Press, 2012), 90.
21. Gurowski quoted in Holzer, *Emancipating Lincoln, 90*.
22. Hay, *Inside Lincoln's White House*, 40.
23. Welles, *Diary*, 1:143.
24. John Hay, *Lincoln's Journalist: John Hay's Anonymous Writings for the Press, 1860–1864*, ed. Michael Burlingame (Carbondale: Southern Illinois University Press, 1998), 311.

25. Henry Halleck to George Thomas (undelivered), September 23, 1862, in US War Department, *The War of the Rebellion: A Compilation of the Official Records of the Union and Confederate Armies*, series 1, vol. 16, pt. 2, p. 539. The *Official Records*, as they are commonly called, will be hereafter referred to as *OR*.
26. Don Carlos Buell to Henry Halleck, September 25, 1862, *OR*, vol. 16, pt. 2, p. 542.
27. Hay, *Inside Lincoln's White House*, 41.
28. For starters, try James Garfield Randall's classic *Lincoln the President*, vol. 1 (New York: Da Capo, 1997) and, more contemporarily, John Waugh's *Lincoln and McClellan: The Troubled Partnership between a President and His General* (New York: Palgrave Macmillan, 2010).
29. McClellan to Ellen McClellan, August 9, 1861, in *Civil War Papers*, 374.
30. McClellan to Ellen McClellan, August 9, 1861, in *Civil War Papers*, 81.
31. James McPherson, "The Commander Who Would Not Fight," in *The War That Forged a Nation: Why the Civil War Still Matters* (New York: Oxford University Press, 2015), 146.
32. McClellan to Ellen McClellan, July 27, 1861, in *Civil War Papers*, 70.
33. Hay, *Inside Lincoln's White House*, 30.
34. Stephen W. Sears, *George B. McClellan: The Young Napoleon* (New York: Ticknor and Fields, 1988), 141.
35. Welles, *Diary*, 1:100.
36. Welles, *Diary*, 1:104.
37. Welles, *Diary*, 1:105.
38. Hay, *Inside Lincoln's White House*, 38–39.
39. McClellan to Ellen McClellan, September 5, 1862, in *Civil War Papers*, 435.
40. McClellan to Samuel L. M. Barlow, November 8, 1861, in *Civil War Papers*, 128.
41. Quoted in Sears, *McClellan*, 325.
42. Shaw quoted in Sears, *McClellan*, 245.
43. Welles, *Diary*, 1:158.
44. McClellan to William Aspinwall, September 26, 1862, in *Civil War Papers*, 482.
45. McClellan to Ellen McClellan, October 5, 1862, in *Civil War Papers*, 490.

46. *OR*, vol. 19, pt. 2, pp. 395–96.

47. *OR*, vol. 19, pt. 2, pp. 395–96.

48. Doris Kearns Goodwin, *Team of Rivals: The Political Genius of Abraham Lincoln* (New York: Simon and Schuster, 2005), 459. For a concise examination of the Emancipation Proclamation as a turning point of the war, see Kevin Pawlak's "'The Heavyest Blow Yet Given the Confederacy': The Emancipation Proclamation Changes the Civil War," in *Turning Points of the Civil War, ed. Chris Mackowski and Kristopher D. White* (Carbondale: Southern Illinois University Press, 2018).

Chapter 1

1. James McPherson points out that "several versions of this anecdote exist." See *War that Forged a Nation*, 2207n37.

2. Welles, *Diary*, 1:104.

3. Francis Fisher Browne, *The Every-Day Life of Abraham Lincoln: A Narrative and Descriptive Biography with Pen-Pictures and Personal Recollections by Those Who Knew Him* (Chicago: Browne and Howell, 1913), 418, http://www.gutenberg.org/files/14004/14004-h/14004-h.htm.

4. George McClellan to Ellen McClellan, October 5, 1862, in *Civil War Papers*, 490.

5. George Gordon Meade, *The Life and Letters of George Gordon Meade*, ed. George Meade Jr. (New York: Charles Scribner's Sons, 1913), 1:317.

6. Fehrenbacher and Fehrenbacher, *Recollected Words of Abraham Lincoln*, 132.

7. Hay, diary entry, September 25, 1864, *Inside Lincoln's White House*, 232.

8. *OR*, vol. 19, pt. 1, p. 72.

9. McClellan to Ellen McClellan, October 7, 1862, in *Civil War Papers*, 492.

10. Charles Wainwright, *A Diary of Battle: The Personal Journals of Colonel Charles S. Wainwright, 1861–1865*, ed. Allan Nevins (Boston: DaCapo, 1998), 115.

11. George Meade to Margaretta Meade, October 12, 1862, in *Life and Letters*, 1:320.

12. Meade, in *Life and Letters*, 1:319.

13. Abraham Lincoln to McClellan, October 13, 1862, *OR*, vol. 21, p. 97.

14. McClellan to Lincoln, October 17, 1862, in *Civil War Papers*, 499.

15. Lincoln to McClellan, October 24, 1862, in *Lincoln: Speeches and Writings*, 379–80.

16. McClellan to Ellen McClellan, October 25, 1862, in *Civil War Papers*, 507.
17. McClellan to Ellen McClellan, October 26, 1862, in *Civil War Papers*, 511.
18. Meade, in *Life and Letters*, 1:320.
19. Meade, in *Life and Letters*, 1:321.
20. Meade, in *Life and Letters*, 1:321.
21. Wainwright, *Diary of Battle*, 114–15.
22. Wainwright, *Diary of Battle*, 115.
23. Ethan Rafuse, *McClellan's War* (Indianapolis: Indiana University Press, 2005), 353.
24. Rafuse, *McClellan's War*, 357.
25. Sears, *McClellan*, 333.
26. McClellan to Henry Halleck, October 11, 1863, in *Civil War Papers*, 496; Stephen W. Sears, *Lincoln's Lieutenants: The High Command of the Army of the Potomac* (New York: Mariner, 2017), 427.
27. Welles, *Diary*, 1:176.
28. Hay, diary entry, September 26, 1862, *Inside Lincoln's White House*, 41.
29. Hay, diary entry, September 25, 1864, *Inside Lincoln's White House*, 232.
30. Salmon P. Chase, diary entry, October 10, 1862, in *The Salmon P. Chase Papers*, ed. John Niven, *vol. 1: Journals, 1829–1872* (Kent, OH: Kent State University Press, 1993), 416.
31. Hay, diary entry, September 25, 1864, *Inside Lincoln's White House*, 232.
32. Wainwright, *Diary of Battle*, 117.
33. Meade, in *Life and Letters*, 1:320.
34. Halleck to Don Carlos Buell, *OR*, vol. 16, pt. 2, p. 638.
35. Halleck to William Rosecrans, October 24, 1862, *OR*, vol. 16, pt. 2, p. 641.
36. Rafuse, *McClellan's War*, 355.
37. Meade to Margaretta Meade, November 22, 1863, in *Life and Letters*, 1:330.
38. McClellan to Halleck, October 25, 1862, in *Civil War Papers*, 510; McClellan to Lincoln, October 27, 1862, in *Civil War Papers*, 511.
39. Welles, *Diary*, 1:177.
40. McClellan to Ellen McClellan, October 29, 1862, in *Civil War Papers*, 515.
41. Hay, *Inside Lincoln's White House*, 232.

42. Meade, in *Life and Letters*, 1:318.
43. Sears, *McClellan*, 139.
44. Welles, *Diary*, 1:124.
45. Shaw quoted in Sears, *McClellan*, 246.
46. Wainwright, *Diary of Battle*, 117.
47. Quoted in G. A. Taylor, "Major-General Joseph Hooker and His Proper Place in History," *The Journal of the Military Service Institution*, ed. T. F. Rodenbough (Governors' Island, NY: Military Service Institution, 1910), 277.
48. McClellan to Joseph Hooker, September 20, 1862, in *Civil War Papers*, 474.
49. Marsena Patrick, *Inside Lincoln's Army: The Diary of Marsena Rudolph Patrick, Provost Marshal General, Army of the Potomac*, ed. David S. Sparks (New York: Thomas Yoseloff, 1964), 164.
50. Meade, in *Life and Letters*, 1:318.
51. Meade, in *Life and Letters*, 1:319.
52. Fitz John Porter to Marble, quoted in Sears, *Lincoln's Lieutenants*, 431.
53. Welles, *Diary*, 1:124.
54. Welles, *Diary*, 1:192.
55. Welles, *Diary*, 1:126.
56. McClellan to Halleck, October 25, 1862, *OR*, vol. 14, pt. 2, pp. 483–84.
57. Welles, *Diary*, 1:108.
58. Welles, *Diary*, 1:115.
59. Quoted in a story by Henry J. Raymond, *Scribner's Monthly*, vol. 19, p. 438.
60. Welles, *Diary*, 1:145.
61. Josiah Favill, *Diary of a Young Officer* (Chicago: R. R. Donnelly and Sons, 1909), 196.
62. Francis P. Blair to Montgomery Blair, November 7, 1862, in *The Francis Preston Blair Family in Politics*, ed. William E. Smith (New York: Macmillan, 1933), 2:144.
63. Welles, *Diary*, 1:183.
64. William Marvel, *Burnside* (Chapel Hill: University of North Carolina Press, 1991), 160.
65. McClellan to Ellen McClellan, November 7–8, 1862, in *Civil War Papers*, 520.

66. McClellan to Ellen McClellan, November 7–8, 1862, in *Civil War Papers*, 520.
67. McClellan to Ellen McClellan, November 8, 1862, in *Civil War Papers*, 521.
68. McPherson, *Tried by War*, 141.
69. David W. Judd, *The Story of the Thirty-Third N.Y.S. Vols; or, Two Years Campaigning in Virginia and Maryland* (Rochester, NY: Benton and Andrew, 1864), 215.
70. Patrick, *Inside Lincoln's Army*, 173.
71. Wainwright, *Diary of Battle*, 124, 125.
72. Wainwright, *Diary of Battle*, 125.
73. Lieut. Robert S. Robertson to parents, November 10, 1862, Bound Volume 219-01, Fredericksburg and Spotsylvania National Military Park archives, Fredericksburg, VA. The archive will hereafter be referred to as "FSNMP archives," and the Bound Volumes as "BV."
74. McClellan to Army of the Potomac, November 7, 1862, in *Civil War Papers*, 521.
75. McClellan to Ellen McClellan, November 9, 1862, November 10, 1862, in *Civil War Papers*, 522, 523.
76. Oliver Otis Howard, *The Autobiography of Oliver Otis Howard* (New York: Baker and Taylor, 1907), 313.
77. Darius Couch, "Sumner's 'Right Grand Division,'" in *Battles and Leaders of the Civil War*, ed. Robert Underwood Johnson et al. (New York: Century, 1884), 3:106.
78. Wainwright, *Diary of Battle*, 124.
79. Raymond, *Scribner's Monthly*, 19:438.
80. Raymond, *Scribner's Monthly*, 19:438.
81. Meade, in *Life and Letters*, 1:325.
82. Meade, in *Life and Letters*, 1:351.
83. Meade, in *Life and Letters*, 1:326.
84. Meade, in *Life and Letters*, 1:332.
85. Patrick, *Inside Lincoln's Army*, 175.
86. William Bolton, *The Civil War Journal of Colonel Bolton, 51st Pennsylvania*, ed. Richard A. Sauers (Conshohocken, PA: Combined Publishing, 2000), 96.
87. Favill, *Diary of a Young Officer*, 201.

88. William Taylor, letter, November 27, 1862, BV 361, FSNMP archives.
89. Isaac Morrow, November 26, 1862, BV 44, FSNMP archives.
90. J. Henrie B., "From the Fifteenth," *Danbury (CT) Times,* November 27, 1862, BV 313, FSNMP archives.
91. John Haley, *The Rebel Yell & the Yankee Hurrah: The Civil War Journal of a Maine Volunteer*, ed. Ruth L. Silliker (Camden, ME: Down East Books, 1985), 50.

Chapter 2

1. Herman Haupt, *Reminiscences of General Herman Haupt* (Milwaukee, WI: Wright and Joys, 1901), 156–57.
2. George McClellan to Henry Halleck, October 7, 1862, *OR,* vol. 19, pt. 2, pp. 492–93.
3. McClellan to Halleck, October 7, 1862, *OR,* vol. 19, pt. 2, pp. 492–93.
4. On November 4, 1862, Haupt estimated that it would take 550 cars to effectively move 1,500 tons of supplies per day. That equates to roughly 2.7 tons of supplies per car. By that calculation, 60 cars per day would furnish only 162 tons of supplies. See Haupt, *Reminiscences,* 154.
5. Haupt, *Reminiscences,* 145.
6. McClellan to Halleck, October 7, 1862, *OR,* vol. 19, pt. 2, pp. 492–93.
7. Abraham Lincoln to McClellan, October 13, 1862, *OR,* vol. 21, pt.1, pp. 97–99.
8. McClellan to Herman Haupt, October 26, 1862, *OR,* vol. 19, pt. 2, p. 511.
9. Haupt, *Reminiscences*, 158–59.
10. Haupt, *Reminiscences*, 146.
11. Favill, *Diary of a Young Officer,* 203.
12. Ambrose Burnside testimony, in *Report of the Joint Committee on the Conduct of the War* (Washington, DC: Government Printing Office, 1863), pt. 1, p. 649. Hereafter referred to as *JCCW.*

13 *OR,* vol. 19, pt. 2, p. 546.

14. Burnside testimony, *JCCW,* pt. 1, p. 650.
15. Ambrose Burnside, *OR,* vol. 21, pt. 1, p. 99.
16. Francis A. O'Reilly, *The Fredericksburg Campaign: Winter War on the Rappahannock* (Baton Rouge: Louisiana State University Press, 2002), 13.
17. Burnside testimony, *JCCW,* pt. 1, p. 650.

18. Orlando Willcox, *Forgotten Valor: The Memoirs, Journals, and Civil War Letters of Orlando B. Willcox* (Kent, OH: Kent State University Press, 1999), 394.
19. Lincoln to McClellan, October 13, 1862, *OR,* vol. 21, pt. 1, pp. 97–99.
20. Jomini was a staple of the West Point curriculum, and General-in-Chief Henry Halleck was probably the army's foremost authority on Jomini's theories. There's no evidence that Lincoln had ever read Jomini himself, though.
21. Haupt, *Reminiscences,* 158–59.
22. Burnside report, *OR,* vol. 21, pt. 1, p. 99.
23. Burnside testimony, *JCCW,* pt. 1, p. 651.
24. Burnside testimony, *JCCW,* pt. 1, p. 651; Burnside report, *OR,* vol. 21, pt. 1, p. 99.
25. Burnside testimony, *JCCW,* pt. 1, p. 651.
26. Burnside, *OR,* vol. 21, pt. 1, p. 101.
27. Burnside quoted in *The Conduct of the War: Report of the Congressional Committee on the Operations of the Army of the Potomac, Causes of Its Inaction and Ill Success, Its Several Campaigns, Why M'Clellan Was Removed, the Battle of Fredericksburg, Removal of Burnside* (New York: Tribune Association, 1863), 24.
28. Burnside, *OR,* vol. 21, pt. 1, p. 99.
29. Haupt to Burnside, *OR,* XIX, vol. 19, pt. 2, p. 565.
30. Burnside, *OR,* vol. 21, pt. 1, pp. 83–84.
31. Haupt, *Reminiscences,* 159.
32. Burnside, *OR,* vol. 21, pt. 1, p. 84.
33. Halleck, *OR,* vol. 21, pt. 1, p. 47. It's worth noting Halleck wrote his report on November 15, 1863, almost a year to the day after the conference with Burnside.
34. Halleck, *OR,* vol. 21, pt. 1, p. 47.
35. O'Reilly, *Fredericksburg Campaign,* 22.
36. Halleck, *OR,* vol. 19, pt. 1, p. 579.
37. Haley, *Rebel Yell,* 57.
38. Burnside, *OR,* vol. 21, pt. 1, p. 102.
39. Robert E. Lee to George Randolph, November 7, 1862, in *The Wartime Papers of Robert E. Lee,* ed. Clifford Dowdey (Boston: Da Capo, 1961), 328.

40. Halleck to George Meade, November 3, 1863, *OR*, vol. 29, pt. 2, p. 412.
41. Burnside to G. W. Cullum, *OR*, XIX, vol. 19, pt. 2, pp. 552–53.
42. Lee to Stonewall Jackson, November 14, 1862, in *Wartime Papers*, 335.
43. Lee to George Randolph, November 10, 1862, in *Wartime Papers*, 332.
44. Lee, in *Wartime Papers*, 324.
45. Lee to Stonewall Jackson, November 12, 1862, in *Wartime Papers*, 334; Lee to Jackson, November 14, 1862, in *Wartime Papers*, 335.
46. Lee to Jackson, November 14, 1862, in *Wartime Papers*, 335.
47. Lee to W. H. F. Lee, November 15, 1862, in *Wartime Papers*, 337.
48. Lee to W. H. F. Lee, November 15, 1862, in *Wartime Papers*, 337.
49. Lee to George Randolph, November 17, 1862, in *Wartime Papers*, 337.
50. Lee to Jefferson Davis, November 17, 1862, in *Wartime Papers*, 338.
51. Lee to Randolph, November 17, 1862, in *Wartime Papers*, 337.
52. Wainwright, *Diary of Battle*, 132.
53. Lee to Samuel Cooper, November 22, 1862, in *Wartime Papers*, 341–42.
54. Henry A. White, *Robert E. Lee and the Southern Confederacy, 1807–1870* (New York: Putnam, 1897), 239–40.
55. James Longstreet, *From Manassas to Appomattox: Memoirs of the Civil War in America* (Philadelphia: J. B. Lippincott, 1896), 293.
56. William Miller Owen, *In Camp and Battle with the Washington Artillery of New Orleans* (Boston: Rockwell and Churchill, 1885), 173.
57. Lee to Mary Lee, November 22, 1862, in *Wartime Papers*, 343.
58. Lee to Jefferson Davis, November 25, 1862, in *Wartime Papers*, 345.
59. Lee to Jefferson Davis, November 25, 1862, in *Wartime Papers*, 345.
60. Meade, in *Life and Letters*, 1:331.
61. Walter H. Taylor, *Four Years with General Lee* (Bloomington: Indiana University Press, 1996), 80.
62. *OR*, vol. 36, pt. 3, p. 166.
63. See Chris Mackowski, *Strike Them a Blow: Battle along the North Anna* (El Dorado Hills, CA: Savas Beatie, 2015) for a full account.
64. Burnside memo, May 24, 1863, BV 225-01, FSNMP archives (original from General Burnside Papers, box 7, entry 159, National Archives, Washington, DC).
65. Joseph Hooker testimony, *JCCW*, pt. 1, pp. 665–66.

66. Burnside, *OR*, vol. 21, p. 84.
67. Burnside, *OR*, vol. 21, p. 84.
68. *OR*, vol. 19, pt. 2, p. 581.
69. *OR*, vol. 19, pt. 2, p. 572.
70. *OR*, vol. 21, pp. 86–87.
71. Burnside testimony, *JCCW*, pt. 1, p. 651.
72. Burnside testimony, *JCCW*, pt. 1, p. 652.
73. Wesley Brainerd, *Bridge Building in Wartime: Colonel Wesley Brainerd's Memoir of the 50th New York Volunteer Engineers*, ed. Ed Malles (Knoxville: University of Tennessee Press, 1997), 94.
74. Brainerd, *Bridge Building in Wartime*, 96.
75. "Of our march from Washington to Fredericksburgh [*sic*] much might be written," Wesley Brainerd later said. The account in his *Bridge Building in Wartime* provides an excellent rundown, pp. 94–97.
76. *OR*, vol. 21, p. 87.
77. Hooker testimony, *JCCW*, pt. 1, 669.
78. Burnside testimony, *JCCW*, pt. 1, p. 654.
79. Burnside testimony, *JCCW*, pt. 1, p. 652.
80. Brainerd, *Bridge Building in Wartime*, 101.
81. Brainerd, *Bridge Building in Wartime*, 98.
82. Brainerd, *Bridge Building in Wartime*, 99–100.
83. Edwin Sumner testimony, n *JCCW*, pt. 1, p. 659. Note, too, that the average height of a Civil War soldier was five feet eight, so a six- to eight-foot-deep hole would be no shallow consideration.
84. Rusty Dennen, "I-95 of the 1800s," *Fredericksburg Free Lance-Star*, May 25, 2003, A10, accessed October 25, 2020, https://news.google.com/newspapers?nid=1298&dat=20030525&id=jfAyAAAAIBAJ&sjid=mwgGAAAAIBAJ&pg=3685,7125013.
85. Sumner testimony, *JCCW*, pt. 1, 657.
86. Sumner to Burnside, November 23, 1862, Burnside Papers, National Archives, quoted in O'Reilly, *Fredericksburg Campaign*, 50.
87. Burnside testimony, *JCCW*, pt. 1, p. 652.
88. Sumner testimony, *JCCW*, pt. 1, p. 658.
89. McAllister, 238–39.
90. William Franklin testimony, *JCCW*, pt. 1, p. 660.

91. Sumner quoted in O'Reilly, *Fredericksburg Campaign,* 50, from a private letter from Sumner to Burnside, Burnside Papers, National Archives.
92. Burnside testimony, *JCCW,* pt. 1, p. 652.
93. Burnside, message to Halleck, December 9, 1862, *OR,* vol. 21, p. 64.
94. Burnside testimony, *JCCW,* pt. 1, p. 654.
95. Franklin testimony, *JCCW,* pt. 1, p. 660.
96. Burnside testimony, *JCCW,* pt. 1, p. 654.
97. Brainerd, *Bridge Building in Wartime*, 107.
98. Meade to Margaretta Meade, in *Life and Letters*, 1:330.
99. Franklin testimony, *JCCW,* pt. 1, p. 657.
100. Franklin testimony, *JCCW,* pt. 1, p. 662.
101. Daniel Woodbury testimony, *JCCW,* pt. 1, p. 665.
102. Brainerd, *Bridge Building in Wartime*, 122.
103. For more on this, see Chris Mackowski, "Hey, General Burnside, Why Don't We Just Wade Across?," September 16, 2011, Emerging Civil War, https://emergingcivilwar.com/2011/09/16/hey-general-burnside-why-dont-we-just-wade-across/.

Chapter 3

1. Brainerd, *Bridge Building in Wartime*, 108.
2. Brainerd, *Bridge Building in Wartime*, 109.
3. Brainerd, *Bridge Building in Wartime*, 111.
4. Brainerd, *Bridge Building in Wartime*, 111.
5. Brainerd, *Bridge Building in Wartime*, 111.
6. Brainerd, *Bridge Building in Wartime*, 111.
7. Robert E. Lee to Mary Lee, November 22, 1862, in *Wartime Papers*, 343.
8. Lee to Stonewall Jackson, November 27, 1862, in *Wartime Papers*, 347.
9. Lee to Jefferson Davis, November 27, 1862, in *Wartime Papers*, 349.
10. Lee to Jackson, November 28, 1862, in *Wartime Papers*, 349.
11. Lee to Jackson, December 2, 1862, in *Wartime Papers*, 347.
12. Longstreet, *From Manassas to Appomattox*, 300.
13. Lee to Jackson, December 2, 1862, in *Wartime Papers*, 347.
14. Lee to Davis, December 6, 1862, in *Wartime Papers*, 352.

15. Lee to Davis, December 6, 1862, in *Wartime Papers*, 353.
16. Lee to Davis, November 6, 1862, in *Wartime Papers*, 353.
17. Lee to Davis, November 8, 1862, in *Wartime Papers*, 356.
18. James Longstreet, "The Battle of Fredericksburg," in *Battles and Leaders of the Civil War*, ed. Robert Underwood Johnson et al. (New York: Century, 1884), 3:71–72.
19. Robert E. Lee, *OR*, vol. 21, p. 552.
20. O'Reilly, *Fredericksburg Campaign*, 63.
21. Longstreet, *From Manassas to Appomattox*, 300.
22. Owen, *Washington Artillery of New Orleans*, 176–77.
23. Lafayette McLaws, "The Confederate Left at Fredericksburg," in *Battles and Leaders of the Civil War, ed. Robert Underwood Johnson et al. (New York: Century, 1884), 3:*86.
24. Edward Porter Alexander, *Fighting for the Confederacy: The Personal Recollections of General Edward Porter Alexander*, ed. Gary Gallagher (Chapel Hill: University of North Carolina Press, 1998), 170.
25. Longstreet, "Battle of Fredericksburg," 3:79.
26. Longstreet, *From Manassas to Appomattox*, 301.
27. Longstreet, *From Manassas to Appomattox*, 301.
28. Owen, *Washington Artillery of New Orleans*, 177.
29. James Longstreet, *OR*, vol. 21, p. 569.
30. Longstreet, *From Manassas to Appomattox*, 303.
31. McLaws, "Confederate Left at Fredericksburg," 3:86.
32. Brainerd, *Bridge Building in Wartime*, 111.
33. McLaws, "Confederate Left at Fredericksburg," 3:87.
34. Alexander, *Fighting for the Confederacy*, 170.
35. Brainerd, *Bridge Building in Wartime*, 112.
36. Alexander, *Fighting for the Confederacy*, 170.
37. Brainerd, *Bridge Building in Wartime*, 110.
38. Brainerd, *Bridge Building in Wartime*, 113.
39. McLaws, "Confederate Left at Fredericksburg," 3:87.
40. Johnson et al., *Battles and Leaders of the Civil War*, 113.
41. Burnside testimony, *JCCW*, pt. 1, p. 655.
42. Sumner testimony, *JCCW*, pt. 1, p. 656.

43. Alexander, *Fighting for the Confederacy*, 171.
44. Longstreet, *From Manassas to Appomattox*, 302.
45. Brainerd, *Bridge Building in Wartime*, 119.
46. Howard, *Autobiography*, 320.
47. A. S. Pendleton to D. H. Hill, December 11, 1862, *OR*, vol. 21, p. 1057.
48. Alexander, *Fighting for the Confederacy*, 170.
49. Alexander, *Fighting for the Confederacy*, 171.
50. Owen, *Washington Artillery of New Orleans*, 180.
51. Quoted in O'Reilly, *Fredericksburg Campaign*, 65.
52. Longstreet, *From Manassas to Appomattox*, 302.
53. Longstreet, "*Battle of Fredericksburg*," 3:73.
54. O'Reilly, *Fredericksburg Campaign*, 78.
55. Longstreet, "*Battle of Fredericksburg*," 3:73.
56. Lafayette McLaws, *OR, vol. 21*, p. 578.
57. McLaws, "Confederate Left at Fredericksburg," 3:87.
58. Longstreet, *From Manassas to Appomattox*, 303.
59. McLaws, "Confederate Left at Fredericksburg," 3:88.
60. Longstreet, *OR, vol. 21*, p. 569.
61. Howard, *Autobiography*, 325.
62. Couch, "Sumner's 'Right Grand Division,'" 3:108.
63. Longstreet, *From Manassas to Appomattox*, 302.
64. James W. Beaty, letter, December 16, 1862, BV 268-05, FSNMP archives.
65. Longstreet, *OR*, vol. 21, p. 569.
66. Longstreet, *OR*, vol. 21, p. 571.
67. Sumner testimony, *JCCW*, pt. 1, p. 655.
68. Haley, *Rebel Yell*, 56.
69. Ambrose Burnside, *OR*, vol. 21, *p.* 89.
70. Patrick, *Inside Lincoln's Army*, 189.
71. John Hennessy, "For All Anguish, for Some Freedom: Fredericksburg in the War," *Blue & Gray*, Winter 2005, p. 50. For additional discussion of population figures, see Joan M. Zenzen, *At the Crossroads of Preservation and Development: A History of Fredericksburg and Spotsylvania National Military Park; Administrative History* (Washington, DC: National Park Service, 2011), 13.

72. Hennessy, "For All Anguish," 50.
73. Haley, *Rebel Yell*, 57.
74. Wainwright, *Diary of Battle*, 132.
75. Ambrose Burnside to Edwin Sumner, *OR*, vol. 21, p. 106.
76. Burnside, *OR*, vol. 21, p. 89.
77. Burnside to William Franklin, *OR*, vol. 21, *p*. 107.
78. Haley, *Rebel Yell*, 55.
79. Henry Halleck to Burnside, December 11, 1862, *OR*, vol. 21, *p*. 65.
80. Haley, *Rebel Yell*, 56, 55.
81. James Longstreet forwarded a similar rationale to Robert E. Lee on July 1, 1863, at Gettysburg. If the Federals remained in position on the morning of July 2, Longstreet argued, it was because they *wanted* Lee to attack them there. For that reason, the Confederate commander should consider a move around the Federals rather than a direct assault against them. Lee, of course, didn't listen.
82. Burnside to Halleck, December 11, 1862, *OR*, vol. 21, p. 64.
83. Burnside to Halleck, December 11, 1862, *OR*, vol. 21, p. 65.
84. Burnside endorsement, Franklin to John C. Parke, December 12, 1862, *OR*, vol. 21, p. 108.
85. Burnside, *OR*, vol. 21, pp. 89–90.
86. Francis A. Walker, *History of the Second Army Corps in the Army of the Potomac* (New York: Charles Scriber's Sons, 1886), 155.
87. Patrick, *Inside Lincoln's Army*, 188.
88. Patrick, *Inside Lincoln's Army*, 189.
89. Wainwright, *Diary of Battle*, 138.
90. Franklin testimony, *JCCW*, pt. 1, p. 661.
91. Couch, "Sumner's 'Right Grand Division,'" 3:109.
92. Walker, *History of the Second Army Corps*, 154.
93. Walker, *History of the Second Army Corps*, 154.
94. Marvel, *Burnside*, 174.
95. Marvel, *Burnside*, 174.
96. Daniel R. Larned to Henry, November 22, 1862, BV 225-05, FSNMP archives (original from the Library of Congress).
97. See Patrick, *Inside Lincoln's Army*, 187, 189.

98. Franklin to Parke, *OR*, vol. 21, p. 108.
99. Burnside testimony, *JCCW*, pt. 1, p. 653.
100. Burnside testimony, *JCCW*, pt. 1, p. 653.
101. Franklin testimony, *JCCW*, pt. 1, p. 707; William B. Franklin, *A Reply of Maj.-Gen. William B. Franklin to the Report of the Joint Committee of Congress on the Conduct of the War, Submitted to the Public on the 6th of April, 1863* (New York: D. Van Nostrand, 1863), 6.
102. William Smith, "Franklin's 'Left Grand Division,'" in *Battles and Leaders of the Civil War*, ed. Robert Underwood Johnson et al. (New York: Century 1884), 3:133.
103. Smith, "Franklin's 'Left Grand Division,'" 3:133.
104. Smith, "Franklin's 'Left Grand Division,'" 3:133.
105. Stonewall Jackson to D. H. Hill, December 12, 1862, *OR*, vol. 21, p. 1060. For the normally secretive Jackson, this is one of the few instances in which he ever bothered to explain himself to a subordinate, even to Hill, who was his brother-in-law.
106. Lee to Gustavus Smith, December 12, 1862, *OR*, vol. 21, p. 1060.
107. Walker, *History of the Second Army Corps*, 156.
108. Smith, "Franklin's 'Left Grand Division,'" 3:131.
109. Haley, *Rebel Yell*, 56.
110. Haley, *Rebel Yell*, 57.

Chapter 4

1. George McClellan, *OR*, vol. 19, pt. 1, p. 45.
2. George Michael Neese, quoted in Brian Matthew Jordan, *Unholy Sabbath: The Battle of South Mountain in History and Memory, September 14, 1862* (El Dorado Hills, CA: Savas Beatie, 2012), 259.
3. William Franklin, *OR*, vol. 19, p. 375.
4. Jordan, *Unholy Sabbath*, 263.
5. Joseph Bartlett, *OR*, vol. 19, p. 389.
6. Bartlett, *OR*, vol. 19, p. 389.
7. Franklin, *Reply*, 6.
8. Ambrose Burnside, *OR*, vol. 21, p. 90; Burnside, May 24, 1863, memo, pp. 14–15.

9. Franklin testimony, *JCCW*, pt. 1, p. 707.
10. Smith, "Franklin's 'Left Grand Division,'" 3:133.
11. O'Reilly, *Fredericksburg Campaign*, 136.
12. In his official report of the battle, written January 2, 1863, Franklin cited a 7:45 a.m. arrival time. In testimony before the Joint Committee on the Conduct of the War on March 28, 1863, he referenced a time of "about 7 o'clock." In his reply to the committee's report, published April 6, 1863, he cited the hour as half past seven. Smith, in his account in *Battles & Leaders*, noted the time as follows: "I think, at 7:45 a.m." Neither Smith nor Reynolds mentioned the time in their official reports. However, Hardie sent a telegram back to Burnside with a time stamp of 7:40 a.m., indicating Meade had been selected to make the attack, so discussion had been wrapped up a few minutes before that point at the latest.
13. Parke to William Franklin, *OR*, vol. 21, p. 71.
14. O'Reilly, *Fredericksburg Campaign*, 137.
15. Wainwright, *Diary of Battle*, 147–48.
16. Smith, "Franklin's 'Left Grand Division,'" 3:134.
17. Franklin, *Reply*, 7.
18. Franklin, *Reply*, 10.
19. Franklin testimony, *JCCW*, pt. 1, p. 708.
20. Franklin testimony, *Reply*, 9.
21. John Reynolds testimony, *JCCW*, pt. 1, p. 698.
22. Wainwright, *Diary of Battle*, 143.
23. Meade, in *Life and Letters*, 1:362.
24. Franklin testimony, *JCCW*, pt. 1, p. 708.
25. Franklin testimony, *JCCW*, pt. 1, p. 661.
26. Walker, *History of the Second Army Corps*, 157.
27. James Hardie telegram, quoted in Burnside's report, *OR*, vol. 21, p. 91.
28. Franklin, *Reply*, 10.
29. Burnside, *OR*, vol. 21, p. 91.
30. Burnside testimony, *JCCW*, pt. 1, p. 653.
31. Burnside, *OR*, vol. 21, p. 91.
32. Franklin, *Reply*, 7.
33. Franklin, *Reply*, 16.

34. Burnside memo, May 24, 1863, pp. 9, 10, BV 225-01, FSNMP archives.
35. Burnside, *OR,* vol. 21, p. 91.
36. Meade, in *Life and Letters*, 1:365–66.
37. Meade, in *Life and Letters*, 1:360, 361.
38. Meade, in *Life and Letters*, 1:361–62.
39. Isaac Rusling Pennypacker, *General Meade* (New York: D. Appleton, 1901), 105.
40. John Esten Cooke, "The Right at Fredericksburg," *Philadelphia Weekly Times*, April 26, 1879, FSNMP archives, BV 143-01.
41. Heros von Borcke, *Memoirs of the Confederate War for Independence* (London: William Blackwood and Sons, 1938), 2:112.
42. von Borcke, *Memoirs,* 87.
43. Cooke, "Right at Fredericksburg."
44. von Borcke, *Memoirs,* 112.
45. von Borcke, *Memoirs,* 113.
46. von Borcke, *Memoirs,* 114.
47. Stapleton Crutchfield, *OR,* vol. 21, p. 636.
48. von Borcke, *Memoirs,* 114.
49. Crutchfield, *OR,* vol. 21, p. 636.
50. von Borcke, *Memoirs,* 114.
51. Jennings Cropper Wise, *The Long Arm of Lee: The History of the Artillery of the Army of Northern Virginia* (Lynchburg, VA: J. P. Bell, 1915), 1:382; O'Reilly, *Fredericksburg Campaign,* 143.
52. Wainwright, *Diary of Battle,* 142.
53. Wise, *Long Arm of Lee,* 382.
54. von Borcke, *Memoirs,* 118.
55. Cooke, "Right at Fredericksburg."
56. George Meade, *OR,* vol. 21, p. 511.
57. Robert E. Lee, *OR,* vol. 21, p. 553.
58. Charles Wainwright, *OR,* vol. 21, p. 458.
59. John G. Simpson, *OR,* vol. 21, p. 514.
60. Meade, *OR,* vol. 21, p. 511.
61. Doubleday, 462.
62. Cooke, "Right at Fredericksburg."

63. Cooke, “Right at Fredericksburg.”
64. Cooke, “Right at Fredericksburg.”
65. J. Churchill Cooke, “Vet Describes Big Battle Here,” Fredericksburg newspaper, ca. 1929–30, BV 189-04, FSNMP archives.
66. Cooke, “Right at Fredericksburg.”
67. von Borcke, *Memoirs,* 118.
68. Wainwright, *OR,* vol. 21, p. 458.
69. Lee, *OR,* vol. 21, p. 553.
70. O’Reilly, *Fredericksburg Campaign,* 149.
71. Wise, *Long Arm of Lee*, 404.
72. Jedediah Hotchkiss, *Make Me a Map of the Valley: The Civil War Journal of Stonewall Jackson’s Topographer*, ed. Archie P. McDonald (Dallas: Southern Methodist University Press, 1973), 100.
73. Lee, *OR,* vol. 21, p. 553.
74. von Borcke, *Memoirs,* 117.
75. von Borcke, *Memoirs,* 119.
76. Chris Mackowski and Kristopher D. White, *Simply Murder: The Battle of Fredericksburg* (El Dorado Hills, CA: Savas Beatie, 2012), 57.
77. James Archer, *OR,* vol. 21, p. 657.
78. Jubal Early, *OR*, vol. 21, p. 663–64.
79. For a rundown of Jackson’s arrest-prone demeanor, see A. Cash Koeniger, “The Garnett Controversy Revisited,” in *The Shenandoah Valley Campaign of 1862*, ed. Garry W. Gallagher (Chapel Hill: University of North Carolina Press, 2003), 225–29.
80. James A. Walker, excerpt from testimony, “James Walker Court Martial,” Virginia Military Institute online archives, accessed January 10, 2020, https://www.vmi.edu/archives/stonewall-jackson-resources/professor-jackson-at-vmi/james-walker-court-martial/.
81. Robert Lewis Dabney, *Life and Campaigns of Lieutenant General Thomas J. Stonewall Jackson* (Harrisonburg, VA: Sprinkle, 1983), 189–90.
82. For an account of frozen-to-death sentries, see Sam Watkins, *Co. Aytch: A Side Show of the Big Show*, 2nd ed. (Chattanooga, TN: Times Printing Company, 1900), 29–30.
83. James I. Robertson Jr., *Stonewall Jackson: The Man, The Soldier, The Legend* (New York: Macmillan, 1997), 643.

84. Early, *OR*, vol. 21, p. 664.
85. Early, *OR*, vol. 21, p. 664.
86. Early, *OR*, vol. 21, p. 664.
87. Jubal Early, *Autobiographical Sketch and Narrative of the War between the States* (Philadelphia: J. B. Lippincott, 1912), 174.
88. Early, *Autobiographical Sketch*, 172.
89. A. P. Hill, *OR*, vol. 21, p. 647.
90. Early, *OR*, vol. 21, p. 667.
91. Stonewall Jackson, *OR*, vol. 21, p. 632.
92. Robert E. Lee to James Seddon, *OR*, vol. 21, p. 547.
93. Quoted in Early, *Autobiographical Sketch*, 468, 469.
94. George Meade to Margaretta Meade, December 2, 1862, in *Life and Letters*, 1:334.
95. John Reynolds, *OR*, vol. 21, p. 454.
96. Jackson, *OR*, vol. 21, p. 631.
97. Reynolds, *OR*, vol. 21, p. 454.
98. Thanks to Greg Mertz for articulating this particular point in this particular way.
99. O'Reilly, *Fredericksburg Campaign*, 501.
100. Frank P. Amsden, *OR*, vol. 21, p. 517.
101. Reynolds, *OR*, vol. 21, p. 456.
102. Wainwright, *Diary of Battle*, 109.
103. Wainwright, *Diary of Battle*, 147.
104. Meade, in *Life and Letters*, 1:337.
105. Meade, in *Life and Letters*, 1:337.
106. Meade, in *Life and Letters*, 1:338.
107. Meade, *OR*, vol. 21, p. 512.
108. Pennypacker, *General Meade*, 102.
109. Frederick L. Hitchcock, *War from the Inside* (Philadelphia: J. B. Lippincott, 1904), 134.
110. Hitchcock, *War from the Inside, 134*.
111. Hitchcock, *War from the Inside*, 135.
112. David Bell Birney, *OR*, vol. 21, p. 362.
113. Pennypacker, *General Meade*, 103.

114. Meade, *OR*, vol. 21, p. 513.

115. Meade quoted in Edward J. Nichols, *Toward Gettysburg: A Biography of General John F. Reynolds* (Richmond, VA: Butternut, 1988), 153.

116. Meade, in *Life and Letters*, 1:340.

117. Pennypacker, *General Meade*, 103.

118. Pennypacker, *General Meade*, 102.

119. Kristopher D. White, "Reynolds Reconsidered," in *Fight Like the Devil: The First Day at Gettysburg—July 1, 1863, by Chris Mackowski, Kristopher D. White, and Daniel T. Davis* (El Dorado Hills, CA: Savas Beatie, 2015), 139. White offers a number of examples to illustrate his point.

120. Burnside, *OR*, vol. 21, p. 93.

121. Meade, in *Life and Letters*, 1:340.

122. Burnside, *OR*, vol. 21, p. 90.

123. William Owen, Washington Artillery, "A Hot Day on Marye's Heights," in *The Blue and the Gray, ed. Henry Steele Commager* (New York: New American Library, 1973), 239.

124. William Landon, December 19, 1862, letter, published in "Letters to the Vincesses Sun," *Indiana Magazine of History* 33, no. 3 (September 1937), BV 117, FSNMP archives.

125. Owen, "Hot Day on Marye's Heights," 237.

126. Favill, *Diary of a Young Officer*, 211.

127. John R. Brooke to St. Clair Mulholland, August 1, 1881, Mulholland Papers, Civil War Library and Museum, Philadelphia, PA, BV 198-05, FSNMP archives.

128. Alexander Hunter, *Johnny Reb and Billy Yank* (New York: Neale Company, 1905), 316.

129. Charles Haydon, diary entry, December 13, 1862, BV 35, FSNMP archives.

130. Hooker testimony, *JCCW*, pt. 1, p. 668.

131. Hitchcock, *War from the Inside*, 113.

132. Burnside, *OR*, vol. 21, p. 93.

133. P. M. Lydig, *OR*, vol. 21, p. 127.

134. Lydig, *OR*, vol. 21, p. 128.

135. J. M. Cutts, *OR*, vol. 21, p. 128.

136. Cutts quoting Burnside, *OR*, vol. 21, p. 128.

137. Cutts quoting Burnside, *OR*, vol. 21, p. 128.
138. R. H. I. Goddard, *OR*, vol. 21, p. 128.
139. James Hardie to Ambrose Burnside, *OR*, vol. 21, p. 92.
140. Hardie to Burnside, *OR*, vol. 21, p. 92.
141. Goddard, *OR*, vol. 21, p. 128.
142. Hardie to Burnside, *OR*, vol. 21, p. 92.
143. Burnside, *OR*, vol. 22, p. 93.
144. Franklin, *OR*, vol. 21, p. 451.
145. Burnside, *OR*, vol. 22, p. 93.
146. Franklin, *Reply*, 14.
147. Hardie to Burnside, *OR*, vol. 21, p. 92.
148. Burnside, *OR*, vol. 21, p. 95.
149. Couch, "Sumner's 'Right Grand Division,'" *3*:113.
150. Franklin, *OR*, vol. 21, p. 451.
151. Reynolds, *OR*, vol, 21, p. 455.
152. Burnside memo, May 24, 1863, p. 22, BV 225-01, FSNMP archives.
153. Burnside memo, May 24, 1863, p. 16.

Chapter 5

1. Ambrose Burnside, *OR*, vol. 21, p. 95.
2. Francis Walker, *History of the Second Army Corps*, 189.
3. Burnside testimony, *JCCW*, pt. 1, p. 653.
4. Couch, "Sumner's 'Right Grand Division,'" 3:117.
5. Rush Hawkins, "Why Burnside Did Not Renew the Attack at Fredericksburg," in *Battles and Leaders of the Civil War*, ed. Robert Underwood Johnson et al. (New York: Century, 1884), 3:127.
6. Hawkins, "Burnside Did Not Renew the Attack," 3:127.
7. Hawkins, "Burnside Did Not Renew the Attack," 3:127.
8. Hawkins, "Burnside Did Not Renew the Attack," 3:127.
9. Hawkins, "Burnside Did Not Renew the Attack," 3:127.
10. Burnside testimony, *JCCW*, pt. 1, p. 653.
11. Hawkins, "Burnside Did Not Renew the Attack," 3:127. Accounts of this council of war differ. It's worth noting that Hawkins, a onetime

member of the New York State Assembly, published his piece in August 1886 for the wide audience afforded by *Century Magazine* and the magazine's subsequent *Battles and Leaders. Unsurprisingly,* he might have inflated his role in the event. Portions of his tale included here are only those that do not conflict with other accounts of the evening.

12. Robert E. Lee, *OR,* vol. 21, p. 555.
13. von Borcke, *Memoirs,* 132.
14. Franklin, *Reply,* 15.
15. Hawkins, "Burnside Did Not Renew the Attack," 3:127.
16. Sumner testimony, *JCCW,* 658.
17. Burnside to Abraham Lincoln, *OR,* vol. 21, p. 65.
18. Couch, "Sumner's 'Right Grand Division,'" 3:117.
19. Sumner quoted in Burnside testimony, *JCCW,* pt. 1, p. 653.
20. Burnside testimony, *JCCW,* pt. 1, p. 653.
21. Burnside testimony, *JCCW,* pt. 1, p. 653
22. Marvel, *Burnside,* 198.
23. Burnside testimony, *JCCW,* pt. 1, pp. 656, 653.
24. Walker, *History of the Second Army Corps,* 180.
25. Burnside, *OR,* vol. 21, *p.* 95.
26. Couch, "Sumner's 'Right Grand Division,'" 3:117.
27. Sumner testimony, *JCCW,* 659.
28. Early, *Autobiographical Sketch,* 182.
29. Hooker testimony, *Joint Committee,* 669.
30. Hooker quoted in Couch, "Sumner's 'Right Grand Division,'" 3:117.
31. McAllister, 242.
32. Cooke, "Right at Fredericksburg," 12.
33. von Borcke, *Memoirs,* 128.
34. Stonewall Jackson, *OR,* vol. 21, p. 634.
35. O'Reilly, *Fredericksburg Campaign,* 425.
36. Jackson, *OR,* vol. 21, p. 634.
37. Cooke, "Right at Fredericksburg," 13.
38. von Borcke, *Memoirs,* 129.
39. Early, *Autobiographical Sketch,* 178.

40. O'Reilly, *Fredericksburg Campaign*, 426.
41. Jackson, *OR*, vol. 21, p. 634.
42. Early, *Autobiographical Sketch*, 178.
43. von Borcke, *Memoirs*, 129.
44. Taylor, *Four Years with General Lee*, 149.
45. Longstreet, *From Manassas to Appomattox*, 316.
46. Lee to James Seddon, in *Wartime Letters*, 362.
47. Alexander, *Fighting for the Confederacy*, 180.
48. Cooke, "Right at Fredericksburg," 14.
49. Robert E. Lee to Mary Lee, in *Wartime Letters*, 365.
50. Lee, *OR*, vol. 21, p. 555.
51. Sorrel, 143.
52. Lee, *OR* 22, 555.
53. Alexander, *Fighting for the Confederacy*, 172.
54. Sorrel, 143.
55. Sorrel, 143.
56. Alexander, *Fighting for the Confederacy*, 184.
57. Lee to Mary Lee, in *Wartime Letters*, 365.
58. von Borcke, *Memoirs*, 132.
59. von Borcke, *Memoirs*, 132.
60. Early, *Autobiographical Sketch*, 180.
61. Early, *Autobiographical Sketch*, 183.

Conclusion

1. Hotchkiss, *Make Me a Map of the Valley*, 101.
2. Stiles, 137.
3. Brainerd, *Bridge Building in Wartime*, 121.
4. Robert E. Lee to James Seddon, in *Wartime Letters*, 365.
5. Lee to Seddon, in *Wartime Letters*, 363.
6. Lee to Seddon, in *Wartime Letters*, 364.
7. Early, *Autobiographical Sketch*, 183.
8. Lee to Seddon, in *Wartime Letters*, 363.

9. For more on self-emancipation in Fredericksburg, start with John Hennessy's work at *Mysteries & Conundrums*, the unofficial blog of Fredericksburg and Spotsylvania National Military Park: "The Exodus Begins: John Washington's Greatest Journey," May 2, 2012, https://npsfrsp.wordpress.com/2012/05/02/the-exodus-begins-john-washingtons-greatest-journey/.
10. Stiles, 132.
11. Taylor, *Four Years with General Lee*, 81.
12. Edward Porter Alexander, *Military Memoirs of a Confederate: A Critical Narrative* (New York: Charles Scribner's Sons, 1907), 302.
13. Lincoln, in *Lincoln: Speeches and Writings*, 419.
14. Wainwright, *Diary of Battle*, 148–49.
15. Wainwright, *Diary of Battle*, 149.
16. Longstreet, "Battle of Fredericksburg," 3:85.
17. Longstreet, "Battle of Fredericksburg," 3:85.
18. Marvel, *Burnside*, 174–75.
19. Wainwright, *Diary of Battle*, 147.
20. Meade, in *Life and Letters*, 1:340.
21. Meade, in *Life and Letters*, 1:338.
22. Meade, in *Life and Letters*, 1:341.
23. Wainwright, *Diary of Battle*, 149.
24. Wainwright, *Diary of Battle*, 150.
25. Haley, *Rebel Yell*, 65.
26. Alexander, *Military Memoirs*, 313.
27. Meade, in *Life and Letters*, 1:344–45.
28. Meade, in *Life and Letters*, 1:345.
29. Lincoln, telegram to Burnside, December 30, 1862, in *Collected Works*, 6:22, quoted in McPherson, *Tried by War*, 147–48.
30. John C. Parke testimony, *JCCW*, pt. 1, 727.
31. Meade, in *Life and Letters*, 1:340.
32. Lee to Gustavus Smith, January 4, 1863, in *Wartime Letters*, 383.
33. Walker, *History of the Second Army Corps*, 199.
34. Meade, in *Life and Letters*, 1:348.
35. Walker, 198.

Appendix I

1. Noel Harrison, *Fredericksburg Civil War Sites, vol. 1, April 1861–November 1862* (Lynchburg, Virginia: H. E. Howard, 1995), 102.
2. See Mackowski and White, *Simply Murder*, 13.
3. Harrison, *Fredericksburg Civil War Sites,* 1:104.
4. Walt Whitman, *The Complete Writings of Walt Whitman: The Complete Prose Works* (New York: G. P. Putman's Sons, 1902), 102.
5. "The Battle of Fredericksburg," *New York Times*, December 17, 1862, quoted in Harrison, *Fredericksburg Civil War Sites,* 1:108.
6. For more on the Chatham slave uprising, see "Chatham Slave Revolt," Fredericksburg and Spotsylvania National Military Park's website, https://www.nps.gov/frsp/learn/historyculture/chatham-slave-revolt.htm and John Hennessy, "The 1805 Slave Revolt at Chatham," *Mysteries & Conundrums*, February 14, 2017, https://npsfrsp.wordpress.com/2017/02/14/the-1805-slave-revolt-at-chatham/. *Mysteries & Conundrums is* the unofficial blog of Fredericksburg and Spotsylvania National Military Park.
7. Whitman, *Complete Prose Works,* 102.
8. Quoted in Harrison, *Fredericksburg Civil War Sites,* 1:108.
9. Harrison, *Fredericksburg Civil War Sites*, 2:167.
10. George F. Noyes, *The Bivouac and the Battle-field; or, Campaign Sketches in Virginia and Maryland* (New York: Harper and Brothers, 1864), 303.
11. Haupt, 183.
12. Noyes, *Bivouac and the Battle-field*, 294.
13. Harrison, *Fredericksburg Civil War Sites,* 2:170.
14. Patrick, *Inside Lincoln's Army*, 214.
15. For more on the Phillips House, see John Hennessy, "Fame, a First, a Fire, Balloons, and a Radio Tower: The Phillips House," *Mysteries & Conundrums*, December 31, 2010, https://npsfrsp.wordpress.com/2010/12/31/fame-a-first-a-fire-balloons-and-a-radio-tower-the-phillips-house/.
16. Noyes, *Bivouac and the Battle-field,* 41.
17. William McCarter, "Fredericksburg as Seen by One of Meagher's Irish Brigade," *National Tribune*, July 29, 1886, BV 227-58, FSNMP archives.
18. Donald C. Pfanz, *History through Eyes of Stone: A Survey of Civil War Monuments Near Fredericksburg, Virginia*, 103, Fredericksburg and Spotsylvania National Military Park collection.

19. Pfanz, *History through Eyes of Stone,* 22.
20. Brainerd, *Bridge Building in Wartime,* 113.
21. George Macy, letter, December 20, 1862, Massachusetts Military Order of the Loyal Legion Collection, United States Military History Institute, quote in O'Reilly, 93.
22. Brainerd, *Bridge Building in Wartime,* 112.
23. McCarter, "Fredericksburg."
24. Michael McGrath, *OR,* vol. 21, p. 179.
25. Smith, "Franklin's 'Left Grand Division,'" 3:136.
26. Wainwright, *Diary of Battle,* 138.
27. Harrison, *Fredericksburg Civil War Sites,* 2:76.
28. Smith, "Franklin's 'Left Grand Division,'" 3:136.
29. Smith, "Franklin's 'Left Grand Division,'" 3:136; Wainwright, *Diary of Battle,* 138–39.
30. Wainwright, *Diary of Battle,* 139.
31. E. P. Roe, *E. P. Roe: Reminiscences of His Life*, ed. Mary A. Roe (New York: Dodd, Mead, 1899), 36–37.
32. Harrison, *Fredericksburg Civil War Sites,* 2:80.
33. For more on Mannsfield, see John Hennessy, "Digging Mannsfield," *Mysteries & Conundrums, December 3, 2010,* https://npsfrsp.wordpress.com/2010/12/03/digging-mannsfield/.
34. Roe, *Reminiscences*, 36–38.
35. Zenzen, *Crossroads of Preservation and Development,* 82.
36. Zenzen, *Crossroads of Preservation and Development,* 98.
37. Zenzen, *Crossroads of Preservation and Development,* 95.
38. Zenzen, *Crossroads of Preservation and Development,* 39.
39. Zenzen, *Crossroads of Preservation and Development,* 43.
40. Zenzen, *Crossroads of Preservation and Development,* 95.
41. Zenzen, *Crossroads of Preservation and Development,* 46.
42. Chickamauga, Gettysburg, Shiloh, and Vicksburg were the first four parks. "The Antietam Plan" got its name because the new land acquisition strategy was first employed at Antietam, the fifth national battlefield Congress approved.
43. Zenzen, *Crossroads of Preservation and Development,* 98.

44. Zenzen, *Crossroads of Preservation and Development*, 98.
45. Early, *Autobiographical Sketch*, 181.
46. For more on the Medals of Honor at the Slaughter Pen, see Richard P. Mills, "Slaughter Pen Farm Bears Witness to Medal of Honor Day," *Free Lance-Star* (Fredericksburg, VA), March 24, 2018, https://www.fredericksburg.com/opinion/columns/slaughter-pen-farm-bears-witness-to-medal-of-honor-day/article_0c928014-a1c7-577e-98bd-d71a321af328.html.
47. Reynolds testimony, *JCCW*, pt. 1, p. 699.
48. Harrison, *Fredericksburg Civil War Sites*, 2:97.
49. Wyman S. White, quoted in Harrison, *Fredericksburg Civil War Sites*, 2:97.
50. Robert E. Lee, *OR*, vol. 21, p. 553.
51. von Borcke, *Memoirs*, 114.
52. Jubal Early, *OR*, vol. 21, p. 663.
53. Pfanz, *History through Eyes of Stone*, 15.
54. Robert E. Lee to Mary Lee, December 25, 1862, in *Wartime Letters*, 380.
55. von Borcke, *Memoirs*, 117.
56. Mackowski and White, *Simply Murder*, 70.
57. Pfanz, *History through Eyes of Stone*, 68.
58. A. Wilson Green, email to author, July 31, 2020.
59. Sorrel, 143.
60. Walter H. Taylor, *General Lee: His Campaigns in Virginia, 1861–1865, with Personal Reminiscences* (Lincoln: University of Nebraska Press, 1994), 150–51.
61. Donald C. Pfanz, *Where Valor Proudly Sleeps: A History of Fredericksburg National Cemetery* (Carbondale: Southern Illinois University Press, 2018), 181.
62. Early, *Autobiographical Sketch*, 182–83.

BIBLIOGRAPHY

Collections

Fredericksburg and Spotsylvania National Military Park archives. Fredericksburg, VA.

Virginia Military Institute online archives, www.vmi.edu/archives/digital-collections/.

Primary Sources

Compilations

Commager, Henry Steele, ed. *The Blue and the Gray*. New York: New American Library, 1973.

The Conduct of the War: Report of the Congressional Committee on the Operations of the Army of the Potomac, Causes of Its Inaction and Ill Success, Its Several Campaigns, Why M'Clellan Was Removed, the Battle of Fredericksburg, Removal of Burnside. New York: Tribune Association, 1863.

Couch, Darius. "Sumner's 'Right Grand Division.'" In Johnson et al., *Battles and Leaders of the Civil War.*

Fehrenbacher, Don E., and Virginia Fehrenbacher, eds. *Recollected Words of Abraham Lincoln*. Stanford, CA: Stanford University Press, 1996.

Hawkins, Rush. "Why Burnside Did Not Renew the Attack at Fredericksburg." In Johnson et al., *Battles and Leaders of the Civil War.*

Johnson, Robert Underwood, et al., eds. *Battles and Leaders of the Civil War.* Vol. 3. New York: Century, 1884.

Longstreet, James. "The Battle of Fredericksburg." In Johnson et al., *Battles and Leaders of the Civil War.*

McLaws, Lafayette. "The Confederate Left at Fredericksburg." In Johnson et al., *Battles and Leaders of the Civil War.*

Report of the Joint Committee on the Conduct of the War. Pt. 1. Washington, DC: Government Printing Office, 1863.

Smith, William. "Franklin's 'Left Grand Division.'" In Johnson et al., *Battles and Leaders of the Civil War.*

Smith, William E., ed. *The Francis Preston Blair Family in Politics.* Vol. 2. New York: Macmillan, 1933.

US War Department. *The War of the Rebellion: A Compilation of the Official Records of the Union and Confederate Armies.* Series 1. Washington, DC: Government Printing Office, 1888.

Books

Alexander, Edward Porter. *Fighting for the Confederacy: The Personal Recollections of General Edward Porter Alexander.* Edited by Gary Gallagher. Chapel Hill: University of North Carolina Press, 1998.

Alexander, Edward Porter. *Military Memoirs of a Confederate: A Critical Narrative.* New York: Charles Scribner's Sons, 1907.

Bolton, William. *The Civil War Journal of Colonel Bolton, 51st Pennsylvania.* Edited by Richard A. Sauers. Conshohocken, PA: Combined Publishing, 2000.

Brainerd, Wesley. *Bridge Building in Wartime: Colonel Wesley Brainerd's Memoir of the 50th New York Volunteer Engineers.* Edited by Ed Malles. Knoxville: University of Tennessee Press, 1997.

Carpenter, F. B. *Six Months at the White House with Abraham Lincoln.* New York: Hurd and Houghton, 1866.

Chase, Salmon P. *The Salmon P. Chase Papers.* Vol. 1, *Journals, 1829–1872.* Edited by John Niven. Kent, OH: Kent State University Press, 1993.

Cooke, John Esten. "The Right at Fredericksburg." *Philadelphia Weekly Times*, April 26, 1879. BV 143-01. Fredericksburg and Spotsylvania National Military Park archives. Fredericksburg, VA.

Dabney, Robert Lewis. *Life and Campaigns of Lieutenant General Thomas J. Stonewall Jackson*. Harrisonburg, VA: Sprinkle, 1983.

Early, Jubal. *Autobiographical Sketch and Narrative of the War between the States*. Philadelphia: J. B. Lippincott, 1912.

Favill, Josiah. *Diary of a Young Officer*. Chicago: R. R. Donnelly and Sons, 1909.

Franklin, William B. *A Reply of Maj.-Gen. William B. Franklin to the Report of the Joint Committee of Congress on the Conduct of the War, Submitted to the Public on the 6th of April, 1863*. New York: D. Van Nostrand, 1863.

Haley, John. *The Rebel Yell & the Yankee Hurrah: The Civil War Journal of a Maine Volunteer*. Edited by Ruth L. Silliker. Camden, ME: Down East Books, 1985.

Hay, John. *Inside Lincoln's White House: The Complete Civil War Diary of John Hay*. Edited by Michael Burlingame and John R. Turner Ettlinger. Carbondale: Southern Illinois University Press, 1997.

Haupt, Herman. *Reminiscences of General Herman Haupt*. Milwaukee, WI: Wright and Joys, 1901.

Hay, John. *Lincoln's Journalist: John Hay's Anonymous Writings for the Press, 1860–1864*. Edited by Michael Burlingame. Carbondale: Southern Illinois University Press, 1998.

Hitchcock, Frederick L. *War from the Inside*. Philadelphia: J. B. Lippincott, 1904.

Hotchkiss, Jedediah. *Make Me a Map of the Valley: The Civil War Journal of Stonewall Jackson's Topographer*. Edited by Archie P. McDonald. Dallas: Southern Methodist University Press, 1973.

Howard, Oliver Otis. *The Autobiography of Oliver Otis Howard*. New York: Baker and Taylor, 1907.

Hunter, Alexander. *Johnny Reb and Billy Yank*. New York: Neale, 1905.

Judd, David W. *The Story of the Thirty-Third N.Y.S. Vols; or, Two Years Campaigning in Virginia and Maryland*. Rochester, NY: Benton and Andrew, 1864.

Landon, William. "Letters to the Vincesses Sun." *Indiana Magazine of History* 33, no. 3 (September 1937). Fredericksburg and Spotsylvania National Military Park archives. Fredericksburg, VA.

Lee, Robert E. *The Wartime Papers of Robert E. Lee*. Edited by Clifford Dowdey. Boston: Da Capo, 1961.

Lincoln, Abraham. *Lincoln: Speeches and Writings, 1859–1865*. Edited by Don E. Fehrenbacher. New York: Library of America, 1898.

Lincoln, Abraham. *Recollected Words of Abraham Lincoln*. Edited by Don E. Fehrenbacher and Virginia Fehrenbacher. Stanford, CA: Stanford University Press, 1996.

Longstreet, James. *From Manassas to Appomattox: Memoirs of the Civil War in America*. Philadelphia: J. B. Lippincott, 1896.

McClellan, George B. *The Civil War Papers of George B. McClellan: Selected Correspondence, 1860–1865*. Edited by Stephen Sears. New York: Da Capo, 1992.

Meade, George Gordon. *The Life and Letters of George Gordon Meade*. Edited by George Meade Jr. Vol. 1. New York: Charles Scribner's Sons, 1913.

Noyes, George F. *The Bivouac and the Battle-field; or, Campaign Sketches in Virginia and Maryland*. New York: Harper and Brothers, 1864.

Owen, William Miller. *In Camp and Battle with the Washington Artillery of New Orleans*. Boston: Rockwell and Churchill, 1885.

Patrick, Marsena. *Inside Lincoln's Army: The Diary of Marsena Rudolph Patrick, Provost Marshal General, Army of the Potomac*. Edited by David S. Sparks. New York: Thomas Yoseloff, 1964.

Raymond, Henry J. *Scribner's Monthly* 19.

Roe, E. P. *E. P. Roe: Reminiscences of His Life*. Edited by Mary A. Roe. New York: Dodd, Mead, 1899.

Taylor, Walter H. *Four Years with General Lee*. Bloomington: Indiana University Press, 1996.

von Borcke, Heros. *Memoirs of the Confederate War for Independence*. Vol. 2. London: William Blackwood and Sons, 1938.

Wainwright, Charles. *A Diary of Battle: The Personal Journals of Colonel Charles S. Wainwright, 1861–1865*. Edited by Allan Nevins. Boston: Da Capo, 1998.

Walker, Francis A. *History of the Second Army Corps in the Army of the Potomac*. New York: Charles Scribner's Sons, 1886.

Watkins, Sam. *Co. Aytch: A Side Show of the Big Show*. 2nd ed. Chattanooga: Times Printing Company, 1900.

Welles, Gideon. *Diary of Gideon Welles, Secretary of the Navy Under Lincoln and Johnson*. Vol. 1. New York: Houghton Mifflin, 1911.

Welles, Gideon. "The History of Emancipation." 1872.

Whitman, Walt. *The Complete Writings of Walt Whitman: The Complete Prose Works*. New York: G. P. Putnam's Sons, 1902.

Willcox, Orlando. *Forgotten Valor: The Memoirs, Journals, and Civil War*

Letters of Orlando B. Willcox. Edited by Robert Garth Scott. Kent, OH: Kent State University Press, 1999.

Secondary Sources

Browne, Francis Fisher. *The Every-Day Life of Abraham Lincoln: A Narrative and Descriptive Biography with Pen-Pictures and Personal Recollections by Those Who Knew Him*. Chicago: Browne and Howell, 1913. http://www.gutenberg.org/files/14004/14004-h/14004-h.htm.

Goodwin, Doris Kearns. *Team of Rivals: The Political Genius of Abraham Lincoln*. New York: Simon and Schuster, 2005.

Hennessy, John. "For All Anguish, for Some Freedom: Fredericksburg in the War." *Blue & Gray*, Winter 2005.

Holzer, Harold. *Emancipating Lincoln: The Proclamation in Text, Context, and Memory*. Cambridge, MA: Harvard, 2012.

Jordan, Brian Matthew. *Unholy Sabbath: The Battle of South Mountain in History and Memory, September 14, 1862*. El Dorado Hills, CA: Savas Beatie, 2012.

Koeniger, A. Cash. "The Garnett Controversy Revisited." In *The Shenandoah Valley Campaign of 1862*, edited by Garry W. Gallagher. Chapel Hill: University of North Carolina Press, 2003.

Mackowski, Chris. *Strike Them a Blow: Battle along the North Anna*. El Dorado Hills, CA: Savas Beatie, 2015.

Mackowski, Chris, and Kristopher D. White. *Simply Murder: The Battle of Fredericksburg*. El Dorado Hills, CA: Savas Beatie, 2012.

Mackowski, Chris, Kristopher D. White, and Daniel T. Davis. *Fight Like the Devil: The First Day at Gettysburg—July 1, 1863*. El Dorado Hills, CA: Savas Beatie, 2015.

Marvel, William. *Burnside*. Chapel Hill: University of North Carolina Press, 1991.

McPherson, James. "The Commander Who Would Not Fight." In *The War That Forged a Nation: Why the Civil War Still Matters*. New York: Oxford University Press, 2015.

McPherson, James. *Tried by War: Abraham Lincoln as Commander in Chief*. New York: Penguin, 2008.

Mysteries & Conundrums: The Unofficial Blog of Fredericksburg and Spotsylvania National Military Park. www.mysteriesandconundrums.com.

Nichols, Edward J. *Toward Gettysburg: A Biography of General John F. Reynolds*. Butternut, 1988.

O'Reilly, Francis A. *The Fredericksburg Campaign: Winter War on the Rappahannock*. Baton Rouge: Louisiana State University Press, 2002.

O'Reilly, Francis A. *"Stonewall" Jackson at Fredericksburg: The Battle of Prospect Hill*. H. E. Howard, 1993.

Pawlak, Kevin. "'The Heavyest Blow Yet Given the Confederacy': The Emancipation Proclamation Changes the Civil War." In *Turning Points of the Civil War*, edited by Chris Mackowski and Kristopher D. White. Carbondale: Southern Illinois University Press, 2018.

Pennypacker, Isaac Rusling. *General Meade*. New York: D. Appleton, 1901.

Pfanz, Donald C. *Where Valor Proudly Sleeps: A History of Fredericksburg National Cemetery*. Carbondale: Southern Illinois University Press, 2018.

Rable, George C. *Fredericksburg! Fredericksburg!* Chapel Hill: University of North Carolina Press, 2002.

Rafuse, Ethan. *McClellan's War*. Indianapolis: Indiana University Press, 2005.

Robertson, James I., Jr. *Stonewall Jackson: The Man, the Soldier, the Legend*. New York: Macmillan, 1997.

Sears, Stephen W. *George B. McClellan: The Young Napoleon*. New York: Ticknor and Fields, 1988.

Sears, Stephen W. *Lincoln's Lieutenants: The High Command of the Army of the Potomac*. New York: Mariner, 2017.

Spruill, Matt, III, and Matt Spruill IV. *Decisions at Second Manassas: The Fourteen Critical Decisions That Defined the Battle*. Knoxville: University of Tennessee Press, 2018.

Taylor, G. A. "Major-General Joseph Hooker and His Proper Place in History." In *The Journal of the Military Service Institution*, edited by T. F. Rodenbough. Governors' Island, NY: Military Service Institution, 1910.

Vermilya, Daniel J. *That Field of Blood: The Battle of Antietam, September 17, 1862*. El Dorado Hills, CA; Savas Beatie, 2018.

White, Henry A. *Robert E. Lee and the Southern Confederacy, 1807–1870*. New York: Putnam, 1897.

Wise, Jennings Cropper. *The Long Arm of Lee: The History of the Artillery of the Army of Northern Virginia*. Vol. 1. Lynchburg, VA: J. P. Bell, 1915.

Zenzen, Joan M. *At the Crossroads of Preservation and Development: A History of Fredericksburg and Spotsylvania National Military Park; Administrative History*. Washington, DC: National Park Service, 2011.

INDEX

Page numbers in **boldface** refer to illustrations.